I0459139

BEFORE THE KING

A SEASON OF RENEWAL

SHIRA SCHECHTER

ISRAEL365

Before The King: A Season of Renewal

Copyright © 2025 by Israel365

All rights reserved.

This book, or any portion of it, may not be reproduced or transmitted electronically, mechanically, or by any other means, including but not limited to photocopying, scanning, downloading, etc., without prior written permission of the author.

For sales inquiries, contact: store@israel365.com

Written by Shira Schechter

Cover by Yehudit Weingarten

Interior design by Aharon Mendlowitz

ISBN: 978-1-957109-89-3

First Edition 2025

www.israel365.com

CONTENTS

INTRODUCTION

You know that feeling when you realize you've become someone you don't entirely recognize? When the gap between who you are and who you meant to be feels uncomfortably wide? There's an ancient tradition that built an entire season around that exact moment of recognition.

From the first day of the Hebrew month of *Elul* through the festivals of *Rosh Hashanah* (Jewish New Year), *Yom Kippur* (Day of Atonement), and *Sukkot* (Feast of Tabernacles), Jews around the world embark on one of humanity's most profound spiritual journeys. It's a journey that begins with the piercing sound of an ancient ram's horn calling souls to awakening, continues through days of the most intense self-examination and divine encounter, and culminates in the joyous celebration of living in God's embrace.

This is the season of the Jewish High Holidays, and it may be the most psychologically sophisticated season of renewal and spiritual transformation in any religious calendar.

What makes this season remarkable isn't just its antiquity—these observances stretch back over three millennia—but its startling relevance to the deepest questions of human existence. How do we change? How do we forgive and seek forgiveness? How do we find meaning in a world that often feels fragmented and uncertain? How do we balance celebration with solemnity, individual growth with community responsibility, security with vulnerability?

The High Holiday season doesn't offer easy answers to these questions. Instead, it provides something far more valuable: a carefully crafted spiritual architecture that guides seekers through the actual process of transformation.

At the heart of this transformation lies a profound metaphor: the coronation of God as King. During *Elul*, Jewish tradition teaches that 'the King is in the field'—accessible and approachable. On *Rosh Hashanah*, we formally crown God as sovereign over all creation. Through the Ten Days of Repentance, we stand before the divine court pleading our case. On *Yom Kippur*, we experience the King's ultimate mercy. And during *Sukkot*, by dwelling in fragile temporary shelters, we discover what we've known all along—that this cosmic King has been with us through every moment of vulnerability and uncertainty.

While these observances emerged from the particular history and covenant of the Jewish people, their themes speak to universal human experiences. The call to honest self-examination. The courage required for genuine apology and forgiveness. The recognition that true security comes not from what we can control, but from our relationship with that which transcends our control. The understanding that personal transformation connects to something larger—that our individual growth participates in the ultimate redemption of a broken world. The understanding that joy and meaning often emerge precisely from our willingness to embrace uncertainty and impermanence.

This book invites you into that journey. Whether you are Jewish and seeking to deepen your understanding of these sacred days, or you come from a different background but find yourself drawn to the wisdom of the Torah, you'll discover practices and perspectives that have sustained millions of people through history's greatest challenges.

You'll learn why a month of spiritual preparation precedes the actual holidays, and how that preparation creates space for transformation that might otherwise remain impossible. You'll explore why *Rosh Hashanah* balances celebration with judgment, and how that paradox reflects the complexity of all meaningful encounters with the Divine. You'll understand why ten additional days of repentance follow the initial judgment, and what those days teach us about human capacity for growth. You'll experience the profound simplicity and shocking depth of *Yom Kippur*, a day when ordinary time stops and extraordinary purification becomes possible. And you'll discover why the season concludes not with solemn reflection, but with the radical vulnerability and surprising joy of dwelling in the *sukkah* (temporary dwelling).

Throughout, you'll encounter not just explanation but invitation—practical guidance for those who want to incorporate these insights into their own spiritual lives, regardless of their religious background. The High Holiday season demonstrates that transformation isn't about perfection; it's about direction. It's not about achieving some impossible standard, but about the willingness to continue growing, changing, and reaching toward our highest selves.

In a world that often feels divided between secular materialism and religious fundamentalism, the High Holiday season offers a third way: a path that honors both reason and mystery, both individual growth and communal responsibility, both celebration and serious moral reflection. It demonstrates that ancient wisdom and contemporary insight can illuminate each other, that ritual and meaning can work together rather than in opposition, that the particular and the universal can each strengthen the other.

As you read these pages, you're invited not just to understand these observances intellectually, but to experience them emotionally and spiritually. You'll find prayers that have sustained people through history's darkest moments, stories that illuminate the deepest questions of human existence, and practices that connect personal growth to the vision of ultimate redemption.

The shofar is about to sound. The season of renewal is about to begin. The question isn't whether you recognize yourself anymore—it's whether you're ready to become who you were always meant to be.

ELUL

I magine you have exactly one month to prepare for the most important meeting of your life - with someone whose opinion matters more than anyone else's, someone who holds your future in their hands. How would you spend that month preparing?

This is the essence of *Elul*.

For thirty days each year, the Jewish calendar creates space for something incredible: the chance to completely reinvent yourself. Not through self-help mantras or life coaching seminars, but through a tried and true holy process that acknowledges both our deepest flaws and our highest potential.

Rosh Hashanah, which literally means the "Head of the Year," falls on the first and second days of the Hebrew month of *Tishrei* (usually in September). It is the day when, according to Jewish tradition, Man was created, and each year it marks the anniversary of that creation. It is also regarded as the Day of

Judgment, when God reviews the deeds of all humanity and determines what the coming year will bring for each person. On this day, He recalls all of His creations and their deeds from the past year, and we sound the *shofar* in order to stir the soul and awaken the heart to repentance

However, the spiritual preparation for *Rosh Hashanah* begins much earlier, during the preceding Hebrew month of *Elul*. This is a time specifically set aside for self-examination and repentance. *Elul* is often viewed as a month of divine closeness, a time when God makes Himself particularly accessible, inviting His people to draw near and seek forgiveness before the solemn days of judgment. This period is marked by special spiritual practices including the daily sounding of the *shofar*, additional prayers, and increased focus on charity and acts of kindness.

Elul is the month when we reaffirm that change is possible. *Elul* reminds us that the person I was yesterday need not be the person I am tomorrow. Most important of all, *Elul* reminds us that God not only expects us to change, but He actively partners with us to make it happen.

Elul is not about perfection. It's about return. The Hebrew word *teshuvah*, often translated as "repentance," more correctly and literally means "to return." To return to being the people we were always meant to be.

Every morning during this month, the sound of the shofar pierces the air in synagogues around the world. It's not a gentle wake-up call but an urgent alarm: *Wake up! Time is running out. The opportunity to return is here, but it won't last forever.*

The month takes its name from the Hebrew letters "אלול", which form an acronym for the verse "I am my beloved's and my beloved is mine" (Song of Songs 6:1). Even in our moments of deepest spiritual reckoning, we are reminded that *Elul* is ultimately a love story; not the love of judgment and condemnation, but the love of a Creator who believes so deeply in our capacity for growth that He has built transformation into the very fabric of the calendar.

As the summer sun begins to fade and autumn approaches, millions of people around the world begin to prepare. They examine their hearts, repair their relationships, and ready themselves to stand before the Eternal with honesty and hope.

This is more than just religious observance. This is about recognizing both our failures and our potential - admitting our shortcomings while reaching toward something higher, acknowledging our limitations while refusing to be defined by them.

The journey of *Elul* asks the most fundamental questions any human being can face: Who are you, really? Who do you want to become? And what are you willing to do to close the gap between the two?

For the thirty days of *Elul*, these questions aren't philosophical abstractions. They become the blueprint for daily living, the lens through which every action is viewed, the compass pointing toward a better version of ourselves.

The prophet Ezekiel offers a powerful metaphor for this process: *"I will give you a new heart, and a new spirit I will put within you; I will remove the heart of stone from your flesh and give you a heart of flesh"* (Ezekiel 36:26).

A "heart of stone" represents spiritual numbness, going through life without truly feeling the presence of God or the impact of our actions. *Elul* is about softening that heart, making it receptive once again to faith, kindness, and holiness.

Picture a blacksmith working on a piece of iron. If the metal is cold, it cannot be shaped. But if it is heated, it becomes soft and moldable. *Elul* is the time to "heat up" our spiritual lives so that when we enter *Rosh Hashanah*, we are ready to be shaped into the best version of ourselves. The practices and spiritual opportunities of this month provide us with the tools to undertake this holy work of transformation.

While the practices described in this book are distinctly Jewish, rooted in centuries of tradition, the themes they address - self-reflection, forgiveness, personal growth, and spiritual renewal - speak to universal human experiences. According to Jewish teaching, the entire world stands in judgment on *Rosh Hashanah*, making the preparatory work of *Elul* not just personally significant but universally meaningful. *Elul* offers insights into how intentional spiritual preparation can transform not just religious observance, but our entire approach to living with purpose and meaning. Whether Jewish or not, readers will find wisdom in *Elul*'s emphasis on taking time for honest self-examination, seeking reconciliation in relationships, and approaching life's most significant moments with deliberate preparation rather than leaving important things to chance.

The invitation has been extended. The month of preparation has begun.

The only question remaining is: What will we do with this opportunity?

THE MONTH OF *ELUL* – A TIME OF PREPARATION

Biblical and Historical Background

Why does *Elul* hold such deep significance? How did it come to be associated with return and renewal? And what are we actually meant to *do* during these weeks leading up to the High Holidays? To answer these questions, we must turn to the Bible and examine the historical and spiritual origins of this extraordinary month.

Elul's significance as a time of repentance and preparation traces back to one of the most pivotal moments in Israel's history: the giving of the Torah on Mount Sinai. While Moses was receiving the Torah from God on Mount Sinai, the Israelites, fearing that he would not return, fashioned a golden calf and worshiped it, violating the covenant they had just made with God (Exodus 32:1-6). When Moses descended from the mountain and saw the people's sin, he shattered the Tablets of the Law (Exodus 32:19).

Realizing the gravity of the situation, Moses ascended the mountain again to seek atonement on behalf of the people. This ascent lasted forty days, beginning on the first day of the month of *Elul* and ending on the tenth day of the month of *Tishrei*, the date of *Yom Kippur* (Day of Atonement). It was on this day that God granted forgiveness and gave Moses the second set of tablets (Exodus 34:1-2, 27-28).

These forty days became a time of divine mercy and an opportunity for spiritual renewal. Just as Moses sought atonement for the nation, we too use this time to seek forgiveness and return to God with a renewed commitment. And just as Moses ascended Mount Sinai on the first of *Elul* to receive the second tablets, *Elul* is a time when we can climb back up spiritually, knowing that God will forgive us for our mistakes.

What's in a Name?

The name *Elul* itself hints at its purpose. The four Hebrew letters that make up the name of the month, אלול, form an acronym for a verse in Song of Songs: אֲנִי לְדוֹדִי וְדוֹדִי לִי, *"I am my beloved's, and my beloved is mine"* (Song of Songs 6:3). This verse expresses the closeness between us and God during this time. Throughout the year, we may feel distant, distracted, or spiritually lacking. But in *Elul*, God reaches out to us, inviting us to renew our relationship with Him. All this in preparation for the High Holidays, when we coronate God as King and sit in judgment before His throne.

Another lesson of *Elul* can also be found within its name. Spelled backward, Elul (אלול) forms the Hebrew word "*Lulei*" (לולא), meaning "if not for."

Throughout the year, many of us live in "*Lulei*" mode, dwelling on missed possibilities and imagined outcomes: *"If not for that mistake I made... if not for the chances I missed... if not for the hand I was dealt..."*

Elul challenges us to break free from these limiting beliefs. Though we cannot change the past, *Elul* reminds us that we can shape the future. Instead of lamenting over what could have been, we must focus on what we can become. We must break free from regret and wishful thinking, and embrace our current reality. God believes in us; it's time that we begin to believe in ourselves.

"The King is in the Field" – God's Special Closeness During *Elul*

One of the most enduring metaphors for the month of Elul comes from Rabbi Isaac Luria, the Arizal, and was later elaborated upon by Rabbi Shneur Zalman of Liadi: Elul is the time when "the King is in the field."

Most of the time, a king remains in his palace, distant from the common people. Anyone who wishes to approach him must go through layers of guards and protocols. However, when the king leaves the palace and travels through the fields, he becomes accessible to everyone. At that moment, even the simplest farmer can approach the king directly.

This, explains Rabbi Shneur Zalman, is the essence of *Elul*. Throughout the year, many people struggle to feel close to God. But in *Elul*, God is "in the field." He is close to us, making Himself available to every person who seeks Him.

Unlike the awe-filled days of *Rosh Hashanah* and *Yom Kippur*, *Elul* is a time of divine closeness that is gentle and loving. We are not approaching God as a strict judge, but as a compassionate father who longs for His children to return.

The message is clear: No matter how far we may have drifted, God is always ready to welcome us back. During *Elul*, He is reaching out, inviting us to reconnect.

PREPARATION FOR DIVINE ENCOUNTER -
PRACTICAL GUIDE TO THE MONTH OF *ELUL*

Elul is a time for spiritual preparation. Just as one would not enter the presence of a great king without preparing properly, we cannot expect to stand before God on the High Holidays of *Rosh Hashanah* and *Yom Kippur* without preparing ourselves.

In order to prepare ourselves for these meetings with the King, we engage in a process of *Teshuvah*, or repentance. *Teshuvah* is not an instant transformation, it is a process, requiring deep reflection and sincere effort. The month of *Elul* is set aside for this purpose. It is a month of soul-searching, where we examine our actions, our words, and our thoughts. Have we lived up to our potential? Have we fulfilled our responsibilities toward God and our fellow human beings?

To help us focus on this task, several customs are observed during the month of *Elul*:

- Blowing the *shofar* daily
- Reciting Psalm 27
- Recitation of penitential prayers called *Selichot*
- Introspection
- Giving Charity and performing good deeds

Together, these practices provide us with concrete ways to take full advantage of this season of spiritual opportunity. These customs are designed to awaken our hearts, guide us in repentance, and prepare us for our encounter with God, so that when we stand before Him on the High Holidays, we do so with sincerity and readiness.

The Daily Blowing of the Shofar

One of the most striking and well-known customs of the month of *Elul* is the daily blowing of the *shofar*. From the first day of *Elul* until the day before *Rosh Hashanah*, the *shofar* is sounded each day after the morning prayer.

The basis for blowing the shofar in *Elul* is not explicitly mentioned in the Bible, but it is derived from the verse in Amos:

"Shall a shofar be blown in a city, and the people not tremble?" (Amos 3:6).

The sound of the shofar serves as a spiritual wake-up call, reminding us that the Day of Judgment is approaching. Like a spiritual alarm clock, it stirs the soul and encourages us to reflect on our actions. Maimonides describes the message of the shofar as follows:

"Awake, you sleepers, from your sleep! Arise, you slumberers, from your slumber! Examine your deeds, return in repentance, and remember your Creator!"[1]

The traditional pattern for blowing the *shofar*, which consists of both long blasts as well as mid-sized and broken blasts, symbolizes both the call to attention and the crying out of the soul as we prepare for judgment and renewal.

The long, steady *tekiah* blasts shake us awake. They cut through the noise of everyday life and demand our attention. Then come the *shevarim* - three broken, sigh-like sounds that reflect the first cracks in our defenses as we begin to face where we've fallen short. The Kabbalists teach that these blasts are

---

1. Laws of Repentance 3:4

the cry of our souls reaching out - not just sorrow over mistakes, but a deep desire to come closer to God. The quick, trembling *teruah* blasts follow, capturing the raw, urgent cry of that longing.

Unlike the blasts of *Rosh Hashanah*, which are part of the commandment of the day, the shofar blowing in *Elul* is a custom rather than an obligation. Still, its call stirs the soul, helping us ready our hearts for the Days of Awe.

Prayer Additions

Elul is a time of increased prayer. There are two special additions that we make to our daily prayers.

1. Reciting Psalm 27

From the beginning of *Elul* until the end of *Sukkot* (Feast of Tabernacles), it is customary to recite Psalm 27 twice daily, once in the morning and once in the evening. This psalm expresses trust in God's protection and our deep longing to be close to Him, as David writes:

"One thing I have asked from the Lord, that I shall seek: That I may dwell in the house of the Lord all the days of my life, to behold the beauty of the Lord and to meditate in His Temple." (Psalm 27:4).

The sages see a reference to the High Holidays in the words of the psalm itself:

He is "my light" on the New Year, for this is a day of judgment, as it is written (Psalms 37:6), "He will reveal your righteousness like a light, and your justice like the high noon";

and "my salvation" on the Day of Atonement, that He should save us and pardon us for all of our transgressions.[2]

What makes Psalm 27 particularly fitting for this season is its honest portrayal of the fluctuating emotions that characterize our relationship with God during these days. David presents faith not as a static condition but as a dynamic journey. Its opening verses convey confidence and trust, the middle section shifts to yearning and supplication, while the final verses reveal fear and desperation. This three-part movement captures the authentic human experience of faith and how we move between certainty and doubt, between feeling God's presence and fearing His absence. Ultimately, despite the psalm's honest acknowledgment of our shifting emotions and spiritual struggles, it concludes with unwavering faith and trust: "Look to the LORD; be strong and of good courage! O look to the LORD!" (Psalm 27:14).

Elul brings out the same mix of emotions found in Psalm 27. We stand before God in judgment, aware of our flaws and failures - but at the same time, we're invited to draw closer, to seek mercy and return. It's a month of both trembling and hope, and that tension is exactly what Psalm 27 gives voice to, which is why we return to it again and again during this season.

The psalm's final line reminds us that no matter how much we struggle or shift during these weeks, our trust in God's goodness holds steady. That quiet hope is what carries us from the first shofar blast of *Elul* through the closing moments of *Yom Kippur*.

---

2. Midrash Tehillim on Psalm 27

PSALM 27

l'-da-VID a-do-NAI o-REE v'-yish-EE
mi-MEE ee-RA a-do-NAI ma-OZ
kha-YAI mi-MEE ef-KHAD bik-ROV
a-LAI m'-ray-EEM le-e-KHOL et b'-
sa-REE tza-RAI v'-o-y'-VAI LEE HAY-
mah kha-sh'-LU v'-na-FA-lu im ta-
kha-NEH a-LAI ma-kha-NEH lo yee-
RA li-BEE im ta-KUM a-LAI mil-kha-
MAH b'-ZOT a-NEE vo-TAY-akh a-
KHAT sha-AL-tee may-AYT a-do-
NAI o-TAH a-va-KAYSH shiv-TEE b'-
vayt a-do-NAI kol y'-MAY kha-YAI
la-kha-ZOT b'-NO-am a-do-NAI ul-
va-KAYR b'-hay-kha-LO kee yitz-p'-
NAY-nee b'-su-KOH b'-YOM ra-AH
yas-tee-RAY-nee b'-SAY-ter a-ho-LO
b'-TZUR y'-ro-m'-MAY-nee v'-a-TAH
ya-RUM ro-SHEE al o-y'-VAI s'-vee-
vo-TAI v'-ez-b'-KHAH v'-a-ho-LO
ziv-KHAY t'-ru-AH a-SHEE-rah va-
a-za-m'-RAH la-do-NAI sh'-ma a-
do-NAI ko-LEE ek-RA v'-kho-NAY-
nee va-a-NAY-nee l'-KHA a-MAR li-
BEE bak-SHU fa-NAI et pa-NE-kha
a-do-NAI a-va-KAYSH al tas-TAYR
pa-NE-kha mi-ME-nee al tat b'-AF
av-DE-kha ez-ra-TEE ha-YEE-ta al
ti-t'-SHAY-nee v'-al ta-az-VAY-nee
e-lo-HAY yish-EE kee a-VEE v'-i-
MEE a-za-VU-nee va-do-NAI ya-as-
FAY-nee ho-RAY-nee a-do-NAI dar-
KE-kha un-KHAY-nee b'-O-rakh

mee-SHOR l'-MA-an sho-r'-RAI al ti-
t'-NAY-nee b'-NE-fesh tza-RAI kee
KA-mu VEE ay-day SHE-ker vee-
FAY-akh kha-MAS lu-LAY he-e-
MAN-tee lir-OT b'-tuv a-do-NAI b'-
E-retz kha-YEEM ka-VAY el a-do-
NAI kha-ZAK v'-ya-a-MAYTZ li-BE-
kha v'-ka-VAY el a-do-NAI

Of David. The LORD is my light and my
help; whom should I fear? The LORD
is the stronghold of my life, whom
should I dread? When evil men
assail me to devour my flesh— it is
they, my foes and my enemies, who
stumble and fall. Should an army
besiege me, my heart would have no
fear; should war beset me, still
would I be confident. One thing I
ask of the LORD, only that do I seek:
to live in the house of the LORD all
the days of my life, to gaze upon the
beauty of the LORD, to frequent His
temple. He will shelter me in His
pavilion on an evil day, grant me the
protection of His tent, raise me high
upon a rock. Now is my head high
over my enemies round about; I
sacrifice in His tent with shouts of
joy, singing and chanting a hymn to
the LORD. Hear, O LORD, when I cry
aloud; have mercy on me, answer
me. In Your behalf my heart says:

"Seek My face!" O LORD, I seek Your
face. Do not hide Your face from me;
do not thrust aside Your servant in
anger; You have ever been my help.
Do not forsake me, do not abandon
me, O God, my deliverer. Though my
father and mother abandon me, the
LORD will take me in. Show me Your
way, O LORD, and lead me on a level
path because of my watchful foes.
Do not subject me to the will of my
foes, for false witnesses and unjust
accusers have appeared against me.
Had I not the assurance that I would
enjoy the goodness of the LORD in
the land of the living... Look to the
LORD; be strong and of good
courage! O look to the LORD!

2. Selichot – Penitential Prayers

During *Elul*, Jewish communities begin reciting *Selichot*, a collection of penitential prayers which seek divine forgiveness. The Sephardic tradition is to recite *Selichot* throughout the entire month of *Elul*, beginning on the first day of the month. In Ashkenazic communities, *Selichot* usually begin on the Saturday night before *Rosh Hashanah*.[3]

The ideal time for reciting *Selichot* prayers is late at night or

---

3. Sephardic Jews trace their heritage to the Jewish communities of Spain, Portugal, North Africa, and the Middle East, while Ashkenazic Jews originate from Central and Eastern Europe. These groups developed distinct liturgical customs, languages, and religious practices, including variations in holiday observances and prayer rituals.

very early in the morning. According to Jewish mystical tradition, this pre-morning period is considered a time of enhanced divine mercy.

The central theme of the *Selichot* prayers is the invocation of God's Thirteen Attributes of Mercy, which were revealed to Moses as he sought atonement for the sin of the Golden Calf. These attributes, recorded in Exodus 34:6-7, include God's proclamation: "The Lord, the Lord, God, compassionate and gracious, slow to anger, and abundant in lovingkindness and truth, preserving kindness for thousands, forgiving iniquity, transgression, and sin." According to the Talmud,[4] God Himself taught Moses these words, promising that whenever the Jewish people sincerely recite them, He will forgive their sins. The *Selichot* prayers are offered with humility and sincerity, seeking to invoke God's mercy and forgiveness.

But what is it about reciting these thirteen attributes that grants forgiveness? Do they possess a kind of magical power? And why thirteen? Rabbi Mordechai Hacohen explains that the number thirteen signifies infinity, transcending the boundaries of order and structure represented by the number twelve. While twelve denotes limitations, such as the twelve months of the year, thirteen stands for boundlessness and the immeasurable. This is reflected in the thirteen Attributes of Mercy, which demonstrate that God's mercy is limitless and unconditional. No matter how far we fall, God will always extend His mercy to help and forgive.[5]

However, it is not enough to merely recite these thirteen attributes. The sages phrase God's instruction to Moses in an unusual way: "they shall do before Me according to this order."

---

4. Babylonian Talmud, Rosh Hashanah 17b
5. Siftei Cohen al HaTorah, p.578

The word "do" is key here. The act of reciting them must be coupled with the intention to live by them.

Maimonides explains that we are called to imitate God's attributes: "Just as He is called 'Gracious,' you shall be gracious; just as He is called 'Merciful,' you shall be merciful; just as He is called 'Holy,' you shall be holy."[6] The divine attributes we invoke - "Slow to anger," "Abundant in kindness," "Righteous," "Just," "Perfect" - are not merely descriptions of God's nature but a moral blueprint for human behavior. A person is obligated to internalize these attributes and reflect them in their own conduct to the extent that they are able.

In this way, the Thirteen Attributes of Mercy are not only a means of seeking God's forgiveness but also a guide for how we should strive to act in the world. By living in accordance with these attributes, we align ourselves with the Divine and bring God's mercy into our own lives.

Self-Examination and Spiritual Inventory

Elul is a time for deep introspection, a chance to reconnect with our purpose and strengthen our relationship with God. It is an opportunity to engage in spiritual accounting. Just as a business owner periodically reviews their financial records, ensuring that nothing is overlooked, we too must periodically assess our deeds, our speech, and our thoughts.

The Bible teaches us, "Let us search and examine our ways, and return to the Lord" (Lamentations 3:40). A relationship with God, like any meaningful relationship, cannot thrive on autopilot. It requires active engagement, intentional reflection,

---

6. Laws of Personal Development 1:6

and consistent effort. Just as we nurture our connections with family and friends through communication and understanding, we must also devote time and energy to our relationship with God.

During the month of *Elul*, we are encouraged to pause and reflect on the past year. We ask ourselves important questions: Have I truly fulfilled my potential? Have I treated others with kindness, integrity, and honesty? Have I deepened my connection with God and adhered more closely to His commandments? We take stock of our actions and intentions, learn from the past, and make meaningful changes that will allow us to grow in the year ahead.

Many people keep a written record of their reflections, making a list of areas in which they need improvement. This helps to ensure that their repentance is focused and sincere. The more honest we are in our self-examination, the more meaningful our repentance will be.

This spiritual accounting is a step in the process of repentance. In Hebrew, we call it *teshuvah*, which literally means "return." Repentance is often misunderstood as merely expressing regret for past actions. In reality, *teshuvah* is about restoring our connection or returning to God and to our soul's pure essence.

The Sages recount an allegorical "conversation" in which Wisdom and Prophecy are asked, "What is the punishment for a sinner?" Wisdom responds with the verse from Proverbs 13:21, "and evil shall pursue sinners." The natural consequence of sin is misfortune or punishment, as evil inevitably pursues those who choose a path of wickedness. Prophecy answers that the punishment is death. However, when the same question is posed to God, He responds, "Let him repent, and I will forgive him."[7]

Justice is real - our choices matter, and there are consequences. But punishment is not what God wants. What He truly desires is our return. That's the mystery of *teshuvah*. Logically, a person who sins should face the results of their actions. But God goes beyond logic. He offers us something undeserved: a way back. *Teshuvah* is a gift; an invitation to come home, to reclaim our truest selves, and to renew our bond with the One who never stopped waiting for us.

This is reflected in the High Holiday prayer in which we recite, "until his last day, He waits for him. If he returns, He will immediately accept him." This teaching illustrates the depth of God's patience and mercy: no matter how far we have strayed, God never gives up hope for our return. He waits for us patiently and with open arms until the very end of our lives. This is the essence of God's mercy: He does not want us to suffer; He wants us to repent and return to Him. The gift of *teshuvah* is not bound by rational limits or timelines, and it is available to us whenever we are ready to come home.

The Sages tell the story of Eleazar ben Dordaya, a man known for chasing every form of physical pleasure. His reputation was so notorious that there wasn't a prostitute he hadn't visited. One day, he heard of a courtesan renowned for both her beauty and her price, and he traveled a great distance to reach her.

During their meeting, she made an offhand remark that struck like a blow: "Just as a breath once exhaled can never return, so too, someone like you can never truly repent." She meant it as a

---

7. Pesikda D'rav Kahana 25:7

comment in passing - but for Eleazar, it shattered something inside.

In that moment, he was overwhelmed with a sense that he had gone too far, that he was lost. Desperate, he fled to a quiet place between the mountains and pleaded for help - not from people, but from the world itself. He called out to the mountains, the heavens, the sun and moon, the stars - begging them to intercede for him. But each one, in turn, reminded him: *We too are not eternal. We also need mercy.*

That's when the truth hit him: *It depends on me. No one else can do this for me.* Alone, broken, and overwhelmed, he wept so deeply that his soul left his body.

And then a voice from heaven declared: "Rabbi Eleazar ben Dordaya is welcomed into eternal life." When Rabbi Judah heard what happened, he cried and said, "Some people earn their place in the World to Come after a lifetime of work - and some in a single moment."[8]

No matter how far a person has fallen, there is always a path back to God. It also shows that true repentance can be immediate, no matter how distant or sinful one may feel. Even the most extreme cases of sinfulness are not beyond the reach of repentance. God does not want us to suffer; He wants us to return to Him and experience the fullness of His mercy.

The Process of Teshuvah

The process of *teshuvah* is outlined by Maimonides[9] and involves four essential steps: 1) taking an honest look at our actions and recognizing what we have done wrong; 2) feeling

---

8. Babylonian Talmud, Avoda Zara 17a
9. Laws of Repentance 2:2

sincere regret over what we have done, not just because of the consequences, but because we understand the spiritual damage caused; 3) resolving firmly not to repeat the mistake; and 4) verbalizing our repentance through confession before God.

Teshuvah goes beyond simply acknowledging mistakes. It is not about guilt or punishment, but about restoration and coming home to one's true self and relationship with God. The four-step process outlined by Maimonides creates a complete journey from recognition through regret to resolution and confession, leading us toward the goal of return, renewal, and becoming who we were meant to be.

This process is deeply psychological. It requires self-awareness, humility, and the courage to face one's imperfections. The Sages[10] teach that when *teshuvah* is done out of love for God, not only are past sins forgiven, but they are transformed into merits.

When a person takes one step toward God, He comes running to meet them.[11] During this month of divine closeness, each effort we make in *teshuvah* is amplified, helping us uncover our own potential for holiness and genuine transformation.

Seeking and Granting Forgiveness

The Bible repeatedly teaches that before we can have a close relationship with God, we must treat others properly. A clear example of this is in Isaiah 1:11-17, where God expresses His frustration with sacrifices and rituals that are not accompanied by justice and kindness. "To what purpose is the multitude of your sacrifices unto Me? ... Wash yourselves,

---

10. Babylonian Talmud, Yoma 86b
11. Shir HaShirim Rabbah 5:3

make yourselves clean; put away the evil of your doings from before My eyes; cease to do evil; learn to do good, seek justice, help the oppressed." (Isaiah 1:11, 16-17). God values righteous actions and caring for others more than merely performing religious rituals.

One key aspect of *Elul* is making amends with those we've wronged. Before asking God for forgiveness, we must first seek forgiveness from the people we've hurt. True repentance involves both repairing our relationship with God and ensuring that we treat others with fairness, kindness, and respect.

Maimonides elaborates on this principle: "For sins between a person and God, Yom Kippur atones. But for sins between one person and another, Yom Kippur does not atone until one seeks forgiveness from his fellow."[12] *Elul* is therefore the time to reach out to friends, family, colleagues, and anyone we may have hurt - whether intentionally or unintentionally.

The spiritual work of making amends includes both asking for forgiveness and granting forgiveness to others. Granting forgiveness is just as important as seeking it. Holding onto grudges weighs down the soul, while releasing them allows us to enter the High Holidays with a pure heart. It also has an equally important benefit; if God sees that we are willing to forgive others, He will be more willing to forgive us.

The Torah itself commands this practice of reconciliation: "You shall not hate your brother in your heart; you shall surely rebuke your neighbor, and not bear sin because of him." (Leviticus 19:17). Letting go of resentment and making peace

---

12. Laws of Repentance 2:9

with others becomes one of the most powerful forms of preparation for *Rosh Hashanah* and *Yom Kippur*.

Charity and Good Deeds

Elul is a time for waking up - spiritually, emotionally, and morally. As we prepare for the Days of Awe, Jewish tradition encourages us to take concrete steps toward change. One of the most powerful of these is giving *tzedakah* - charity. Rabbi Moshe Isserles points to the custom of giving *tzedakah* on the eve of *Rosh Hashanah* as a way of entering the new year with a clean slate,[13] but the practice of increasing charitable giving throughout *Elul* has long been part of our tradition.

This emphasis finds support in the verse from Isaiah (1:27): "Zion shall be redeemed with justice, and her returnees with righteousness (*tzedakah*)." Though not originally tied to *Elul*, many commentators read this verse as highlighting the central role of charity in achieving both personal and national redemption.

The Lubavitcher Rebbe, Rabbi Menachem Mendel Schneerson, deepened this idea by noting the Torah portion of *Re'eh*, which is always read just before *Elul*. In this portion, we are commanded to "open your hand generously" (Deuteronomy 15:8). The timing of this Torah portion is no coincidence. *Elul* is a time when divine mercy is near, and we are asked to reflect that mercy in our own actions.

But giving charity in *Elul* is about more than hoping to earn divine favor. As the Rebbe taught, it's about becoming more like God. When we give freely and with compassion, we mirror the divine trait of mercy and invite that same mercy into our

---

13. Orach Chaim 581:1

lives. It's a way to repair what's broken, open our hearts, and step into the new year ready to be kinder - to others and to ourselves.

Conclusion

The month of *Elul* tackles some of life's most challenging questions: How do we become better people? How do we repair damaged relationships? How do we break free from patterns that hold us back?

The practice of taking a spiritual inventory provides a model for honest self-reflection that anyone can adapt, whether examining relationships, professional conduct, or personal character. The emphasis on seeking forgiveness and making amends addresses our deep need for reconciliation and healing in our relationships. *Elul*'s focus on character refinement - working on traits like patience, kindness, and integrity - offers practical wisdom for anyone seeking personal growth. The month's call to draw closer to the Divine resonates with seekers of all faiths who long for deeper spiritual connection and purpose.

Most significantly, *Elul* demonstrates that meaningful transformation requires intentional preparation and sustained effort over time, rather than expecting instant change. The rhythm of daily spiritual practices, regular self-examination, and gradual character development provides a roadmap for anyone committed to becoming their best self. Real growth requires honest self-assessment, relationships take ongoing work to maintain and repair, and spiritual development needs both our own effort and divine grace.

Elul is not just a month of preparation; it is a month of transformation. *Elul* is a time when the barriers between human beings and God are lowered, allowing us to reconnect with our Creator in a more personal and immediate way.

The month of *Elul* is a gift. It is a time of divine closeness, an opportunity to return to God, and a chance to repair our relationships with others. Through the *shofar*, prayer, self-examination, forgiveness and charity, we prepare ourselves to stand before God on *Rosh Hashanah* with sincerity and humility.

God's promise is clear:

"Return to Me, and I will return to you." (Malachi 3:7).

The question is not whether God is ready to welcome us back, but whether we are ready to take the first step.

COLLECTED INSIGHTS

Spires and Towers

Rabbi Elie Mischel

In his spiritual memoir, *Surprised by Joy*, C.S. Lewis describes his first trip to Oxford University as a young man in 1916. A scholarly boy, Lewis traveled to this fabled center of learning, known as the "city of dreaming spires," with tremendous anticipation. But upon leaving the train station, Lewis became more and more bewildered; could this succession of "mean shops" and unimpressive streets really be Oxford? Lewis walked through the shabby town until he reached open country; only then did he turn around and look. "There, behind me... never more beautiful since, was the fabled cluster of spires and towers. I had come out of the [train] station on the wrong side and been all this time walking into the mean and sprawling suburb of Botley. I did not see to what extent this little adventure was an allegory of my whole life." The glories of Oxford, its spires and towers, were right behind Lewis, after all. All he had to do was turn around.

The spiritual seekers of our community – and there are more than we realize! – are frustrated; they are yearning for "spires and towers," but finding none. Though we fill our days with rituals and obligations – religious, communal and social – we are left with a gnawing feeling that somehow, we are missing the main course. For too many people, Judaism is perceived and experienced as a set of ritual and ethical practices; practices that may make us better people, but which have little relevance to our deep, inner yearning for a relationship with God. We know that there must be something deeper, something far more extraordinary – if only we knew where to look.

According to the Sages, the Hebrew letters of the word *Elul* (אלול), the name of the Hebrew month leading up to the High Holidays, is an acronym for the words found in Song of Songs (6:3). The Hebrew words for "I am my beloved's and my beloved is mine" are אני לדודי ודודי לי. The first letter of each of these four words spell *Elul* (אלול). *Elul* is the "big picture" month when we remember that the ultimate goal of all the rituals and obligations is to achieve a real, personal - and even romantic - relationship with our Creator. "I am my beloved's and my beloved is mine" - *Elul* is the antidote to "transactional" service of God; it is our opportunity, finally, to see the spires and towers that we long for.

The first step towards a deeper connection with God is to acknowledge that something fundamental, something essential, is missing from our religious lives. In other words, the first step is to *yearn* for something deeper; to feel a deep emptiness in our lives, an emptiness that can only be filled by a personal relationship with our Creator. This, fundamentally, is the theme of the month of *Elul*.

The English poet and painter William Blake once wrote: "I wander through each chartered street, Near where the chartered Thames does flow, And mark in every face I meet, Marks of weariness, marks of woe. In every cry of every Man, In every Infant's cry of fear, In every voice, in every ban, The mind-forged manacles I hear."[14]

In every face he meets, Blake finds "marks of weakness, marks of woe." Every community has its share of woes – political,

---

14. William Blake, "London," in Songs of Experience (1794).

financial and more. No one has ever lacked difficulties and challenges. But worst of all are the "mind-forged manacles," the mental prisons of our own creation – the tragic ways in which we limit our religious experience to the technical and superficial.

Rabbi Abraham Isaac HaCohen Kook, the first Ashkenazi Chief Rabbi of Israel, wrote that the people who live during the final generations before the Messiah arrives will no longer be satisfied with the details of religion. They will demand to see the forest, the panoramic view.[15]

We are in a generation where people are searching. Young people are not rejecting God, but rather seeking a form of faith that is deeper than what they grew up with. They yearn for a profound connection with the Divine, a glimpse of those "spires and towers" that C.S. Lewis so poignantly described. The month of *Elul* is a reminder that the essence of faith lies not in the minutiae of religious practice, though they are important, but in cultivating a personal, transformative relationship with our Creator.

As we approach the High Holidays, let us take a moment to turn around, like Lewis did in Oxford, and behold the spiritual magnificence that has been behind us all along. Let us break free from our "mind-forged manacles" and embrace the opportunity to deepen our faith, to see beyond the "mean shops" of routine observance and discover the awe-inspiring vistas of genuine spiritual connection. And as more and more people search for the forest beyond the trees, for the panoramic view of faith rather than just its details, we may dare to hope that we are witnessing the dawn of redemption.

---

15. Rabbi Abraham Isaac HaCohen Kook, Orot HaTeshuva [The Lights of Repentance], ch. 4, sec. 10.

What's Next?

Sara Lamm

As we look back on the 23rd anniversary of September 11th and simultaneously approach the first anniversary of October 7th, this question weighs heavily on our minds. Time has moved swiftly since these respective tragedies, yet in many ways, it feels as though it has stood still. We continue to wait - for answers, for peace, for the release of the hostages. The uncertainty of what comes next lingers in the air, leaving us searching for something to hold on to, some assurance of what the future might bring. In times like these, the Bible offers us a unique kind of comfort. Not by revealing what lies ahead, but by guiding us on how to live meaningfully in the present.

Human nature often compels us to seek certainty about the future. We want to know what is coming so we can prepare, protect ourselves, or find solace in the idea that everything is part of a predetermined plan. As a mega planner, I sometimes feel like the queen of needing to know what will be, both in the big picture and the little picture. And I'm positive I'm not alone with this thought. If only we had a magic eight ball to look into the future. But the Bible takes a different stance. It explicitly discourages turning to such practices, reminding us that the pursuit of certainty about what lies ahead is not the way to find peace or clarity.

Instead, the Bible teaches us a deeper truth in the verse (Deuteronomy 18:13): "You must be wholehearted with the Lord your God"

This verse challenges us to avoid becoming consumed by what we cannot know. Instead of worrying about the future, we are encouraged to live with sincerity, integrity, and a wholehearted commitment to the present. Rather than trying to uncover what is hidden or predict the unpredictable, the Bible urges us to focus on our actions and intentions here and now.

This message is particularly significant in the context of Jewish thought, which emphasizes the power of free will. Judaism does not see the future as an unchangeable script; rather, it is something we co-create through our choices and behaviors. The future is open-ended, shaped by our deeds, our values, and our willingness to change. It's here in the words of the Bible that we find a sense of agency and responsibility. In the midst of uncertainty, we hold the power to influence what happens next.

The concept of free will becomes especially poignant during the Hebrew month of *Elul*, a time of reflection, repentance, and renewal in the Jewish calendar. As we prepare for the High Holy Days, we engage in *teshuvah* - returning to our true selves, seeking forgiveness, and committing to change. *Elul* reminds us that each year, we are granted an opportunity to start anew, to learn from the past, and to make different choices for the future. It is a time when we are encouraged to ask, "What will I do next?" rather than "What will happen next?"

During *Elul*, we are reminded that God believes in our capacity for growth and transformation. The Bible teaches us that in these days, God extends a hand to those who sincerely seek to come closer to Him. It is a period of divine openness, where our efforts to return, renew, and repair are met with divine assistance. This idea is a profound comfort in uncertain times: while we may not know what lies ahead, we are assured that our efforts to improve and change are never in vain.

Thus, the question of "What's next?" is reframed. Instead of allowing fear of the unknown to paralyze us, we are called to take action in the present. The Bible guides us to trust that by living with integrity, compassion, and wholeheartedness today, we contribute to shaping a future that is meaningful and just. Our deeds, no matter how small or seemingly insignificant, have the potential to make a real impact on the world around us.

Ultimately, it's what we choose to do in the face of uncertainty, whether we choose fear or faith, resignation or resolve, that will make all the difference in *what is next*.

Growth, Faith and New Beginnings

Shira Schechter

The start of a new school year always feels like the beginning of a new chapter - a moment filled with anticipation, excitement, and a hint of uncertainty. This year is especially poignant for me as my oldest child begins high school, a milestone that feels like a giant leap toward adulthood. As the doors of the school open, they usher in not only a new academic year but also a new stage in life for us as a family.

For parents, these transitions evoke a blend of pride and nostalgia. We look at our children, once so small and dependent, now growing into independent, thoughtful individuals. Watching them step into a new phase of their lives is thrilling, yet also tinged with a sense of loss. Their childhood seems to slip a little further away with each passing day. But within that bittersweet mix lies a deep sense of hope and possibility, as each new beginning carries the promise of discovery, growth, and transformation.

New beginnings are often filled with mixed emotions. For my child, high school is an exciting but intimidating adventure - new teachers, new subjects, new friendships, and in his case, dorm life. As parents, we want to protect them from the hardships of growing up, yet we also recognize that the struggles they face will shape them into resilient, capable adults. We know that with each new challenge, they learn something invaluable about themselves, building confidence, resilience, and self-awareness.

In the Torah, the journey of the Israelites from Egypt to the Promised Land is filled with similar emotional complexity. After being freed from slavery, they faced an uncertain future in the desert. Their journey was long and filled with moments of doubt, fear, and complaint. They didn't always know what lay ahead, and at times, they even longed for the familiarity of their old life in Egypt. But throughout that journey, they were growing as a people, learning to trust themselves and their relationship with God.

One of the key lessons of the Israelites' journey is the importance of embracing the unknown with faith. As they stood at the shores of the Sea of Reeds, not knowing how they would cross as the Egyptians rapidly approached from behind, panic set in:

And they said to Moses, "Was it for want of graves in Egypt that you brought us to die in the wilderness? What have you done to us, taking us out of Egypt? Is this not the very thing we told you in Egypt, saying, 'Let us be, and we will serve the Egyptians, for it is better for us to serve the Egyptians than to die in the wilderness'?" (Exodus 14:11-12)

In that moment of fear, Moses responded:

But Moses said to the people, "Have no fear! Stand by, and witness the deliverance which the Lord will work for you today; for the Egyptians whom you see today you will never see again. The Lord will battle for you; you hold your peace!" (Exodus 14:13-14)

He taught them to trust in divine guidance and to believe that even in the face of uncertainty, they were not alone. Similarly, we too must have faith that the new beginnings in our lives will lead us to where we are meant to be. This story reminds us that while the path forward may not always be clear, every step we take is part of a greater journey of personal and spiritual growth.

The beginning of the school year always coincides with the Hebrew month of *Elul*, a time of renewal on the Jewish calendar. *Elul* is the final month of the year, leading us into *Rosh Hashanah*, the Jewish New Year. In Jewish tradition, *Elul* is a time of introspection, preparation, and rebirth. It's a month when we reflect on the year gone by, assess our actions, and think about how we want to grow in the year ahead.

The resonance between the personal journey of starting a new school year and the spiritual journey of *Elul* is striking. Both involve stepping into the unknown, carrying lessons from the past while preparing for the opportunities and challenges that lie ahead. Just as students sharpen their pencils and prepare their minds for the year to come, during *Elul*, we sharpen our souls, reflecting on who we are and who we want to be in the coming year.

Every new beginning is a gift. It's an opportunity to start fresh, to build on what we've learned, and to set new intentions for the future. Whether it's a new school year, a new life stage, or the start of a new spiritual year, these moments invite us to pause, reflect, and embrace the possibilities ahead.

As we navigate these new beginnings, whether in school, in life, or in our spiritual journey, we carry with us the lessons of the past but remain open to the surprises and opportunities of the future. In the balance between reflection and anticipation, between holding on and letting go, we find the true gift of new beginnings: the chance to grow, to explore, and to become the best versions of ourselves.

May this season of new beginnings bring growth, courage, and joy to all of us as we move forward with hope and faith.

A Beloved Relationship

Sara Lamm

One of my favorite songs is "Dodi Li" by Peter, Paul, and Mary. Their music was the soundtrack of my youth, and "Dodi Li" resonated with me so deeply that it was the song I chose to walk down the aisle to at my wedding. Aside from its beautiful melody and words which originate from the *Song of Songs*, it felt incredibly timely — I got married just two days before the Hebrew month of *Elul*. The Hebrew letters of *Elul*, Aleph (א), Lamed (ל), Vav (ו), Lamed (ל), form an acronym for "Ani L'dodi V'dodi Li" (אני לדודי ודודי לי), meaning "I am my beloved's and my beloved is mine" (Song of Songs 6:3).

It was a sweet and lovely coincidence that made the song even more meaningful for my wedding.

Did you know that this love-infused verse is also incredibly relevant to the Hebrew month of *Elul*? *Elul* is the last month of the Jewish year and marks the formal beginning of the High Holiday season, perhaps the most important period in the Jewish calendar. But what do loving relationships have to do with this month, and how do they connect to the High Holidays in general?

The High Holidays begin on the first day of the Hebrew month of *Tishrei*, typically falling in September or October. *Rosh Hashanah*, the Jewish New Year, kicks off this festive month, followed by *Yom Kippur*, the Day of Atonement. Then comes *Sukkot*, the Festival of Booths, and finally *Shemini Atzeret* and *Simchat Torah*, which mark the conclusion of *Sukkot* and the celebration of completing the annual cycle of reading the Torah. It's a lot to keep track of! However, the days leading up to these holidays, including the month of *Elul*, are considered incredibly meaningful and auspicious.

The phrase "*Ani L'dodi V'dodi Li*" captures the spirit of *Elul*. Rather than seeing this period as one solely of solemnity, the *Song of Songs* invites us to view it through the lens of love. *Elul* is traditionally considered a time of *teshuva*, or repentance, where we reflect on our actions over the past year and strive to return to our best selves. But it's also a time to renew and deepen our relationship with God. The phrase reminds us that our bond with the Divine is not based on fear or obligation but on a reciprocal, loving connection — like that of two partners who cherish one another.

One practical aspect of the month of *Elul* is the recitation of *Selichot*, prayers asking for forgiveness. These prayers are designed to evoke God's mercy and remind us of His compassionate nature, always ready to welcome us back.ˆAt the heart of the *Selichot* prayers are the Thirteen Attributes of Mercy, a set of divine qualities revealed to Moses on Mount Sinai after the sin of the Golden Calf:

"The Lord passed before him and proclaimed: "Lord! Lord! a God compassionate and gracious, slow to anger, abounding in kindness and faithfulness, extending kindness to the thousandth generation, forgiving iniquity, transgression, and sin; yet He does not remit all punishment, but visits the iniquity of parents upon children and children's children, upon the third and fourth generations" (Exodus 34:6-7).

These attributes — including compassion, grace, patience, kindness, and truth — tell us *who* God is. They reveal a God who is not just a distant judge but a loving partner, eager to forgive and embrace us.

Throughout the month of *Elul*, we repeat these attributes over and over, allowing them to sink into our consciousness. They remind us of the kind of relationship we have with God, one rooted in love and mercy. As we meditate on these qualities, we begin to understand that "*Ani L'dodi V'dodi Li*" is not just a poetic verse but a real description of our bond with God. Just as in any loving relationship, knowing the qualities of the one we love helps us to connect more deeply with them.

In this way, the Thirteen Attributes serve as a bridge to connect us with God throughout *Elul*. By repeating them, we are reminded of His forgiving and compassionate nature. If God, who is all-knowing and omnipotent, is always ready to welcome us back with love, how much more should we strive to return to Him with open hearts? It is this understanding that transforms our relationship with God from one of fear to one of love and intimacy.

The idea that "I am for my beloved, and my beloved is for me" is more than just a romantic sentiment. It is a call to action. *Elul* invites us to view our relationship with God not as a contract but as a dynamic and evolving relationship. God is not only a judge or ruler but also a beloved who desires our presence, connection, and our return. This shift from a fearful relationship to a loving, reciprocal one helps us understand that repentance is not about mere compliance but about deepening our connection with the Divine.

A Time to Forget

Rabbi Elie Mischel

Tony LaRussa, the the all-time-great manager of the St Louis Cardinals, wrote a book called One Last Strike, in which he tells the story of the Cardinals' amazing and unlikely run to the World Series in 2011 and offers lessons on leadership based on his experiences. As a manager, LaRussa was famous for his extreme attention to detail, and this book is true to form. He spends pages and pages elaborating on tiny details of baseball strategy – mind-numbing stuff!

Something strange happens when La Russa gets to the more controversial parts of his story. Take the time he famously sent in the wrong pitcher because of a bad phone connection - a major blunder. When he writes about it, he offers only a few vague, unsatisfying lines. The same goes for his DUI arrest. It's mentioned, but barely.

It makes you wonder: is there a double standard here? La Russa insists that great leaders must sweat the small stuff, and he recalls every detail of his triumphs with razor-sharp clarity. But when it comes to his failures, his memory seems to go fuzzy - and all we're left with is a brief mention before he moves on.

Perhaps nothing in the beginning of the Bible is as shocking as the first murder in the history of mankind. No matter how many times we read the story, Cain's act of murder remains appalling. You would think that God would use this opportunity to make an example of Cain. The Bible itself says that we should take an eye for an eye, so why wasn't Cain punished with death?

But that is not what happens.

"The Lord said to Cain, 'Where is your brother Abel?' And he said, 'I do not know. Am I my brother's keeper?' 'What have you done? Hark, your brother's blood cries out to Me from the ground! Therefore, you shall be more cursed than the ground, which opened its mouth to receive your brother's blood from your hand. If you till the soil, it shall no longer yield its strength to you. You shall become a ceaseless wanderer on earth'" (Genesis 4:9-12).

God allows Cain to live, and instead of death, he is punished with exile and wandering.

Was Cain being let off the hook? He murdered his brother, exile does not seem like a severe enough punishment for such a despicable act.

As a father, I know that little children possess an extraordinary, almost magical characteristic. Young children have the ability to hit the reset button every five minutes. They could be yelling and screaming about some injustice one minute, and then five minutes later they've completely forgotten what just happened. They don't stew over things. They get upset and frustrated and then they move on.

Rabbi Nachman of Breslov, the founder of the Breslov Hasidic movement, explained that young children hold the secret to a successful approach to life. We generally find it frustrating that we are constantly forgetting things, but Rabbi Nachman says that forgetting is one of the great blessings in life that we simply don't appreciate; it's what enables us to move on and start over. If we didn't forget, we would spend our lives weighed down by memories of our failures.

Based on this explanation, we can appreciate Cain's punishment. God did not punish Cain with the death penalty.

Instead, he punished him with something much worse. For the rest of his life, Cain would never be able to settle down. He would never be permitted to "move on" and forget his sin. He lived the rest of his days with his sin directly in front of his eyes, and nothing could be worse than that.

This brings us back to Tony LaRussa. Is he a hypocrite for encouraging us to dive into details and yet refusing to do just that when it comes to his own failings? Maybe so. But Tony LaRussa's "selective memory" may very well be the secret to his success as a manager. Baseball is famously a game of failure. Even the best players and managers constantly mess up. Tony LaRussa achieved incredible success specifically because he mastered the art of forgetting. He controlled as much of the game as he could, and simply dissociated himself from what he couldn't control.

The Hebrew month of *Elul* and the High Holidays are times to remember. They are the times of year set aside for reflecting on our past and remembering our sins. But when they are over, we must master the art of forgetting. We need to learn how to start fresh and not allow ourselves to be weighed down by memories of our past failures. If you do something that you are ashamed of you should apologize to whomever you've wronged and apologize to God. But then you have to move on.

There is a time to remember and a time to forget. Following the High Holidays is the time to forget.

The Month of Return

Adam Eliyahu Berkowitz

Anticipation and preparation are two words I have always had difficulty with. When I studied in *yeshiva*,[16] my rabbi called me "do-ish." I have a tendency to jump right in and figure things out as I go along.

Objectively speaking, the Jewish calendar seems poorly designed. Instead of being spread evenly throughout the year, the holidays are clustered together. My rabbi used to joke that you have to be half-crazy to be an observant Jew and if you weren't already there, the High Holidays would take you all the way. *Rosh Hashana*, which begins on the first of the Hebrew month of *Tishrei*, is intense. Ten days later we get hit with *Yom Kippur,* a day of fasting and prayer . And as soon as *Yom Kippur* ends, Jews rush outside and begin building their *sukkot* (booths for the Feast of Tabernacles), which starts only five days later.

Tishrei is an intense month of repentance and closeness to God. But it doesn't begin in *Tishrei*. Already 30 days prior, at the beginning of the preceding month known as *Elul*, we begin the process of repentance. Starting on the first of the month, we blow the *shofar* at the end of the morning prayer service as a wake-up call to repent, and we add Psalm 27 at the end of the morning and evening services.

Why do we need to start to prepare so far in advance? Can't we just show up at the High Holidays and pour out our hearts to God? Why do we need to spend a whole month getting ready?

When I was a line cook, I made hundreds of trips to the

---

16. A *yeshivah* is a traditional Jewish educational institution devoted primarily to the study of the Torah and rabbinic literature

refrigerator and pantry for ingredients or equipment. I got fast
- really fast - racing to the back of the kitchen at breakneck
speed few could match. Then I went to work for David
Waltuck, one of the top chefs in Manhattan. At first, I couldn't
figure out what made him such a great chef. He never yelled,
and he never, ever ran. Yet food seemed to magically appear on
the plate, perfectly prepared.

One day, after a particularly hectic dinner service, David
handed me a prep list - and my life changed. The work didn't
get easier, but everything shifted. Instead of running around
during dinner service, I ran around before it. Instead of three
frantic hours while waiters were screaming for food, I had two
frantic hours beforehand.

It may not sound like much of a tradeoff, but it made all the
difference. When everything was prepped, my cooking was
more thoughtful. I had the time - and the peace of mind - to
focus on what was actually going on the plate and to make
adjustments as needed. Part of me resisted David's method. It
seemed to go against the magic of being "in the moment,"
watching everything come together in a flash of creativity, as if
the dish had assembled itself. But his method worked. It
worked consistently. And it made me a better chef.

Rosh Hashanah and *Yom Kippur* mark a process of *teshuvah*, a
return to God, that dominates much of the Hebrew month of
Tishrei. But the preparation for that intense spiritual period
begins earlier, in the month of *Elul*. By the end of *Elul*, we're
meant to reach some level of reconciliation with our Creator.
That kind of transformation would be impossible without a
prep list.

Rosh Hashanah kicks off *Tishrei*. But jumping straight into it
without preparation is a recipe for an overwhelming, chaotic

Yom Kippur. Judaism anticipates this. That's why we're given *Elul* - a full month to get ready. It's the secret to a well-prepared *teshuvah*.

Jewish tradition teaches that *Elul* is an acronym for *Ani L'Dodi v'Dodi Li* - "I am my beloved's and my beloved is mine" (Song of Songs 6:3). This verse describes our relationship with God like a romance. And every romance needs spontaneity - a spark, something alive and unplanned. But even spontaneity, I've learned, takes preparation.

As a man, I'll admit this was not instinctive for me. But watching my wife get ready for a quick, 'spontaneous' date has taught me otherwise. Even the magical moments take planning.

The same is true in our relationship with God. The most meaningful prayers are rarely the ones that go according to script. The best prayers are real conversations - a give-and-take where both sides speak from the heart. But that kind of prayer doesn't happen by accident. It takes preparation.

I usually spend *Elul* preparing my talking points - thinking through what I'll say in my defense when I stand before God on *Yom Kippur*. *Rosh Hashanah* is the day to reflect on the past year and crown God as King. *Yom Kippur* is when we stand in judgment and confess. But for me, it all starts in *Elul*.

The most powerful *Rosh Hashanah* I ever had was the year I carried a notebook with me throughout *Elul*. I wrote down everything that had happened over the past year. That year, *Rosh Hashanah* felt a little less frantic, a little more focused. I missed the last-minute adrenaline rush - scouring my memory for one more act of kindness, one more commandment I could mention in my defense. But the preparation gave me space to really reflect on my journey toward God: how far I had come, how much it had enriched my life, and how I planned to grow even more in the year ahead.

Hear the Lion Roar

Rabbi Elie Mischel

The following scenario is probably familiar to many of us: Summer was great, but with a couple of weeks between the end of camp and the first day of school, we find our kids becoming restless and ready to return to routine. They miss the structured days and the company of classmates.

Finally, the much-awaited first day of school arrives. With backpacks ready and new shoes shining, the drive to school is filled with anticipation. But as the school gates approach, the hesitation sets in. The familiarity of home seems far more appealing than the daunting school corridors.

What changes in those few moments between leaving home and arriving at school, transforming eagerness into hesitation?

"A lion has roared, Who can but fear? My God has spoken, Who can but prophesy?" (Amos 3:8)

The prophet Amos declares that there is no one who wouldn't fear a lion's roar. He's clearly talking about a lion in the wild - not one behind a thick wall of glass at the zoo. There, we watch safely, even eat lunch while the lions pace. But if that barrier were gone, if nothing stood between us and the lion, we'd be filled with fear. And rightly so.

Rabbi Isaiah Horowitz taught that on a deeper level, the letters of the Hebrew word for lion, אַ-רְ-יֵ-ה (aryeh), stand for *Elul* (אלול), *Rosh Hashana* (ראש השנה), *Yom Kippur* (יום כיפור) and the last day of *Sukkot* (Feast of Tabernacles) known as *Hoshana Rabba* (הושענא רבה); the Days of Awe and the month leading up to them. According to Rabbi Horowitz, Amos was really saying, "who does not fear and tremble during this time of year?" Just as everyone fears the roar of a lion, we fear the Days of Awe.[17]

This insight holds the key to truly experiencing the High Holidays. Just as a lion's roar only strikes fear when there's nothing separating us from the lion, we can only be moved by these days if we lower the emotional walls that keep us at a distance.

The Days of Awe aren't just rituals - they're a confrontation with life's biggest questions. We ask God for life, for health, for happiness, for meaning. These are days when we face our own mortality, our frailty, the reality of life and death - head-on.

Our gut reaction, when confronted with this kind of heaviness, is to evade the intensity. Human nature makes us uncomfortable with the intensity of *Rosh Hashanah* and *Yom Kippur*, so we do everything we can to distract ourselves from the fundamental themes of the High Holidays. We create walls between ourselves and these holy days, between us and God.

Rabbi Abraham Joshua Heschel writes: "Disregard of the ultimate dimension of human existence is a possible state of mind as long as man finds tranquility in his dedication to partial objectives."[18] All year long we occupy ourselves with partial objectives. "I'm going to nail down that new client"; "I'm going to lose 20 pounds"; or even spiritual objectives like "I'm going to study the Bible for half an hour every day." All of these are good goals, but at the end of the day, they are only partial objectives that allow us to evade the biggest questions of life: What is my life really about? What am I here for?

---

17. Rabbi Isaiah Horowitz (Shelah HaKadosh), *Shnei Luchot HaBrit*, Sha'ar HaKavvanot, 85
18. Abraham Joshua Heschel, *Man Is Not Alone: A Philosophy of Religion*, 210.

Heschel explains that we human beings can successfully avoid the big issues most of the time. But inevitably, something drastic happens in our lives, and evasion is no longer a possibility. Maybe, God forbid, someone we love is taken from us, or we are struck with a health problem. When things like this happen, the walls that we set up come crashing down. All of our partial objectives, all of our goals and projects that we get so immersed in – all of it seems vapid and small compared to the big issues of life.

During the month of *Elul* and the High Holiday season, our goal has to be to think about the big issues. To lift the veil that stands between our hearts and the essential questions of life. To remove the separation between us and God.

Why do kids beg to go to school one day, only to freeze in fear the moment they arrive? Because before school actually starts, it's just an idea - something distant and abstract. In the same way, concepts like "judgment," "repentance," and "life and death" stay abstract for us most of the year. They don't feel real - until we're standing right in front of them.

But when they pull up in front of the building and they see the teachers, the big yellow school buses, kids with backpacks, all of a sudden school is no longer just an idea, it is real. The wall of separation between the reality of school and the children is gone. The idea becomes a reality and in that moment they are struck with fear – they hear the lion roar!

The month of *Elul*, leading up to the Days of Awe, is about removing the separation and tearing down the barriers. During this month we set aside all of our "partial objectives" and we think about the big questions of life, so that we can tremble when we hear the lion roar on the High Holidays.

If we are successful, the lion's roar will foster a fear that is not paralyzing, but exhilarating; a fear that compels us to live more passionately, more purposefully and more connected to the Divine. We pray that the lion's roar awakens us to the real purpose of the High Holidays and serves as a call to live every day with purpose, passion, and genuine connection.

In the *selichot* prayers recited on the days leading up to the Days of Awe we say: "Everyone wants to fear Your name!" Everybody wants to feel, to be in awe of God during these incredible days. But will we remove the separation? Will we lift the veil? That is up to us.

A Time to Stand Still

Rabbi Elie Mischel

At the height of his popularity, Rabbi Abraham Joshua Heschel spoke in London to an overflow crowd. The crowd was there, waiting, when Rabbi Heschel walked quickly over to the speaker's podium and made the following announcement: "My friends, I have just witnessed the most extraordinary event in the history of the world. Just 20 minutes ago!"

The crowd started to buzz: "What happened? 20 minutes ago?" After the buzz died down, Rabbi Heschel explained: "20 minutes ago, I saw the sun set!"[19]

The setting of the sun is an open miracle that happens every evening - but do any of us even notice it?

For children, everything is new. When my kids were younger and we'd drive down the New Jersey Turnpike, my youngest daughter would suddenly start screaming: "Airplane! Airplane!" We'd respond, of course, with a yawn: "Yes, sweetie, it's an airplane."

But who are the real chumps here? Our children, who are captivated by wonders we've come to take for granted? Or us - jaded adults who feel like we've seen it all?

Sadly, it's an almost inevitable part of life that we become world-weary. The first time you're handed the keys to your own car, the world opens up. That sense of freedom is incomparable. And yet, before long, driving becomes just another part of your routine.

The same thing can happen to our connection to God. Whether

---

19. Edward K. Kaplan, *Rabbi Abraham Joshua Heschel: Mystic in a Time of Crisis*

it's reciting prayers or lighting candles on Friday night, what once stirred our hearts can become unremarkable. We still go through the motions, but something essential begins to fade.

What can we do to break out of this spiritual dullness? Thankfully, our sages built a remedy right into the Jewish calendar.

In preparation for the High Holidays, the Days of Awe, we recite communal prayers for divine forgiveness called *selichot*. These begin at least four days before *Rosh Hashanah* and continue through *Yom Kippur*. They help us enter the proper mindset for the High Holidays - but they are exhausting! Recited in the middle of the night or early in the morning, and always said while standing, they demand real effort. Which makes me wonder: Why must they be recited standing? We're already getting up early or staying up late - can't we at least sit down?

The answer lies in Psalm 122, which states: "Our feet are standing within your gates, Jerusalem!" (Tehillim 122:2)

According to Hasidic tradition, Jerusalem - the holiest place in the world - symbolizes *Yom Kippur*, the holiest day of the year. If Jerusalem represents *Yom Kippur*, what, then, is its gate? *Selichot*. These prayers are the gateway to reaching the awesome holiness of *Yom Kippur*.

But how exactly are *selichot* a gateway?

Look again at the beginning of the verse: "Our feet are standing." In Hebrew, the word for "feet" is *ragleinu*, which shares a root with the word *hergelim*, meaning "habits." On a deeper level, the verse isn't just talking about our physical legs - it's a call to pause our routines. To truly arrive in Jerusalem, to genuinely prepare for Yom Kippur, we need to stop moving on autopilot. Our habits must come to a standstill. Our habits must "stand", and come to a stop.

Selichot shake us out of autopilot. They disrupt our routine and wake us up spiritually, emotionally, and even physically.

The Torah portion of *Nitzavim* (Deuteronomy 29:9–30:20), read right before *Rosh Hashanah*, begins with the words: "You are all standing this day before God." This is the season when we're meant to pause. To stop and notice sunsets. To linger before reciting a prayer or lighting *Shabbat* candles.

Why do we stand during *selichot*? Because standing wakes us up. When we're tired and need to jolt ourselves back to life, we stand. It's almost impossible to fall asleep on your feet. Standing is not just a posture - it's a statement. It's physical, psychological, and spiritual alertness.

Standing, like *selichot* themselves, is designed to shock us out of spiritual complacency. As the great Bob Marley once sang: "You better get up, stand up, don't give up the fight!" You can't lead a revolution from your couch. And you can't break free of habit while sitting on your couch.

As we stand in prayer, legs aching and minds slowly awakening, may we shake off the numbness. May we rediscover wonder in the everyday and feel the presence of God with renewed intensity. And may we walk through the "gates of Jerusalem" - and the High Holidays - with renewed life..

King David's Lesson in Faith

Shira Schechter

The late Rabbi Lord Jonathan Sacks, former Chief Rabbi of the British Commonwealth, told the following story:

"It happened in one synagogue in London on *Shemini Atzeret* (Eight Day of Assembly) that the cantor began reciting Psalm 27. The warden said, "Sha!" The *chazzan* (cantor) kept going. The warden said, "You don't say Psalm 27 on *Shemini Atzeret*." The cantor said, "You do." The warden said, "You don't!" The cantor said, "But I'm the cantor." And the warden then said, "But I'm the warden. You're fired." And he sacked him on the spot.

When the holiday was over, the cantor took his case to an English civil court on grounds of unfair dismissal. The case came before a non-Jewish judge, obviously. And he had to rule whether the cantor had been dismissed with cause or without cause, which in turn depended on the question, "Do you or don't you recite Psalm 27 on *Shemini Atzeret*?"

How was the judge supposed to know? How is he supposed to rule on something that is in fact an argument in Jewish law? The judge did something absolutely brilliant. He had the psalm read out, in full, in English, in court. And then he turned to the litigants and said, 'That psalm is so beautiful that I think it should be said every day.' The cantor got his job back, and peace and order was restored."

Rabbi Sacks concluded the story as follows: "It's a lovely story. And of course if you read the psalm in its entirety, you'll see exactly why it should be said every day. Because no other psalm breathes so beautifully the quiet confidence of faith."

We don't read Psalm 27 every day of the year - but for the entire month of *Elul* and through the High Holidays, we say it *twice* a day, every day.

It's always a good thing to recite Psalms - after all, as the British judge said, Psalm 27 is so beautiful it ought to be read daily. But why was this particular psalm chosen for *Elul*? And why the double reading - morning and night?

Rabbi Amnon Bazak explains that this psalm captures three spiritual states: complete trust and joy in God; fear and doubt that shake that trust; and the sense of loneliness and struggle when we feel surrounded by enemies.

What's striking is that King David holds on to his faith through *all* of these moments - not just in joy, but also in fear, even in darkness. That's the heart of Psalm 27, and the reason we read it now.

Faith isn't only for the good times. When life is sweet, we thank God for it. When we feel uncertain, we cry out to Him. And when we suffer, we cling to the hope that we'll one day see His goodness "in the land of the living" (v. 13).

During *Elul*, our spiritual state also shifts. This is the month of preparation - a time for soul-searching and repentance as we approach Rosh Hashanah, the Day of Judgment. The fear is real: according to tradition, all of humanity passes before God, who decides our fate for the coming year. But so is the faith. Alongside David's desperate plea - "Do not hide Your face from me" (v. 9) - we also hear his quiet confidence: "The Lord is my light and my salvation" (v. 1).

So why morning *and* night?

Because those two times represent two different types of faith. Morning is faith when things are clear and hopeful, when the path is visible. Night is faith in the dark, when we can't see what's ahead and have to remember what light once looked like.

By reciting Psalm 27 at both ends of the day, we remind ourselves to hold on to God not just when it's easy, but when it's hard. Faith is not a mood; it's a commitment.

May *Elul* move us forward in that commitment, and may we all be blessed with a year of light, clarity, and peace.

The Paradox of Trusting God

Shira Schechter

King Solomon instructs us, "Trust in the Lord with all your heart" (Proverbs 3:5). We repeat that verse in moments of joy and especially in times of crisis. But what does it really mean to trust in God? Are we supposed to believe that everything will turn out all right just because God is watching over us? And what about when it doesn't?

On October 7, Hamas terrorists murdered 1,200 innocent people, raped and tortured hundreds more, and kidnapped 240 hostages. Clearly, not everything ends well. So what does trust in God look like when the world feels broken?

To answer that, let's turn to the words of King David in Psalm 27.

David opens the psalm with unshakable confidence:

"The Lord is my light and my salvation - whom shall I fear? The Lord is the stronghold of my life - of whom shall I be afraid?" (verses 1–3)

He boldly proclaims that he is unafraid because God is with him. It's a stirring expression of faith. David seems certain that no matter what, he will be protected - that everything will turn out all right.

But as the psalm continues, a dramatic shift occurs:

"Hear my voice when I call, O Lord... do not hide your face from me... do not reject me or forsake me, O God my Savior." (verses 7–9)

What happened to that fearless trust? Why is David now

begging God not to abandon him? Didn't he just say he had nothing to fear because God was his light and salvation?

At first glance, this feels like a contradiction. But it's actually something much deeper.

Rabbi Aharon Lichtenstein explained that there are two distinct ways of trusting in God.

"According to the first approach," he writes, "trust is expressed by the certainty that God stands at your side and will assist you... This approach is fundamentally optimistic, saturated with faith and with hopeful expectation for the future. On the field of battle, the warrior who can adopt this trust feels that he is on the threshold of victory; in moments of crisis, one feels that salvation is on the way; during a night of terrors, this type of trust heralds the break of dawn. In short, this approach is expressed in the familiar formula: 'With God's help, everything will be all right.'"

Rabbi Lichtenstein calls this first kind of trust "faithful trust." This is what David expresses in the opening verses of Psalm 27 - a bold confidence that God is present and victory is near.

But there is a second kind of trust.

"Also included in the matter of trust," Rabbi Lichtenstein writes, "is that a person must surrender his soul to God, and should constantly occupy his thoughts with this matter: If brigands should come to kill him or to force him to abrogate the Torah, he should prefer to give up his life rather than go against the Torah. Concerning this, David said, 'To You, God, I shall offer up my soul' (Psalm 25:1), and it further states, 'My God, in You I have trusted, let me not be disgraced' (ibid. 2)... This approach does not attempt to scatter the clouds of misfortune, try to raise expectations, or whitewash a dark future. It does not claim that 'it will all work out for the best,' either individually or nationally. On the contrary, it expresses a steadfast commitment - *even if* the outcome is tragic, we remain reliant on and connected to God. We will remain faithful until the end and shall not exchange our trust in God for dependence on man. This approach does not claim that God will remain at our side; rather, it asks us to remain at His side."[20]

This second kind of trust - *loving trust* - is what we find in the second half of Psalm 27.

David knows that life doesn't always go according to plan. He's no stranger to suffering and betrayal. He's experienced loss and loneliness. And so, even as he pleads with God not to abandon him, he accepts that things may not turn out the way he hopes. But he also knows that *whatever happens* comes from God. Even in pain, even in fear, David remains loyal. He may not feel that God is on his side - but he will stay on God's side.

That's why the psalm ends with these words of strength:

"Look to the Lord; be strong and of good courage! O look to the Lord!" (verse 14)

Trusting God doesn't mean denying our pain or pretending things are fine. It means staying faithful *even when they're not.*

As Rabbi Lichtenstein explains, both types of trust are necessary. *Faithful trust* is the belief that everything will turn out well—that God is on our side. This is the kind of trust a soldier needs before going into battle, or a parent clings to

---

20. Rabbi Aharon Lichtenstein, *By His Light: Character and Values in the Service of God*

while praying for a sick child. Without it, we couldn't move forward with hope or purpose.

But *faithful trust* alone is not enough—because sometimes, what we want is not what God wills. Sometimes, like on October 7, tragedy strikes. Sometimes the soldier doesn't return. Sometimes the child doesn't get better. In those moments, *loving trust* must carry us. The trust that says, like Job:

"Though He may slay me, still I will trust in Him." (Job 13:15)

That, Rabbi Lichtenstein wrote, "expresses the essence of Jewish trust in the face of tragic situations."

No one lived this truth more fully than Rabbi Akiva.

Rabbi Akiva, one of the greatest sages in Jewish history, lived in the aftermath of the destruction of the Second Temple. He was full of *faithful trust* - believing that redemption was on its way, that the Jewish people would be restored to sovereignty and spiritual greatness in their land. He even believed that Bar Kokhba might be the Messiah.

But his life also became a paradigm of *loving trust*. When the Romans outlawed the teaching of Torah, he continued anyway, knowing the consequences. When they arrested him and tortured him to death, he rejoiced that he could finally fulfill the command to love God "even if He takes your soul." As his flesh was raked with iron combs, he died reciting the *Shema*:

"Hear, O Israel: The Lord our God, the Lord is One" (Deuteronomy 6:4).

Rabbi Akiva never gave up hope. He believed until the very end. And when that end came, he did not despair. He smiled - not because he was naive or numb, but because he remained *faithful.* As he explained to the Roman governor, Turnus Rufus, his smile was not a sign of indifference to suffering, but of profound *bittachon*—deep trust in God.

Throughout our lives, we are called to live with both kinds of trust.

We need *faithful trust* - to believe that with God's help, all will be well. This kind of trust gives us strength in battle, resilience in prayer, and optimism in dark times.

But we also need *loving trust* - a fierce, quiet loyalty that holds fast even when the outcome is not what we hoped. A trust that stays rooted in God's will, even when we don't understand it.

To trust in God means not just to celebrate His goodness in moments of light, but to cling to Him in moments of darkness. It means hoping for the best - and remaining faithful even if the worst comes to pass.

It means believing that God is on our side - and promising that we will always be on His.

The Choice is Yours

Shira Schechter

A young boy once accidentally broke his father's most cherished possession, a beautiful vase passed down through generations. Afraid of his father's anger, the boy hid the broken pieces and avoided him for days. He asked his older brother what to do, and the brother warned, "Father will be furious; he may never forgive you." He asked a neighbor, who said, "He'll punish you for sure." Finally, he went to his mother, who said gently, "Just tell him the truth. Your father loves you more than anything. If you're honest and sorry, he'll understand."

Nervously, the boy confessed to his father, expressing remorse and expecting the worst. But instead of anger, his father knelt down, embraced him, and said, "I'm so glad you told me the truth. I see that you truly feel bad about what happened. We'll figure this out together."

This story mirrors the deep lesson the sages teach us about our Father in Heaven: when asked what the punishment for a sinner should be, wisdom answered, "Evil pursues sinners" (Proverbs 13:21), emphasizing the natural consequences of wrongdoing. Prophecy responded, "The soul that sins shall die" (Ezekiel 18:4), conveying a harsh and final judgment. But when God Himself was asked, His response was radically different: "Let him repent and be forgiven." This contrast between wisdom, prophecy, and God reveals a central theme in Judaism: no matter the gravity of our mistakes, repentance - *teshuva* - always offers a path to redemption.

This theme appears vividly in the Torah portion *Nitzavim* (Deuteronomy 29:9–30:20), which contains what is known as the "portion of repentance" (Deuteronomy 30:1-10). Following

a series of harsh consequences for abandoning God's laws—
including exile, suffering, and being scattered among the
nations - the Torah shifts to a message of hope and return.
Even in the darkest moments, the possibility of repentance
remains open. If we choose to return to God, we will be
restored.

Rabbi Isaac Arama draws attention to the structure of these
verses, noting that they move back and forth between the
people returning to God and God returning to the people. For
instance, in Deuteronomy 30:2 it says:

"And you return to the Lord, your God, and you and your
children heed God's command with all your heart and soul,
just as I enjoin upon you this day,"

While in the next verse, it says:

"Then the Lord, your God, will restore your fortunes and take
you back in love. [God] will bring you together again from all
the peoples where the Lord, your God, has scattered you."

This alternating language teaches a crucial lesson: when we
take even the smallest steps toward God, He meets us halfway,
offering divine assistance and guidance. Repentance is not a
one-sided effort; it is a dynamic interaction where God actively
helps us along the path to redemption.

God does not stand back with detached judgment, waiting to
punish sinners. Instead, He eagerly awaits our first steps
toward return, ready to help us rebuild. *Teshuva* is not simply
about confessing past sins; it is about reigniting a relationship
with God, and renewing our bond with Him.[21]

---

21. Rabbi Isaac Arama, *Akeidat Yitzchak*, Deuteronomy 30:1-10

Rabbi Joseph Albo expands on this idea when reflecting on the famous call in Deuteronomy 30:19: "I have set before you life and death... therefore, choose life." Albo explains that this "life" refers to the spiritual vitality that comes from a relationship with God, sustained by the practice of repentance. *Teshuva* is not merely an option; it is a matter of life and death. The "life" Albo speaks of is not just physical existence, but the life of the soul, deeply connected to God. To "choose life" means to seize the opportunity to return to God, renewing the relationship that sustains us.[22]

Ultimately, no matter how far we have strayed, the door to repentance is always open. God does not seek to punish with finality; instead, He offers *teshuva* as the means to return. Repentance is a gift that allows us to confront our failings without being crushed by them. It is a call to growth, transformation, and hope. *Teshuva* teaches that no matter how far we have fallen or how distant we feel from God, the way back is always open. We are never beyond redemption, for God desires our return and is ready to welcome us with compassion.

Through repentance, we reconnect with God and rediscover the meaning and purpose that infuse our existence. Choosing *teshuva* transforms life from mere survival into a relationship of love and devotion to the Divine. In the end, *teshuva* is not just about making amends for past mistakes; it is about choosing life in its fullest, deepest sense.

And that choice is always ours to make.

---

22. Rabbi Joseph Albo, *Sefer HaIkkarim* (The Book of Principles), Part 3

It's Not Too Late to Change Your Narrative

Shira Schechter

When we think of Psalm 92, most of us immediately associate it with *Shabbat*. That makes sense - it opens with the words, "A psalm, a song for *Shabbat* day," and was sung in the Temple every *Shabbat*. It remains a core part of our *Shabbat* prayers today. But beyond that opening line, the psalm doesn't mention *Shabbat* again. So why was it chosen to accompany the holiest day of the week?

Some commentators explore how its themes of justice, gratitude, and divine perspective align with the spiritual atmosphere of *Shabbat*. But Rabbi David Silverberg[23] draws attention to something else - another, often overlooked layer within the psalm: the theme of repentance, or *teshuva*. While the psalm may not seem, at first glance, to speak directly about repentance, Jewish tradition and close reading suggest otherwise. Understanding this hidden theme not only opens a new window into Psalm 92, but also offers a powerful message of hope - on *Shabbat* and particularly during the month of *Elul*.

According to Jewish tradition, Psalm 92 was composed by Adam after a fateful encounter with his son, Cain. Following the murder of Abel, Cain came face to face with his father. When Adam asked what punishment he had received for his terrible crime, Cain replied that he had been forgiven - that God had granted him a reprieve. This revelation stunned Adam. Until that moment, he hadn't grasped the full power of repentance. Overwhelmed by the realization that even such a

23. Rabbi David Silverberg, SALT 2015 - Parashat Bereishit, https://etzion.org.il/en/tanakh/torah/sefer-bereishit/parashat-bereishit/salt-2015-parashat-bereishit

grave sin could be forgiven, Adam composed Psalm 92 as a response.

But this raises an important question: Psalm 92 is filled with gratitude, praise of God, and the ultimate triumph of righteousness. What does this have to do with repentance? As Rabbi Silverberg explains, the Psalm wrestles with the painful reality that, in this world, the wicked often seem to prosper while the righteous suffer. And yet, the psalmist insists that this is not the end of the story. As it says in verse 8, "Though the wicked spring up like grass... they will be destroyed forever." Psalm 92 affirms that God sees all, and in the fullness of time, justice will prevail. In this light, repentance is not just about personal forgiveness - it is about believing in the long arc of divine justice and the possibility of transformation, both for individuals and the world.

At its heart, Psalm 92 is an anthem of hope. It reminds us that life's current frame doesn't capture the entire narrative. Just as the wicked's apparent success is fleeting, the shadows of our past misdeeds don't dictate our ending. This sentiment is the connection to repentance. Repentance isn't just about seeking forgiveness; it's about understanding that our story is dynamic and ongoing. It champions the idea that with introspection and a genuine desire to change, we can redirect our life's narrative. Mistakes can turn into lessons, and regrets can forge a path to redemption.

The journey of repentance, much like the underlying message of Psalm 92, reminds us that the present moment is just that – a moment. Our past errors, no matter how grave, can be repurposed as catalysts for profound growth. Like the evolving chapters of a book, with every act of sincere repentance, we are given a chance to rewrite our story.

Psalm 92 is a testament not just to the sanctity of the *Shabbat* but to the redemptive power of *teshuva*. As long as we breathe, it's never too late to change the narrative, to seek a better, nobler self, and to believe in the possibility of a brighter tomorrow.

Divine Do-Overs

Shira Schechter

Imagine this: God gives Moses a detailed plan for a sacred space where His presence will dwell among the people. The instructions are precise, beautiful, and full of promise. But before a single beam is cut or curtain woven, everything falls apart. The people - just recently redeemed from Egypt - build a Golden Calf and worship it. It's a shocking betrayal, right in the middle of their covenant with God.

And yet, after this collapse, something surprising happens. The plan for the Tabernacle goes forward—exactly as originally given. The Torah doesn't skip a beat. In fact, it repeats almost every detail of the instructions in two separate sections: first, in *Terumah* and *Tetzaveh* (Exodus 25–30), where God gives the commands; then again in *Vayakhel* and *Pekudei* (Exodus 35–40), where the people carry them out. In between is *Ki Tisa* (Exodus 30–34), the story of the Golden Calf.

Why place this sin in the middle? And why repeat so much of the same material?

Rabbi Aharon Lichtenstein offers a helpful analogy. A young couple spends months planning their dream home - every detail carefully chosen. But on their honeymoon, the wife is unfaithful. The husband is crushed. A friend steps in and helps them reconcile. Eventually, they return home, and everything they ordered - furniture, artwork, appliances - arrives as planned. But can the house feel the same?

That's the question the Torah raises. God's plan for the Tabernacle was given before the Golden Calf. The people sinned. Moses pleaded with God. Forgiveness was granted. Then the people built the Tabernacle exactly as God had originally commanded. Same blueprint. Same purpose. But now it's built by the very people who just broke the covenant.[24]

The message is subtle but powerful: even after failure, the relationship isn't thrown out. It's repaired. The Tabernacle is not a backup plan - it's still the plan. God is still willing to dwell among the people.

There's one key shift. In the first version, everything comes from God - it is pure instruction. In the second, it's the people who take action. "See, the Lord has chosen Bezalel... and filled him with the spirit of God, with wisdom, understanding, and skill" (Exodus 35:30–31). God provides the vision, but now human hands bring it to life.

And those hands? They're the same ones that built the Golden Calf.

That's the heart of this story: the same people who failed are the ones called to build something holy. That's what real repentance, real *teshuva*, looks like. Not just regret, but return. Not just forgiveness, but restoration.

This isn't just a story about ancient Israel. It speaks to anyone who's ever asked: Can what was broken ever be whole again?

According to the Torah, the answer is yes.

---

24. Rabbi Aharon Lichtenstein, commentary on Ki Tisa and Pekudei, in *Out of the Depths I Call*

Heart Over Hype: The Truth About King David

Shira Schechter

What made David - the overlooked youngest son of a shepherding family - the one God chose to be the eternal king of Israel?

He wasn't the obvious choice. When the prophet Samuel was sent to anoint the next king, Jesse brought in all his older sons. One by one, they passed before Samuel. Strong, impressive, commanding. But God rejected each of them. David wasn't even invited to the gathering. He was out in the fields tending sheep.

Only after Samuel asked, "Are these all your sons?" did Jesse mention the youngest. When David finally appeared, God said to Samuel, "Arise and anoint him, for this is the one" (1 Samuel 16:12).

But the real answer to why David was chosen comes a few verses earlier, when God told Samuel: "Do not consider his appearance or his height... Man looks at the outward appearance, but the Lord looks at the heart" (1 Samuel 16:7).

That one verse explains everything. God wasn't seeking a polished leader or a powerful warrior. He was looking for someone whose heart was open to Him.

David's greatness didn't come from perfection - it came from his spiritual sensitivity, his honesty, and his deep desire to walk with God. Long before he became king, David was already forging a relationship with the Creator. Alone in the hills of Bethlehem, watching over sheep, he sang songs of praise, reflected on the beauty of creation, and placed his trust entirely in God. The Sages teach that David would rise at midnight to pray and sing, filling the quiet hours of the night with yearning and devotion.[25]

When David stepped onto the battlefield to face Goliath, it wasn't out of arrogance or naivety. It was a bold defense of God's honor. He declared: "You come to me with a sword and spear, but I come to you in the name of the Lord of Hosts, the God of the armies of Israel" (1 Samuel 17:45). David believed that God, who had protected him from lions and bears (1 Samuel 17:37), would also deliver him from this enemy.

David's faith was never just belief - it was action. It shaped the way he fought, ruled, prayed, and repented.

That last quality, repentance, is the most defining part of David's spiritual life. After his sin with Bathsheba, and the arranged death of her husband Uriah, the prophet Nathan confronted him. David didn't argue, justify, or shift blame. He simply said, "I have sinned against the Lord" (2 Samuel 12:13).

From that moment came one of the most powerful prayers in the Bible: "Create in me a clean heart, O God, and renew a right spirit within me..." (Psalm 51). David didn't just repent for himself - he taught generations how to return to God. His words gave language to guilt, sorrow, hope, and healing. He showed that no sin is too great for God's mercy when the heart truly turns back.

David's life wasn't easy. He was betrayed by his own son, hunted by enemies, weighed down by his own failures. But through it all, he kept turning to God. His Psalms, many of

---

25. Babylonian Talmud, Berachot 3b–4a. The Sages teach that King David would rise at midnight to pray and sing, stirred by a north wind playing the strings of his harp, dedicating the quiet hours of the night to yearning and devotion.

them written through tears, express every emotion a human being can feel: joy, fear, gratitude, doubt, awe. And somehow, through all of it, David kept praying.

One line from Psalm 23 may sum him up best: "Even though I walk through the valley of the shadow of death, I will fear no evil, for You are with me" (Psalm 23:4). David didn't expect a life without pain—he expected that God would be with him in the midst of it.

David is the model of someone whose heart belongs to God - not because he never stumbled, but because he never stopped seeking. He teaches us that what God wants most isn't perfection, but truth, humility, and closeness.

And the God who looked into David's heart still looks into hearts today. He still chooses those who are honest, willing, and ready to return.

As the prophet Isaiah wrote, the line of David will rise again. A shoot will grow from the stump of Jesse, and the earth will be filled with the knowledge of God as the waters cover the sea (Isaiah 11:1–9). Until that day, David remains a guide - not just for Israel, but for anyone searching for a way back to God.

Another Shot of Vodka, Please!

Rabbi Elie Mischel

Soon after the Communists gained power in Russia, they began placing restrictions on Jewish practices. Ultimately, all Jewish educational institutions were forced to shutter, while those spotted in synagogues risked being fired from their jobs. As the decades passed, the Soviets' squashing of almost all public Jewish life meant most Jews were raised with little Biblical education and knowledge.

In the early 1970s, Rabbi Shlomo Riskin traveled to the Soviet Union on a secret mission to strengthen and assist Soviet Jewry throughout the Soviet Union. It was a dangerous trip, and he was trailed by suspicious KGB agents most of the time that he was there. One *Shabbat*, Rabbi Riskin prayed in a synagogue in Riga, while Soviet agents sat in the back pews. Rabbi Riskin was honored with opening the Ark and taking out the Torah scroll. As he took out the scroll, the sexton whispered to him in Yiddish: "We're thirsty for Torah study! We will be having some refreshments downstairs after the service, and we want you to share some thoughts with us. Come downstairs after the service – but without your 'friends,'" glancing at the KGB agents.

Fortunately for Rabbi Riskin, when the services were over the KGB agents left the synagogue for a lunch break and Rabbi Riskin went downstairs, through a long dark hallway, until he found a room with 15 men standing around a table with a plate of honey cake and a few bottles of vodka. The sexton smiled at him and poured him a full glass of vodka, and Rabbi Riskin recited the blessing before eating. He shared a teaching from the Torah portion of *Ki Teitzei*, from the Book of Deuteronomy, and they sang a song and danced in honor of *Shabbat*. Then they poured him another glass of vodka, Rabbi Riskin shared more Bible teachings, and everybody sang and danced again. This cycle – a shot of vodka, a Bible study, a song – repeated itself several times.

Eventually, Rabbi Riskin ran out of Bible teachings – he had nothing left to say! But he was feeling good – very good, after all that vodka – and said to one of the men in the room: "Please, I'd like you to share a Bible teaching. I want to hear something I can bring back to New York with me."

The Russian Jew obliged, and cited the following verse about paying a day laborer: "You must pay him his wages on the same day, before the sun sets, for he is needy and urgently depends on it; else he will cry to Hashem against you and you will incur guilt" (Deuteronomy 24:15). If we employ a laborer, we must pay him at the end of the day; we must not delay in paying his wages.

"But God," said the Russian Jew, "seems to be hypocritical on this point. Many righteous people suffer greatly in this world and only receive their rightful rewards when they reach heaven. But how can this be? How can God tell us that we have to pay the day laborer at the end of the day, when God Himself does not pay us for our holy deeds as soon as we perform them?! How can God make us wait until the end of our lives, until we reach the next world? It's hypocritical!"

For these Russian Jews, this wasn't a theoretical question. These Jews were risking their careers, and even their lives, by coming to the synagogue and maintaining their Jewish identity. By being there, at this 'criminal' gathering, drinking vodka and sharing words of Torah, they were placing their lives and their families' lives in danger! Where was their reward?

The Russian Jew answered his own question. "In Biblical law, there is a distinction between a day laborer, a worker hired by the hour or by the day, and a contractor hired by the project. A day laborer is easily replaceable; most day laborers don't bring any particular skills or abilities to their jobs. This kind of laborer must be paid at the end of every day."

"But a contractor is different. A contractor is hired for a unique job; not just anybody can do what he does. The contractor is not hired for a particular amount of time but for as long as the job takes. And so a contractor must be paid only at the end of a project."

"We, vis-à-vis God, are not day laborers. We are contractors! God has "hired" each of us to perform a unique job in a particular place and at a particular time. God has given each of us our unique talents to fulfill this contract. None of us are here by accident; we have each been given a highly specific project! This "project" begins as soon as we are able to make decisions for ourselves, and the "project" ends only when we die. Only then, at the end of our lives, can God judge whether we have successfully completed our project here on earth. And so only then can we be properly paid for our hard work and rewarded for all of the good we do in this world!"

The Russian Jew looked at everyone in the room and said: "The most important thing one can do in this world is to discover his purpose; how each of us can best improve the world even a little bit, given our individual abilities and situation. And we must discharge our divinely given responsibility with as much integrity, devotion and grace as we can possibly muster."[26]

---

26. Rabbi Shlomo Riskin, *Listening to God: Inspirational Stories for My Grandchildren*

Too often, we fall into the trap of acting like day laborers. We punch the clock, go to synagogue or church, and call it a day. We keep our heads down, try to do the right thing, and the years fly by. We forget that we were not born into this world to be "day laborers." That none of us is replaceable! We forget that we all have a unique project that must be completed before time runs out.

As we approach *Rosh Hashanah* and *Yom Kippur*, now is the time to remember why we are here – to reflect upon the unique project that God has contracted with each of us to perform. May we merit to get the job done!

2

ROSH HASHANAH – THE JEWISH NEW YEAR

The moment has arrived.

After thirty days of preparation, after countless shofar blasts piercing the morning air, after honest self-examination and heartfelt attempts at reconciliation, the day we have been preparing for is finally here. All the spiritual work of *Elul*—every prayer whispered in the pre-dawn darkness, every act of charity, every difficult conversation seeking forgiveness—has been leading to this threshold.

On *Rosh Hashanah*, every human being on earth passes before the Divine throne. Kings and commoners, the famous and the forgotten, those who have lived with purpose and those who have drifted through life, all stand before the ultimate Judge.

Yet this is no ordinary courtroom. The Judge is also our King, and more intimately still, our Father. The day that determines our fate is also the day we celebrate with festive meals and sweet symbols of hope. We dress in our finest clothes to stand in judgment. We blow an ancient ram's horn to announce a coronation. We tremble with awe even as we taste apples dipped in honey, expressing our faith in the sweetness of the year to come.

How do we hold such contradictions in our hearts? How do we celebrate while being judged? How do we experience both the terror and the joy of standing before our Creator?

The answer lies in understanding what *Rosh Hashanah* truly represents: not the impersonal mechanics of divine justice, but the most intimate encounter possible between a human soul and its Source. This is the day when the King of the Universe makes Himself available to every person who seeks Him. This is when the gap between heaven and earth narrows to the thickness of a whisper, when the most ordinary human being can speak directly to the One who determines the fate of galaxies.

Rosh Hashanah teaches us that we matter—not only as individuals, but as part of something infinitely larger than ourselves. Our choices ripple through eternity. Our repentance can literally change the world. Our prayers on this day join a chorus that began with the first human beings and will continue until the end of time.

The *shofar* is about to sound. The gates of heaven are opening. The most important time of the year is beginning.

Are we ready to meet our King?

THE MEANING AND SPIRIT OF *ROSH HASHANAH*

When the Jewish New Year begins on the first day of *Tishrei*, something extraordinary happens. *Rosh Hashanah*, literally "Head of the Year," is celebrated not with fireworks or champagne, but with the piercing call of an ancient ram's horn echoing through synagogues worldwide.

This is no ordinary new year. For two days, Jewish communities enter what can only be described as the ultimate paradox: celebrating while standing in divine judgment, feasting while facing the ultimate reckoning of their lives. It's a day when the mundane rhythms of daily existence pause, and every human being stands before their Creator to account for the year that has passed.

The name *Rosh Hashanah* captures something profound about these sacred hours. Just as the head governs the entire body, *Rosh Hashanah* sets the spiritual tone and direction for the rest of the year. These aren't just the first days of a new calendar cycle, they are the source from which the entire year will draw its meaning, its blessings, and its possibilities for growth.

What begins on *Rosh Hashanah* doesn't end there. These two days launch the Ten Days of Repentance, a period of unprecedented spiritual intensity that reaches its climax on *Yom Kippur* (Day of Atonement), when our fate for the coming year is finally sealed. But that reckoning is still eight days away. Today, the gates of heaven swing wide open, and the question becomes: How will we walk through them?

Universal Significance

Rosh Hashanah encompasses something even more profound than the individual encounter with the Divine.

While this day is distinctly Jewish in its observance, Jewish tradition teaches that its significance extends far beyond the Jewish community. Unlike other holidays that focus primarily on Jewish history and destiny, *Rosh Hashanah* is a day of universal judgment when God reviews the actions of all humanity. Every person on earth, whether they know it or not, passes before the same divine throne.

The liturgy powerfully expresses this reality: "All creatures shall parade before You as a herd of sheep. As a shepherd herds his flock, directing his sheep to pass under his staff, so You shall pass, count, and record the souls of all living, and decree a limit to each person's days, and inscribe their final judgment."

This understanding transforms how we approach our spiritual work during these sacred days. When we engage in repentance, when we pour our hearts out in prayer, when we perform acts of kindness, we believe we're not only working toward our own spiritual repair, we're actively participating in the world's healing. The Sages teach that even a single act of righteousness can tip the scales of judgment for the entire world.[1]

This places profound responsibility on each and every one of us. Our spiritual efforts during these Days of Awe are understood to influence the destiny of all humanity. This explains why Jewish communities approach these holidays with such intensity, and why the themes of repentance and renewal extend beyond personal concerns to encompass hopes for universal peace, justice, and divine recognition.

The prayers of *Rosh Hashanah* express this cosmic vision: that all the world's inhabitants will ultimately recognize God as

---

1. Maimonides, Laws of Repentance 3:4

their Creator and King, fulfilling the ancient prophecy that envisions a time when all humanity will acknowledge one God: "And the Lord shall be King over all the earth; on that day the Lord shall be one and His name one" (Zechariah 14:9).

Divine Kingship

On *Rosh Hashanah*, Jewish communities worldwide symbolically crown God as King of the Universe. This coronation represents a meaningful acknowledgment of God's sovereignty and a recognition that our fate—and the fate of the entire world—are in His hands. Yet this coronation carries profound weight, as the King who is being crowned is also the Judge before whom we stand.

Central to this theme is the distinctive sound of the *shofar* (ram's horn) which rings out during these days, serving both as a trumpet fanfare announcing God's coronation and as a wake-up call for introspection and self-reflection, reminding us that we stand in divine judgment.

While *Rosh Hashanah* carries the weight of divine judgment, it also balances solemnity with joy and hope. Alongside the intense focus on prayer and reflection, the holiday is marked by festive meals featuring sweet foods like apples dipped in honey, symbolizing hopes for sweetness in the year ahead.

Biblical Origins

The origins of the holiday of *Rosh Hashanah* are found in the Hebrew Bible, where it is referred to as *Yom Teruah*, "a day when the horn is sounded" (Numbers 29:1), referring to the blowing of the *shofar* (ram's horn). In Leviticus 23:24-25, the Torah similarly commands: "In the seventh month, on the first day of the month, you shall observe complete rest, a sacred occasion commemorated with loud blasts (*zichron teruah*). You shall not work at your occupations; and you shall bring an offering by fire to the Lord."

This foundational biblical text perfectly illustrates both the challenge and beauty of Jewish biblical interpretation. These brief passages give us the essential framework but leave many questions unanswered. The Torah tells us when to observe this day (first day of the seventh month), what to do (blow the shofar, rest from work, bring offerings), and that it is a sacred occasion. But it doesn't explain why this day is significant or how to observe it meaningfully beyond these basic requirements. What kind of horn is supposed to be sounded? How many blasts should be blown, and what should they sound like? What does it mean to "observe complete rest?" How does one "mark a sacred occasion?" The biblical text assumes knowledge that it doesn't provide.

Notice what else is missing from these verses: there's no mention of it being a "new year," no explanation of themes like divine judgment or kingship, no details about specific prayers, foods, or customs. The Torah doesn't even call it "*Rosh Hashanah*," that name developed later through Jewish tradition. It's particularly striking that such a major holiday receives relatively brief treatment in Scripture, especially compared to the detailed instructions given for Passover or the Day of Atonement.

This is where the richness of Jewish tradition becomes essential. According to Jewish understanding, Moses received not only the Written Torah but also an Oral Law - detailed explanations and instructions that were passed down through generations before being recorded in the Talmud and other rabbinic literature. Some of the practices and meanings associated with *Rosh Hashanah* come from this Oral Law tradition, believed to have been taught by Moses himself, while others were developed later by Jewish sages through careful interpretation and application of biblical principles. The themes of divine kingship, judgment, and renewal; the symbolic foods like apples and honey; the special prayers and liturgy - these emerged through this combination of received tradition and faithful interpretation by generations seeking to fulfill God's commandments in meaningful ways. Understanding this interplay between Scripture and tradition helps explain how a few brief biblical verses have given rise to one of Judaism's most profound and beautiful celebrations.

The Birthday of Humanity

Though the Torah does not explicitly refer to this day as *Rosh Hashanah*, the sages identified it as the anniversary of the creation of the world,[2] as we say in the *Rosh Hashanah* prayers, "This day is the beginning of Your works, a remembrance of the first day." More precisely, it is the anniversary of the creation of humanity with the formation of Adam and Eve. The biblical account in Genesis describes this pivotal moment: "And God said: 'Let us make man in our image, after our likeness; and let them have dominion over the fish of the sea, and over the fowl of the air, and over the cattle, and over all the earth'" (Genesis 1:26). The text continues, "And God created man in His own image, in the image of God created He him; male and female created He them" (Genesis 1:27). This creation occurred on the sixth day, when "God saw everything that He had made, and behold, it was very good" (Genesis 1:31).

Rosh Hashanah is not just the start of a new cycle of time, but a moment of renewal for all of creation. It is the day that marks

---

2. Vayikra Rabbah 29:6

the birth of human awareness, responsibility, and relationship with the Divine; a reflection on humanity's unique role and responsibility within creation. The biblical text emphasizes this special status: humans alone are created "in the image of God" (Genesis 1:27) and given dominion over the earth (Genesis 1:28), establishing from the very beginning our accountability to our Creator.

Central to *Rosh Hashanah* is the theme of reaffirming God's sovereignty over creation. The Sages teach that "there is no king without subjects," emphasizing that kingship requires recognition and acceptance by those being ruled. On *Rosh Hashanah*, we commemorate not only the creation of humanity but also the moment when God became King of the universe— for it was only with the creation of conscious beings capable of choice that divine kingship could be meaningfully established. Each year on this anniversary, we renew and reaffirm God's sovereignty over creation, and our commitment to live as His subjects. This is why the liturgy of *Rosh Hashanah* is filled with declarations of God's kingship, proclaiming "The Lord is King, the Lord was King, the Lord will be King forever and ever."

Judgment and Renewal

The day also carries cosmic significance; on *Rosh Hashanah*, the fate of every individual and all nations is inscribed. Just as humanity began on *Rosh Hashanah*, each of us gets a chance to begin again on this day. *Rosh Hashanah* is also called *Yom Hadin*, judgment day, because on this day, all of humanity stands in judgment before God. The timing is not coincidental: on the anniversary of humanity's creation, when we renew God's kingship, we also face the ultimate accounting for how we have fulfilled our role as His subjects and stewards of creation during the past year. This idea is expressed in the

Mussaf (additional) prayer of the day: "Today is the birth of the world; today all creation stands in judgment."

According to traditional Jewish sources,[3] on *Rosh Hashanah*, every human being passes before God like sheep before a shepherd, each one individually considered. God reviews everything we've done—our actions, our speech, even our thoughts and intentions. This includes how we've treated others, how we've acted in private, how faithful we've been to God's commandments, and whether we've worked on becoming better people.

Based on this accounting, on *Rosh Hashanah*, God writes down the judgment, but it is not sealed until the end of *Yom Kippur* (Day of Atonement). These ten days are a gift, an opportunity to reflect, make changes, apologize, and return to the path of goodness before the final judgment is sealed.

One might wonder why a day of judgment falls on the new year. Shouldn't it be a time of joy and celebration? In truth, *Rosh Hashanah* is both serious and hopeful. *Yom HaDin*, the Day of Judgment, means that God evaluates every person and decides their fate for the year to come. But this judgment is not about punishment, it's about growth. We are given the chance to look inward, to return to God, and to become the people we were meant to be. Through sincere reflection and change, we can influence what the new year holds, and draw closer to our Creator in the process.

The *shofar* embodies this dual nature perfectly. As mentioned earlier, it serves both as a trumpet fanfare announcing God's coronation as King and as a spiritual alarm clock. As the great Jewish philosopher Maimonides explained, the *shofar* calls out:

3. Babylonian Talmud, Rosh Hashanah 16a

"Wake up, you who are sleeping, and think about your actions!"[4] *Rosh Hashanah* is a day of awe, accountability, and hope. The tone is serious, but not gloomy. We crown God as our King, recognizing His rule over the world and over our lives, and we trust in His justice and compassion as we stand before Him in judgment.

The Nature of the Day - Joy Amidst Judgment

This trust in divine compassion, even amid the gravity of judgment, points to one of *Rosh Hashanah*'s most remarkable characteristics. At first glance, *Rosh Hashanah* presents a puzzling paradox. We dress in our finest clothes, prepare elaborate festive meals and greet each other with wishes for a "sweet new year." Yet simultaneously, we stand before God in solemn judgment, acutely aware that our very lives hang in the balance as the "Books of Life and Death" are opened before the Divine Judge.

How do we reconcile these seemingly contradictory aspects?

The Book of Nehemiah offers a fascinating glimpse into this tension. After the Jewish people returned from Babylonian exile, they gathered on *Rosh Hashanah* to hear the Torah being read aloud. Recognizing how far they had strayed from their spiritual ideals, they began to weep and wanted to fast as an expression of remorse. Yet their leader Ezra redirected them with these powerful words: "Go, eat choice foods and drink sweet drinks and send portions to whoever has nothing prepared, for the day is holy to our Lord. Do not be sad, for the joy of the Lord is your strength" (Nehemiah 8:10).

This ancient instruction still guides our *Rosh Hashanah*

---

4. Laws of Repentance 3:4

observance today. We are commanded to rejoice even as we face divine judgment.

The Sages further highlight this tension when they ask why we don't recite *Hallel*, the joyous psalms of praise recited on most Jewish holidays, on *Rosh Hashanah*.[5] The answer is striking: "The angels asked God, 'Why don't the Jewish people sing *Hallel* on *Rosh Hashanah*?' God replied, 'When the King sits in judgment with the Books of Life and Death open before Him, would it be appropriate to sing songs of praise?'"

Even the *shofar*'s sounds embody this duality, simultaneously announcing divine coronation with joy while serving as an alarm for the soul's awakening, as noted above.

Rather than trying to resolve this tension, Jewish tradition embraces it. *Rosh Hashanah*'s seemingly contradictory elements actually complement each other. Our joy stems precisely from our confidence that even as we face judgment, we stand before a compassionate King who desires our return. Our solemnity acknowledges the profound stakes involved when confronting our spiritual condition.

The holiday teaches us that genuine joy doesn't require avoiding life's serious dimensions. Instead, true celebration emerges from facing reality honestly while trusting in divine mercy. We rejoice not despite the judgment, but because of the opportunity it presents: the chance to realign ourselves with our highest purpose and strengthen our relationship with the Creator.

On *Rosh Hashanah*, we experience the ultimate paradox of spiritual life, that accountability and celebration, judgment

---

5. Babylonian Talmud, Rosh Hashanah 32a

and joy, can not only coexist but actually deepen and enhance one another.

The Call to Transformation

At its heart, *Rosh Hashanah* is about transformation. Jewish tradition views time as a spiral, not a straight line. Each *Rosh Hashanah* is not simply a repetition of the last, but an opportunity to return to the same spiritual place from a higher perspective. It is a time for *teshuvah*, often translated as "repentance" but which literally means "return." *Rosh Hashanah* is an invitation to recreate ourselves, to become the people we were meant to be.

This concept of intentional spiritual growth resonates deeply with the teachings of Rabbi Kalonymus Kalman Shapira, a 20th-century Hasidic master. He taught that each year one should "clarify a goal and envision the actualized 'you' of next year. Visualize who this 'you' will be: his attainments... his daily life... his character... and his inner essence."

Rabbi Shapira also warned of the consequences of failing to grow: "If next year comes and you have not realized that 'you,' it is as if your life has been cut short. The new 'you' was aborted, it is not alive now, you are still an old 'you' of perhaps years ago." Drawing from the biblical description of Abraham as being "advanced in years" (Genesis 24:1), he explained that true maturity means becoming the most developed version of yourself for this moment in time, "the Abraham of this year, not the Abraham of the past."

This teaching captures the essence of what *Rosh Hashanah* invites us to do. It encourages us to use this annual milestone not just for reflection, but for envisioning and committing to who we can become in the year ahead.

Two Days, Which Are One

Rosh Hashanah is unique among the Jewish festivals in its observance. While other biblical festivals are celebrated for one day in Israel and two days in the diaspora due to historical uncertainties about when the new month began, *Rosh Hashanah* is observed for two days everywhere, even in Israel itself.

Before the Jewish calendar was fixed by calculation, months were declared based on eyewitness reports of seeing the new moon. News of these announcements sometimes took time to reach Jewish communities far from Jerusalem. Because of this delay, communities outside Israel weren't always sure when the new month began, and therefore did not know on which days to celebrate the festivals. Communities outside Israel observed each holiday for two days because news of the new month's declaration might not reach them in time.

This safety measure ensured they would celebrate on the correct day. In Israel itself, where the calendar declaration was known immediately, these holidays required only one day of observance.

Unlike the other festivals which occur later in the month, *Rosh Hashanah* is celebrated on the first day of *Tishrei*, creating a unique timing challenge. Since *Rosh Hashanah* coincides with the very day that the declaration of the new month is made, if witnesses arrived late in the day to report the new moon, this would leave insufficient time to properly observe the holiday.

To address this uncertainty, the early Sages established that *Rosh Hashanah* should be observed for two full days, even in Jerusalem. This ensured the sanctity of the day would not be compromised by confusion about its proper time of observance.

After the calendar was fixed and the start of the new month was known in advance, the two-day practice for other festivals remained outside of Israel, and the two-day observance of *Rosh Hashanah* continued everywhere as an established tradition.

One beautiful way to understand the two days of *Rosh Hashanah* is found in Hasidic teachings, which explain that the two days reflect two different aspects of judgment and, by extension, two dimensions of who we are. This insight suggests that the two days correspond to how each person is seen both as an individual and as a part of their wider community.

Every person lives on two levels at once. There is the personal self, with individual choices, actions, and growth. But there is also the self as a member of a community, connected in purpose and responsibility to those around them.

The two days of *Rosh Hashanah* represent these two intertwined paths of judgment. One day focuses on our personal journey; how we have lived our own lives, faced our challenges, and grown. The other day reflects how we have contributed to, and are part of, the larger community and shared destiny.

This teaches a timeless lesson. Our individual paths are deeply linked to the well-being of those around us. No one stands alone. Our personal fate is connected with the fate of our community. We are not only responsible for ourselves but also for one another.

So the extended celebration of *Rosh Hashanah* is a powerful reminder that true growth and renewal happen both within us and through our relationships, commitments, and contributions to the greater whole.

FROM PREPARATION TO RENEWAL: A JOURNEY THROUGH *ROSH HASHANAH*

As the sun dips below the horizon and *Rosh Hashanah* begins, a unique sense of calm and possibility fills the air. The evening carries a special atmosphere, one of reverence, hope, and new beginnings, inviting us into a space of reflection and renewal. Through time-honored traditions and ritual, we welcome the new year not just with words, but with intention. This moment sets the tone for the holiday to come.

Preparing for the holiday

The Torah's command to "observe complete rest" means that *Rosh Hashanah* follows similar work prohibitions as *Shabbat*. This includes refraining from activities like writing, driving, using electricity, handling money, and other forms of creative labor. However, unlike *Shabbat*, cooking and food preparation are permitted on festivals, as the Torah specifically allows "only what every person is to eat, that alone may be prepared for you" (Exodus 12:16). Therefore, Orthodox Jews make sure to complete preparations like shopping and cleaning before sunset, while knowing they can still prepare fresh, warm meals to honor the festival if necessary.

The goal is to create sacred time set apart from ordinary weekday concerns, allowing us to focus entirely on the spiritual significance of the day. These restrictions, rather than being burdensome, actually enhance the holiday by removing distractions and creating space for prayer, reflection, and meaningful connection with family and community.

The final preparations for *Rosh Hashanah* evening represent the culmination of the spiritual work that has been ongoing throughout the month of *Elul*. As *Rosh Hashanah* draws near, both physical and spiritual preparations intensify to ensure we enter the holiday with proper reverence and readiness.

What to Buy and Prepare

In the days leading up to *Rosh Hashanah*, we make sure to purchase and prepare specific items to properly celebrate the holiday.

For the table: In preparation for the holy day, we purchase or bake round *challah* (ritual bread eaten on *Shabbat* and Jewish holidays), and make sure we have apples, honey, pomegranates, and any other symbolic foods that our family tradition includes (see later section on symbolic foods). We ensure that we have enough wine or grape juice for the *Kiddush* blessing with which we sanctify the holiday. Enough food is prepared for two holiday meals, and many also prepare or purchase sweet foods and desserts such as honey cake or honey cookies, symbolizing the sweet new year we pray for. Before evening, we set our tables with our finest dishes, silverware, and tablecloth to honor the holiday.

For lighting: Prepare candles for the holiday - typically two, though some light additional candles.

For dress: Plan to wear your finest clothing. Many choose white garments, as white is associated with purity, cleanliness, and new beginnings, making it a fitting choice for a time of introspection and renewal. If you have new clothes, this is considered an appropriate time to wear them, symbolizing the fresh start of the new year.

Spiritual Preparations on Rosh Hashanah Eve

The day before *Rosh Hashanah* is marked by several important spiritual practices.

Selichot prayers: Extended penitential prayers called *selichot* are recited, often in the early morning. While these special prayers asking for God's forgiveness and mercy have been recited throughout the month of *Elul*, extended *selichot* are said on the morning before *Rosh Hashanah*, preparing our hearts for the judgment of *Rosh Hashanah*. They serve as a means of awakening repentance and pleading for God's mercy and grace.

No shofar blowing: Notably, although the *shofar* has been blown daily during the month of *Elul* as a call to repentance, it is not blown on *Rosh Hashanah* eve. This deliberate pause serves to distinguish between the *Elul shofar* blasts, which are a custom meant to awaken us spiritually, and the *Rosh Hashanah shofar* blowing, which is a biblical commandment. The silence creates anticipation and emphasizes the sacred nature of the *shofar* calls that will come with the holiday itself.

Final Personal Preparations

As evening approaches, take time for personal reflection on the year that has passed and your hopes for the year ahead. Many people review their spiritual progress during *Elul* and make final preparations of the heart. Some visit the ritual bath for spiritual purification. Others focus on acts of charity or reconciliation with family and friends.

Ensure all work is completed before sunset, as *Rosh Hashanah*, like *Shabbat*, prohibits most forms of labor. Have your prayer book ready if you plan to attend evening services, and prepare mentally to enter this sacred time with focus and intention.

Candle Lighting: Illuminating the New Year

Like all biblical Jewish holidays, *Rosh Hashanah* begins with the kindling of lights. Women traditionally have the honor of bringing the sanctity of the holiday into the home through this sacred act.

As the festival approaches, lighting candles becomes a quiet way to welcome the special day and bring light and joy into the home. Just as candles mark the arrival of *Shabbat*, so too do they honor the beginning of the festival, adding a gentle glow that sets the tone for the meal. Traditionally, two candles are lit, symbolizing husband and wife,[6] though some choose to light more.

Alongside the lighting, a special blessing called *Shehecheyanu* is recited, expressing gratitude for reaching this joyous moment. Though some wait until the beginning of the holiday meal, many choose to say this blessing while lighting candles since the lighting marks the beginning of the festival.

The sages teach that the gates of heaven are particularly open to women's prayers at the moment of candle lighting. Many women use these precious moments after lighting to pray for their families, their communities, and the world.

Prayer after Lighting the Sabbath Candles

> *Yehi ratzon millefanecha, adonai elohai
> elohei yisra'el, shettechonein oti (ve'et
> ishi) ve'et kol kerovai, vetittein lanu
> chayyim tovim va'arukkim,
> vetizkereinu bezichron tovah
> uverachah, vetifkedeinu bifkuddat
> yeshu'ah verachamim, vetashkein
> shechinatecha beineinu, vezakkeinu
> legaddeil banim uvenei vanim*

---

6. *Peninei Halakha*, Festivals, chapter 2

chachamim unevonim ohavei adonai,
yir'ei elohim, anshei emet zera kodesh,
badonai deveikim ume'irim et ha'olam
batorah uvema'asim tovim uvechol
melechet avodat habborei. Anna,
shema et techinnati bizchut sarah
verivkah rachel velei'ah immoteinu,
veha'eir nereinu shello yichbeh le'olam
va'ed, veha'eir panecha
venivvashei'ah. Amen.

May it be Your will, O Lord my God and God of Israel, that You be gracious to me (and my spouse) and all my relatives, and grant us good and long lives. Remember us for good and blessing, and consider us for salvation and compassion. May Your Divine Presence dwell among us, and may we merit to raise children and grandchildren who are wise and understanding, who love the Lord and fear God, people of truth, holy offspring, who cling to the Lord and illuminate the world with Torah and good deeds and all the work of serving the Creator. Please, hear my supplication in the merit of Sarah, Rebecca, Rachel, and Leah, our mothers, and illuminate our light so that it never extinguishes forever and ever. May You shine Your face

upon us and we shall be saved.
Amen.

Evening Prayers

The evening service on *Rosh Hashanah* carries a distinct tone that sets the mood for the entire Ten Days of Repentance. The service opens with a special melody, deep, haunting, and unlike those heard on regular holidays, that immediately draws the congregation into the unique spiritual atmosphere of the day. This melody continues throughout the evening prayers, creating a sense of reverence and reflection.

Starting with the evening services, critical changes are made to the *Amidah*, the standing prayer. On *Rosh Hashanah* and *Yom Kippur* (Day of Atonement), we add a paragraph into the third blessing of the *Amidah* prayer asking for God's awe to spread to all creation. This addition emphasizes the universal nature of God's kingship, reminding us that the Divine reigns over the entire world and is not limited to a specific group of people. Reflecting this theme, the familiar closing words of the blessing change from "The Holy God" to "The Holy King," reinforcing the focus on God's sovereignty.

Additions to the High Holiday *Amidah*

a-TAH ka-DOSH v'-shim-KHA ka-DOSH
uk-do-SHEEM b'-khol YOM y'-ha-l'-
LU-kha SE-lah
uv-KHAYN TAYN pakh-d'-KHA a-do-
NAI e-lo-HAY-nu AL kol ma-a-SE-
kha v'-ay-ma-t'-KHA AL kol MAH
she-ba-RA-ta. v'-yi-ra-U-kha KOL
ha-ma-a-SEEM v'-yish-ta-kha-VU

l'-fa-NEH-kha KOL ha-b'-ru-EEM.
v'-yay-a-SU khu-LAM a-gu-DAH e-
KHAT la-a-SOT r'-tzo-n'-KHA b'-lay-
VAV sha-LAYM. k'-MO she-ya-DA-
nu a-do-NAI e-lo-HAY-nu she-ha-
shil-TON l'-fa-NEH-kha OZ b'-ya-d'-
KHA ug-vu-RAH bee-mee-NEH-kha
v'-shim-KHA no-RA AL kol MAH
she-ba-RA-ta

uv-KHAYN TAYN ka-VOD a-do-NAI l'-
a-ME-kha t'-hi-LAH li-ray-E-kha v'-
tik-VAH to-VAH l'-dor-SHE-kha u-
fit-KHON PEH lam-ya-kha-LEEM
LAKH. sim-KHAH l'-ar-TZE-kha v'-
sa-SON l'-ee-RE-kha utz-mi-KHAT
KE-ren l'-da-VID av-DE-kha va-a-ri-
KHAT NAYR l'-ven yi-SHAI m'-shee-
KHE-kha bim-hay-RAH v'-ya-MAY-
nu

uv-KHAYN tza-di-KEEM yir-U v'-yis-
MA-khu vee-sha-REEM ya-a-LO-zu
va-kha-see-DEEM b'-ri-NAH ya-
GEE-lu v'-o-LA-tah tik-PATZ PEE-
ha. v'-KHOL ha-rish-AH ku-LAH k'-
a-SHAN tikh-LEH KEE ta-a-VEER
mem-SHE-let za-DON MIN ha-A-
retz

v'-tim-LOKH a-TAH a-do-NAI l'-va-
DE-kha AL kol ma-a-SE-kha b'-HAR
tzi-YON mish-KAN k'-vo-DE-kha u-
vee-ru-sha-LA-yim EER ka-d'-SHE-
kha. ka-ka-TUV b'-div-RAY ka-d'-
SHE-kha yim-LOKH a-do-NAI l'-o-

LAM e-lo-HA-yikh tzi-YON l'-DOR
va-DOR ha-l'-lu-YAH
ka-DOSH a-TAH v'-no-RA sh'-ME-kha
v'-AYN e-LO-ah mi-bal-a-DE-kha.
ka-ka-TUV va-yig-BAH a-do-NAI
tz'-va-OT ba-mish-PAT v'-ha-AYL
ha-ka-DOSH nik-DASH bitz-da-
KAH. ba-RUKH a-TAH a-do-NAI ha-
ME-lekh ha-ka-DOSH

You are holy and Your Name is holy and
holy beings praise You every day,
forever.

And so, grant that Your awe, O Lord,
our God, be upon all Your works,
and Your dread upon all You have
created; and [then] all [Your] works
will fear You, and prostrate before
You will be all [Your] created beings.
And may they all form a single band
to do Your will with a perfect heart.
For we know O Lord, our God that
rulership is Yours, strength is in
Your hand, might is in Your right
hand and Your Name is awesome
over all You have created.

And so, grant honor, O Lord, to Your
people, praise to those who fear You,
good hope to those who seek You
confident speech to those who yearn
for You, joy to Your land, gladness to
Your city, flourishing of pride to
David, Your servant and an array of

light to the son of Jesse, Your
anointed, speedily in our days.

And then the righteous will see [this]
and rejoice, and the upright will be
jubilant, and the pious will exult
with joyous song; injustice will close
its mouth, and all the wickedness
will vanish like smoke, when You
remove the rule of evil from the
earth.

And You The Lord will reign alone over
all Your works on Mount Zion,
dwelling place of Your glory, and in
Jerusalem, city of Your Sanctuary, as
it is written in Your holy words,
"The Lord will reign forever; Your
God, Zion, throughout all
generations. Praise God."

Holy are You, and awesome is Your
Name, and there is no God beside
You, as it is written, "And the Lord of
Hosts is exalted through justice and
the Almighty, the Holy One, is
sanctified through righteousness."
Blessed are You, O Lord, the King,
the Holy One.

In addition, four other key passages are
added to the *Amidah* beginning on
Rosh Hashanah and continuing
through *Yom Kippur*. These short
prayers implore God to remember us
favorably and inscribe us in the
Book of Life, recalling the divine

judgment and mercy which
characterize these holy days.

In the first blessing we add:

> zokh-RAY-nu l'-kha-YEEM ME-lekh
> kha-FAYTZ ba-kha-YEEM v'-kha-t'-
> VAY-nu b'-SAY-fer ha-kha-YEEM l'-
> MA-an-kha e-lo-HEEM kha-YEEM

> Remember us for life King, Who desires
> life; and inscribe us in the Book of
> Life, for Your sake, Living God.

In the second blessing add:

> mee kha-MO-kha AV ha-ra-kha-MEEM
> zo-KHAYR y'-tzu-RAV l'-kha-YEEM
> b'-ra-kha-MEEM

> Who is like You merciful Father, Who
> remembers His creatures for life, in
> His mercy.

In the second to last blessing add:

> ukh-TOV l'-kha-YEEM to-VEEM KOL b'-
> nay v'-ree-TE-kha

Inscribe for a good life all the children of
Your covenant.

In the last blessing add:

> b'-SAY-fer kha-YEEM b'-ra-KHAH v'-
> sha-LOM u-far-na-SAH to-VAH ni-
> za-KHAYR v'-ni-ka-TAYV l'-fa-NE-
> kha a-NAKH-nu v'-KHOL a-m'-KHA
> BAYT yis-ra-AYL l'-kha-YEEM to-
> VEEM ul-sha-LOM

> In the book of life, blessing, peace and
> abundant maintenance, may we be
> remembered and inscribed before
> You; we and all Your people, the
> House of Yisrael for a good life and
> peace.

The evening service, like all prayer services, concludes with the
Aleinu prayer, which expresses our hope for a future where all
people will recognize and acknowledge God as the sole ruler of
the universe. This prayer takes on deeper meaning during this
season as we proclaim God's sovereignty and our hope that all
humanity will eventually recognize Him as the one true God.

Aleinu Prayer

> a-LAY-nu l'-sha-BAY-akh la-a-DON ha-
> KOL la-TAYT g'-du-LAH l'-yo-TZAYR
> b'-ray-SHEET she-lo a-SA-nu k'-go-
> YAY ha-a-ra-TZOT v'-LO sa-MA-nu

k'-mish-p'-KHOT ha-a-da-MAH
she-LO SAM khel-KAY-nu ka-HEM
v'-go-ra-LAY-nu k'-KHOL ha-mo-
NAM: she-HAYM mish-ta-kha-
VEEM la-HE-vel va-REEK u-mit-pa-
l'-LEEM el AYL lo yo-SHEE-a, va-a-
NAKH-nu ko-r'-EEM u-mish-ta-
kha-VEEM u-mo-DEEM lif-NAY
ME-lekh mal-KHAY ha-m'-la-
KHEEM ha-ka-DOSH ba-RUKH HU,
she-HU no-TEH sha-MA-yim v'-yo-
SAYD A-retz, u-mo-SHAV y'-ka-RO
ba-sha-MA-yim mi-MA-al, ush-
khee-NAT u-ZO b'-gav-HAY m'-ro-
MEEM, HU e-lo-HAY-nu AYN OD, E-
met mal-KAY-nu E-fes zu-la-TO ka-
ka-TUV b'-to-ra-TO v'-ya-DA-ta ha-
YOM v'-ha-shay-VO-ta el l'-va-VE-
kha KEE a-do-NAI HU ha-e-lo-
HEEM ba-sha-MA-yim mi-MA-al v'-
AL ha-A-retz mi-TA-khat AYN OD:
al KAYN n'-ka-VEH l'-KHA a-do-NAI e-
lo-HAY-nu lir-OT m'-hay-RAH b'-tif-
E-ret u-ZE-kha l'-ha-a-VEER gi-lu-
LEEM min ha-A-retz v'-ha-e-lee-
LEEM ka-ROT yi-ka-ray-TUN l'-ta-
KAYN o-LAM b'-mal-KHUT sha-DAI
v'-KHOL b'-nay va-SAR yik-r'-U
vish-ME-kha, l'-haf-NOT ay-LE-kha
KOL rish-AY A-retz, ya-KEE-ru v'-
yay-d'-U KOL yosh-VAY tay-VAYL
KEE l'-KHA tikh-RA kol BE-rekh ti-
sha-VA kol la-SHON: l'-fa-NE-kha a-

do-NAI e-lo-HAY-nu yikh-r'-U v'-yi-
PO-lu, v'-likh-VOD shim-KHA y'-
KAR yi-TAY-nu, vee-ka-b'-LU khu-
LAM et OL mal-khu-TE-kha, v'-tim-
LOKH a-lay-HEM m'-hay-RAH l'-o-
LAM va-ED, KEE ha-mal-KHUT she-
l'-kha HEE ul-o-l'-MAY AD tim-
LOKH b'-kha-VOD, ka-ka-TUV b'-
to-ra-TE-kha a-do-NAI yim-LOKH
l'-o-LAM va-ED: v'-ne-e-MAR v'-ha-
YAH a-do-NAI l'-ME-lekh al kol ha-
A-retz ba-YOM ha-HU yih-YEH a-
do-NAI e-KHAD ush-MO e-KHAD:

It is our obligation to praise the Master
of all, to ascribe greatness to the
Creator of the world in the
beginning: that He has not made us
like the nations of the lands, and has
not positioned us like the families of
the earth; that He has not assigned
our portion like theirs, nor our lot
like that of all their multitudes. For
they prostrate themselves to vanity
and nothingness, and pray to gods
that cannot deliver. But we bow,
prostrate ourselves, and offer thanks
before the Supreme King of Kings,
the Holy One blessed is He, Who
spreads the heavens, and
establishes the earth, and the seat of
His glory is in heaven above, and the
abode of His invincible might is in

the loftiest heights. He is our God,
there is nothing else. Our King is
true, all else is insignificant, as it is
written in His Bible: And You shall
know this day and take into Your
heart that the Lord is God in the
heavens above and upon the earth
below; there is nothing else.
(Deuteronomy 4:39).

We, therefore, put our hope in You, the
Lord our God, to soon behold the
glory of Your might in banishing
idolatry from the earth, and the
false gods will be utterly
exterminated to perfect the world
as the kingdom of Shadai. And all
mankind will invoke Your Name, to
turn back to You, all the wicked of
the earth. They will realize and
know, all the inhabitants of the
world, that to You, every knee must
bend, every tongue must swear
[allegiance to You]. Before You, O
Lord, our God, they will bow and
prostrate themselves, and to the
glory of Your Name give honor. And
they will all accept [upon
themselves] the yoke of Your
kingdom, and You will reign over
them, soon, forever and ever. For
the kingdom is Yours, and to all
eternity You will reign in glory, as it
is written in Your Bible: the Lord

will reign forever and ever. And it is
said: And the Lord will be King over
the whole earth; on that day the
Lord will be One and His
Name One.

Following the evening service, it is customary to greet others
with a special *Rosh Hashanah* blessing: *Leshana tovah teikatev
v'teichatem* for men, or *Leshana tovah teikatevee v'teichatemee* for
women. This greeting means, "May you be written and sealed
for a good year," expressing the wish that one's fate for the
coming year be inscribed favorably in the Book of Life. This
expression acknowledges the gravity of these days of judgment
while expressing our hope and faith that God will indeed grant
us all a year of blessing, health, and peace.

Festive Meal: Sweetness and Symbolism

Following the evening services, families gather for a festive
meal that combines celebration with symbolism.

Before beginning the meal, the head of the household recites
the festival *Kiddush*, the prayer sanctifying the day, over a cup
of wine. He includes the *shehechiyanu* blessing, thanking God
for bringing us to this time.

Shehechiyanu **Blessing**

> ba-RUKH a-TAH a-do-NAI e-lo-HAY-nu
> ME-lekh ha-o-LAM she-he-khe-YA-
> nu v'-ki-y'-MA-nu v'-hi-gi-A-nu la-
> z'-MAN ha-ZEH

> Blessed are You, Lord our God, King of
> the universe, who has given us life,

sustained us, and brought us to this
time.

The ritual hand-washing is then performed before eating bread. Just as on *Sabbath*, the blessing is recited over two loaves of bread called *challah*.

On *Rosh Hashanah*, Jews traditionally eat round *challah* bread instead of the usual braided loaves. The circular shape symbolizes both the cycle of the year and the crown of God's kingship. Because a circle has no beginning or end, it also represents our hope for a year of unending blessings. We dip the *challah* in honey instead of the usual salt, expressing our hopes for a sweet year ahead.

Simanim: Eating Our Prayers

One of the most beloved traditions of *Rosh Hashanah* evening is eating symbolic foods known as *simanim*. This custom, mentioned in the Talmud[7] and elaborated by medieval authorities, uses wordplay and symbolism to express our deepest hopes for the new year.

Various traditions for *simanim* have developed over time, but they all share the same foundational principle. We select foods whose names suggest or sound similar to blessings we hope to receive in the coming year. The ritual follows a simple pattern: before tasting each symbolic food, we recite a specific prayer expressing our hopes for the year ahead, then savor a small portion with intention, thinking about the wishes and possibilities for the new year.

Traditional simanim include:

---

7. Bablonian Talmud, Keritot 6a

- Apple dipped in honey: "May it be Your will to renew for us a good and sweet year." This most famous *siman* represents our hope for sweetness in the coming year.
- Pomegranate: "May it be Your will that our merits be as numerous as the seeds of a pomegranate." The Talmud teaches that even the "empty ones" among us are as full of good deeds as a pomegranate is full of seeds.
- Head of a fish: "May it be Your will that we be as the head and not as the tail." This expresses our wish to be leaders in doing what is right rather than followers.
- Carrots: "May it be Your will that evil decrees against us be torn up." The Hebrew word for carrot (*gezer*) sounds like the word for decree (*gezeira*).
- Dates: "May it be Your will that our enemies come to their end (*yitamu*)." The Hebrew word for date (*tamar*) is similar to the word *tam*, meaning "to complete" or "finish," from which *yitamu* is derived.

Some families have the custom of adding their own *simanim*, finding creative ways to express in food and word what their hearts yearn for in the year to come.

Following the *simanim* ritual, we enjoy a typical holiday meal with delicious food, words of Torah and song. The evening unfolds with warmth and joy, as families linger around the table sharing hopes for the new year. This combination of ritual symbolism and festive celebration sets the tone for the entire holiday period. The meal ends with the traditional Grace After Meals, recited after a meal that contains bread. On *Rosh Hashanah*, we include a special addition for holidays.

The Morning Prayers of *Rosh Hashanah*

Rosh Hashanah is not only a time of celebration, it is also a time of prayer. The morning hours are spent in the synagogue reciting special prayers that reflect the themes of the day, in addition to the regular holiday prayers.

The prayers recited during *Rosh Hashanah* are both ancient and deeply moving. One of the most well-known is *Avinu Malkeinu* ("Our Father, Our King"), a passionate appeal for mercy, forgiveness, and blessing. According to Jewish tradition, the prayer was first composed by the great sage Rabbi Akiva, who lived at the end of the first century and beginning of the second, during a time of national crisis, when a drought was threatening the people of Israel. Rabbi Akiva stood before the congregation and cried out, *"Avinu Malkeinu,"* "Our Father, our King, we have no king except You. Our Father, our King, for Your sake have mercy on us," and it immediately began to rain. This short plea was expanded into the cherished prayer that we recite today as part of the High Holiday liturgy and on fast days throughout the year. It is an expression of both intimacy and reverence, a recognition that God is both a compassionate father and a sovereign king.

This prayer perfectly encapsulates our relationship with God: we are both His children and His subjects. As our Father, He loves and forgives us, but as our King, He sets rules to guide us. This dual relationship also means that as our Father, God desires to help us, and as our King, He has the power to resolve any issue we face.

Avinu Malkeinu Prayer

Avinu malkeinu chatanu lefanecha:

Avinu malkeinu ein lanu melech ella
attah:
Avinu malkeinu aseih immanu lema'an
shemecha:
Avinu malkeinu chaddeish aleinu
shanah tovah:
Avinu malkeinu battel mei'aleinu kol
gezeirot kashot:
Avinu malkeinu batteil machshevot
sone'einu:
Avinu malkeinu hafeir atzat oyeveinu:
Avinu malkeinu kalleih kol tzar umastin
mei'aleinu:
Avinu malkeinu setom piyyot
mastineinu umekatrigeinu:
Avinu malkeinu kalleih dever vecherev
vera'av ushevi umashchit ve'avon
mibbenei veritecha:
Avinu malkeinu mena maggeifah
minnachalatecha:
Avinu malkeinu selach umechal lechol
avonoteinu:
Avinu malkeinu mecheih veha'aveir
pesha'einu vechattoteinu minneged
einecha:
Avinu malkeinu mechok berachamecha
harabbim kol shitrei chovoteinu:
Avinu malkeinu hachazireinu bitshuvah
sheleimah lefanecha:
Avinu malkeinu shelach refu'ah
sheleimah lecholei ammecha:
Avinu malkeinu kera roa' gezar dineinu:

Avinu malkeinu zachereinu bezikkaron
tov lefanecha:

Avinu malkeinu kateveinu beseifer
chayyim tovim:

Avinu malkeinu kateveinu beseifer
ge'ullah vishu'ah:

Avinu malkeinu kateveinu beseifer
parnasah vechalkalah:

Avinu malkeinu kateveinu beseifer
zechuyyot:

Avinu malkeinu kateveinu beseifer
selichah umechilah:

Avinu malkeinu hatzmach lanu
yeshu'ah bekarov:

Avinu malkeinu hareim keren yisra'el
ammecha:

Avinu malkeinu hareim keren
meshichecha:

Avinu malkeinu mallei yadeinu
mibbirchotecha:

Avinu malkeinu mallei asameinu sava:

Avinu malkeinu shema koleinu chus
veracheim aleinu:

Avinu malkeinu kabbeil berachamim
uveratzon et tefillatenu:

Avinu malkeinu petach sha'arei
shamayim litfillateinu:

Avinu malkeinu zachor ki afar
anachenu:

Avinu malkeinu na al teshiveinu reikam
millefanecha:

Avinu malkeinu tehei hasha'ah hazzot

she'at rachamim ve'eit ratzon
millefanecha:
Avinu malkeinu chamol aleinu ve'al
olaleinu vetappeinu:
Avinu malkeinu aseih lema'an harugim
al sheim kodshecha:
Avinu malkeinu aseih lema'an tevuchim
al yichudecha:
Avinu malkeinu aseih lema'an ba'ei
va'eish uvammayim al kiddush
shemecha:
Avinu malkeinu nekom nikmat dam
avadecha hashafuch:
Avinu malkeinu aseih lema'ancha im lo
lema'aneinu:
Avinu malkeinu aseih lema'ancha
vehoshi'einu:
Avinu malkeinu aseih lema'an
rachamecha harabbim:
Avinu malkeinu aseih lema'an shimcha
haggadol haggibbor vehannora
shennikra aleinu:
Avinu malkeinu chonneinu va'aneinu ki
ein banu ma'asim aseih immanu
tzedakah vachesed vehoshi'einu:

Our Father, our King! we have sinned
before You.
Our Father our King! we have no King
except You.
Our Father, our King! deal with us
[kindly] for the sake of Your Name.

Our Father, our King! renew for us a
good year.

Our Father, our King! annul all harsh
decrees concerning us.

Our Father, our King! annul the designs
of those who hate us.

Our Father, our King! thwart the plans
of our enemies.

Our Father, our King! rid us of every
oppressor and adversary.

Our Father, our King! close the mouths
of our adversaries and our accusers.

Our Father, our King! remove pestilence,
sword, famine, captivity,
destruction and [the burden of]
iniquity from the members of Your
covenant.

Our Father, our King! withhold the
plague from Your inheritance.

Our Father, our King! forgive and
pardon all our iniquities.

Our Father, our King! blot out and
remove our transgressions and sins
from before Your eyes.

Our Father, our King! erase in Your
abundant mercy all records of our
liabilities.

Our Father, our King! bring us back in
wholehearted repentance
before You.

Our Father, our King! send complete
healing to the sick among Your
people.

Our Father, our King! tear up the evil
[parts] of our sentence.

Our Father, our King! remember us
favorably before You.

Our Father, our King! inscribe us in the
Book of Good Life.

Our Father, our King! inscribe us in the
Book of Redemption and
Deliverance.

Our Father, our King! inscribe us in the
Book of Maintenance and
Sustenance.

Our Father, our King! inscribe us in the
Book of Merits.

Our Father, our King! inscribe us in the
Book of Pardon and Forgiveness.

Our Father, our King! cause deliverance
to spring forth for us soon.

Our Father, our King! raise up the might
of Israel Your people.

Our Father, our King! raise up the might
of Your anointed.

Our Father, our King! fill our hands with
Your blessings.

Our Father, our King! fill our
storehouses with abundance.

Our Father, our King! hear our voice,
spare us and have compassion
upon us.

Our Father, our King! accept our prayer
with compassion and favor.

Our Father, our King! open the gates of
heaven to our prayer.

Our Father, our King! remember, that
we are dust.

Our Father, our King! please do not turn
us away empty-handed from You.

Our Father, our King! let this hour be an
hour of compassion and a time of
favor before You.

Our Father, our King! have compassion
upon us, and upon our children and
infants.

Our Father, our King! do it for the sake
of those who were slain for Your
Holy Name.

Our Father, our King! do it for the sake
of those who were slaughtered for
[proclaiming] Your Unity.

Our Father, our King! do it for the sake
of those who went through fire and
water for the sanctification of Your
Name.

Our Father, our King! avenge the spilled
blood of Your servants.

Our Father, our King! do it for Your sake
if not for ours.

Our Father, our King! do it for Your sake
and deliver us.

Our Father, our King! do it for the sake
of Your great mercy.

Our Father, our King! do it for the sake
of Your great, mighty, and awesome
Name which is proclaimed upon us.

Our Father, our King! favor us and
answer us for we have no

accomplishments; deal with us
charitably and kindly and deliver us.

Torah Reading

As on all Jewish holidays, we pause between the morning service and additional *Musaf* prayers to read from the Torah. Each holiday has its own special readings, chosen because they reflect the distinct character and messages of the day. On *Rosh Hashanah*, these ancient stories reflect the themes of: divine judgment, mercy, and the possibility of transformation.

First Day: Sarah's Laughter and Ishmael's Redemption

On the first day of *Rosh Hashanah*, we read from Genesis 21, which tells not one but two remarkable stories that illuminate the holiday's themes. The reading begins with the fulfillment of God's seemingly impossible promise to Sarah that she would have a child and continues with an unexpected tale that offers deep lessons about divine judgment and mercy.

The story opens with the miraculous birth of Isaac to Abraham and Sarah. Sarah, now ninety years old and long past childbearing years, gives birth to the child whose name, Isaac, means "laughter." The reading captures Sarah's wonder and joy: "God has brought me laughter; everyone who hears will laugh with me." According to the Sages, both Sarah and Hannah (whose story we read in the selection from the Prophets known as the *Haftarah*) had their prayers for children answered, and they conceived on *Rosh Hashanah*. This makes the first day's reading a celebration of answered prayer and divine compassion, inspiring us to approach our own prayers on this day with the same faith and intensity that these righteous women demonstrated.

But the Torah reading doesn't end with Isaac's birth. It continues with a much more difficult story, the expulsion of Hagar and her son Ishmael from Abraham's household. At first glance, this seems disconnected from *Rosh Hashanah*'s themes. Why include a story of family conflict and banishment on a day of renewal and hope?

The answer lies in an unexpected source. Ishmael himself becomes a model for repentance and divine mercy. When Ishmael is dying of thirst in the wilderness, the Torah tells us that "God heard the cry of the boy, and a messenger of God called to Hagar from heaven and said to her, "What troubles you, Hagar? Fear not, for God has heeded the cry of the boy where he is" (Genesis 21:17).

The phrase "where he is" is unusual and contains a revolutionary teaching about divine judgment. The medieval commentator Rashi explains that the ministering angels protested to God: "Why save someone whose descendants will one day cause suffering to Your people?" But God responded: "Right now, what is he, righteous or wicked?" When they answered "righteous," God declared: "I judge him according to his actions now, not according to what he might do in the future."[8]

This lesson speaks directly to anyone who feels discouraged about spiritual growth or transformation. Many people approaching *Rosh Hashanah* feel like hypocrites, thinking: "How can I ask for forgiveness when I'll probably make the same mistakes again next year?" Ishmael's story answers this doubt definitively. What matters is not our past failures or our

---

8. Based on the Babylonian Talmud, Rosh Hashanah 16a

fears about future lapses. What matters is our sincere intention right now, in this moment.

Even if you've been confronting the same character flaws for fifteen years, even if you've made and broken the same resolutions repeatedly, that history doesn't disqualify you from genuine repentance today. God judges us "according to where we are now," based on our current resolve, our present sincerity, and our immediate commitment to growth. The fact that we've struggled before only makes our current determination more precious, not less meaningful.

Second Day: The Ultimate Test

The Torah reading for the second day presents one of the most challenging and profound stories in all of Scripture: The Binding of Isaac. Found in Genesis 22, this narrative has been contemplated, debated, and interpreted by countless generations seeking to understand its meaning.

The story begins with God's shocking command to Abraham: "Take your son, your only son Isaac, whom you love, and go to the land of Moriah, and offer him there as a burnt offering" (Genesis 22:2). After waiting decades for this promised child, after seeing God's covenant seemingly fulfilled in Isaac's birth, Abraham now faces an incomprehensible demand that appears to contradict everything he has been promised.

What follows is a journey of three days to Mount Moriah, where Abraham binds Isaac upon an altar and raises the knife. Only at the final moment does an angel call out: "Do not lay your hand on the boy or do anything to him, for now I know that you fear God, since you have not withheld your son, your only son, from me" (Genesis 22:12). Abraham then notices a ram caught in a thicket, which he offers instead of Isaac.

This story resonates powerfully with *Rosh Hashanah*'s themes of judgment and mercy. Abraham faces the ultimate test of faith; not just belief in God's existence, but willingness to trust divine wisdom even when it contradicts human understanding. The story explores the depths of devotion, the nature of sacrifice, and the relationship between divine command and human conscience.

For many readers, the Binding of Isaac raises difficult questions. How can a loving God demand such a sacrifice? What does it mean to "fear God" in the way Abraham demonstrated? Different interpretations have emerged throughout history, but most find in this story a testament to the depth of Abraham's commitment.

The ram that appears at the crucial moment connects directly to *Rosh Hashanah*'s central ritual. The *shofar* blown on this day is traditionally made from a ram's horn, serving as an eternal reminder of the ram that took Isaac's place. Each blast recalls Abraham's willingness to sacrifice everything for his faith and God's provision of another way. In Jewish understanding, the merit of Abraham's devotion continues to benefit his descendants, making this story a powerful petition for divine mercy during the season of judgment.

The Binding of Isaac also speaks to the transformative power of crisis and testing. Both Abraham and Isaac emerge from this experience fundamentally changed. Abraham has demonstrated the ultimate proof of his faith, while Isaac has experienced both the fragility of life and the power of divine intervention. Their story suggests that moments of greatest challenge can become turning points that deepen our relationship with the Divine and strengthen our spiritual resolve.

The *Haftarah* Readings: Prophetic Voices of Hope

Following the Torah reading on each day of *Rosh Hashanah*, we read selected passages from the Prophets known as the *Haftarah*. These readings extend and amplify the themes introduced in the Torah portions and connect to the nature of the day.

First Day *Haftarah*: Hannah's Prayer

The *Haftarah* for the first day is taken from the beginning of I Samuel (1:1-2:10), and tells the story of Hannah, a woman who desperately longed for a child. The connection to the Torah reading is both historical and spiritual. According to the Sages, just as Sarah conceived Isaac on *Rosh Hashanah*, Hannah's prayers were also answered on this day, and she conceived.

Hannah's story begins in heartbreak. Unable to conceive while her husband's other wife has multiple children, she experiences the deep pain of unfulfilled longing. But rather than despair, Hannah channels her anguish into prayer. The text describes her praying at the Tabernacle "in bitterness of soul" (I Samuel 1:10), moving her lips silently with such intensity that the priest Eli initially mistakes her for a drunk woman.

When Hannah explains that she is "pouring out her soul before the Lord" (verse 15), Eli blesses her, and she conceives. True to her promise, she dedicates her son Samuel to God's service, and he becomes one of Israel's greatest prophets and leaders.

By reading about both Sarah and Hannah on the same day, we recall not only their individual greatness but draw inspiration from their examples of persistent, heartfelt prayer. Their stories teach us that even when our situations seem hopeless, sincere supplication can reach heaven and bring about miraculous change. On the day when the entire world stands in judgment, these women's stories offer hope that our prayers matter.

Second Day *Haftarah*: Jeremiah's Vision of Return

The second day's reading from the prophet Jeremiah (31:2-20) offers a beautiful message of hope that perfectly balances the intensity of the Binding of Isaac story. After hearing about Abraham's ultimate test of faith, we need to hear about God's unlimited love.

The passage opens with one of the most comforting promises in all of Scripture: "I have loved you with an everlasting love; therefore have I drawn you to Me with loving-kindness." These words remind us that even when we stand in judgment, we stand before a God whose relationship with us is built on love, not just justice.

Jeremiah's vision includes one of the most heartbreaking images in the Bible: Rachel weeping for her exiled children. "A voice is heard in Ramah, lamentation and bitter weeping. Rachel is weeping for her children; she refuses to be comforted for her children, because they are no more" (Jeremiah 31:15).

But immediately after this scene of despair comes God's promise of hope: "Keep your voice from weeping and your eyes from tears, for there is a reward for your work... and your children shall come back to their own country" (Jeremiah 31:16-17).

The reading ends with words that reveal God's heart like a loving parent: "Is Ephraim my dear son? Is he my darling child? For as often as I speak against him, I do remember him still. Therefore my heart yearns for him; I will surely have mercy on him, declares the Lord" (Jeremiah 31:20).

This reading gives us exactly what we need after the challenging story of Isaac's binding. While the Torah portion shows us the demands of faith and the weight of divine testing, Jeremiah reveals God's tender, parental love and deep desire for reconciliation. Together, they show us the complete picture of our relationship with God: one that includes both challenge and comfort, testing and tenderness, judgment and mercy.

Jeremiah's message also speaks directly to *Rosh Hashanah*'s call for *teshuvah* (return/repentance). No matter how far we've wandered from where we should be, the path back remains open. The weeping that Jeremiah describes, both Rachel's and our own, isn't the end of the story. It's part of the journey toward healing and joy.

This vision of return points toward something even greater. Just as Rachel's tears will give way to her children's homecoming, the *shofar* we hear on *Rosh Hashanah* carries the promise of an ultimate homecoming when all of humanity will recognize God's love and the scattered will be gathered. Our personal return to God during these days connects to this larger hope for the world's healing, reminding us that when we grow spiritually, we're part of something much bigger than ourselves.

Musaf: The Additional Prayer

Following the reading from the Torah and the Prophets, we recite the *Musaf* prayer, the additional *Amida* (standing) prayer that is recited on Jewish festivals.

One of the most haunting prayers of *Rosh Hashanah* comes to us from a story of incredible courage. In 11th-century Germany, a rabbi named Amnon faced an impossible choice. The local bishop repeatedly pressured him to convert to Christianity, and when Rabbi Amnon asked for time to consider, he immediately regretted even suggesting he might abandon his faith.

When soldiers dragged him before the bishop for his answer, Rabbi Amnon said, "My tongue should be cut out for failing to refuse you immediately." The enraged bishop took him literally, ordering that the rabbi's hands and feet be severed. Rabbi Amnon was carried home, broken in body but unbroken in spirit.

On *Rosh Hashanah*, as he lay dying, Rabbi Amnon asked to be brought to the synagogue. There, with his final breath, he composed one of the most powerful prayers in Jewish liturgy: *Unetaneh Tokef*.

The prayer captures both the terror and hope of standing before God in judgment. It paints a vivid picture: the divine court opening the Book of Life, every person's fate hanging in the balance. "Who will live and who will die," it asks, "who will have rest and who will wander, who will be serene and who tormented?"

But just when the prayer threatens to overwhelm us with life's fragility, it offers hope. Three actions, it teaches, can change even the harshest decree: repentance, prayer, and charity. Not because they earn us anything, but because they transform us. When we truly examine our hearts, reach out to God, and care for others, we become different people—people worthy of a different fate.

The prayer ends with perhaps the most honest words ever written about human existence: "We come from dust, and return to dust... we are like broken shards, like dry grass, like a withered flower, like a passing shadow and a vanishing cloud." Yet even in acknowledging our frailty, we find strength: "But You are the King who lives eternal. There is no end to Your years and there is no limit to the length of Your days...." *Unetaneh Tokef* holds space for both our deepest fears and our highest hopes, reminding us that even when everything else fails, our connection to the Divine endures.

Unetaneh Tokef

> u-n'-ta-NEH TO-kef k'-du-SHAT ha-
> YOM, kee HU no-RA v'-a-YOM, u-VO
> ti-na-SAY mal-khu-TE-kha, v'-yi-
> KON b'-KHE-sed kis-E-kha, v'-tay-
> SHAYV a-LAV be-e-MET. e-MET, e-
> MET a-TAH HU da-YAN u-mo-
> KHEE-akh, v'-yo-DAY-a va-AYD, v'-
> kho-TAYV v'-kho-TAYM, v'-so-FAYR
> u-mo-NEH, v'-tiz-KOR kol ha-nish-
> ka-KHOT. v'-tif-TAKH et SAY-fer ha-
> zikh-ro-NOT, u-may-ay-LAV yi-ka-
> RAY, v'-kho-TAM yad kol a-DAM BO.
> u-v'-sho-FAR ga-DOL yi-ta-KA, v'-
> KOL d'-ma-MAH da-KAH yi-sha-
> MA, u-mal-a-KHEEM yay-kha-fay-
> ZUN, v'-KHEEL ur-a-DAH yo-khay-
> ZUN, v'-yo-m'-RU, hi-NAY yom ha-
> DEEN, lif-KOD al tz'-VA ma-ROM
> ba-DEEN, kee lo yiz-KU v'-ay-NE-
> kha ba-DEEN. v'-khol ba-AY o-LAM
> ya-av-RUN l'-fa-NE-kha kiv-NAY
> ma-RON: k'-va-ka-RAT ro-EH ed-
> RO, ma-a-VEER tzo-NO TA-khat

shiv-TO, KAYN ta-a-VEER v'-tis-POR
v'-tim-NEH v'-tif-KOD NE-fesh kol
KHAI, v'-takh-TAYKH kitz-VAH l'-
khol b'-ri-yo-TE-kha, v'-tikh-TOV et
g'-ZAR di-NAM
b'-ROSH ha-sha-NAH yi-ka-tay-VUN,
uv-YOM tzom ki-PUR yay-kha-tay-
MUN: ka-MAH ya-av-RUN v'-kha-
MAH yi-ba-ray-UN, mee yikh-YEH
u-mee ya-MUT, mee v'-kitz-O u-
mee lo v'-kitz-O. mee va-MA-yim u-
mee va-AYSH. mee ve-KHA-rev u-
mee va-kha-YAH. mee va-RA-av u-
mee va-tza-MA. mee va-RA-ash u-
mee va-ma-gay-FAH. mee va-kha-
nee-KAH u-mee va-s'-kee-LAH. mee
ya-NU-akh u-mee ya-NU-a. mee
yish-KOT u-mee yi-ta-RAYF. mee yi-
sha-LAYV u-mee yit-ya-SAYR. mee
yay-a-NEE u-mee yay-a-SHAYR.
mee yush-PAL u-mee ya-RUM
ut-shu-VAH ut-fi-LAH utz-da-KAH ma-
a-vee-REEN et RO-a ha-g'-zay-RAH
kee kh'-shim-KHA KAYN t'-hi-la-TE-
kha, ka-SHEH likh-OS v'-NO-akh
lir-TZOT, kee lo takh-POTZ b'-mot
ha-MAYT, kee im b'-shu-VO mi-dar-
KO v'-kha-YAH. v'-ad yom mo-TO t'-
kha-KEH LO, im ya-SHUV mi-YAD
t'-ka-b'-LO: e-MET, kee a-TAH hu
yo-tz'-RAM, v'-a-TAH yo-DAY-a
yitz-RAM, kee HAYM ba-SAR va-
DAM. a-DAM y'-so-DO may-a-FAR

v'-so-FO le-a-FAR, b'-naf-SHO ya-
VEE lakh-MO, ma-SHUL k'-KHE-res
ha-nish-BAR, k'-kha-TZEER ya-
VAYSH, ukh-TZEETZ no-VAYL, ukh-
TZAYL o-VAYR, ukh-a-NAN ka-LAH,
ukh-RU-akh no-SHA-vet, ukh-a-
VAK po-RAY-akh, v'-kha-kha-LOM
ya-UF
v'-a-TAH HU ME-lekh AYL KHAI v'-ka-
YAM
AYN kitz-VAH lish-no-TE-kha, v'-AYN
KAYTZ l'-O-rekh ya-ME-kha. v'-AYN
l'-sha-AYR mar-k'-VOT k'-vo-DE-
kha, v'-AYN l'-fa-RAYSH ay-LUM sh'-
ME-kha. shim-KHA na-EH l'-KHA,
v'-a-TAH na-EH lish-ME-kha. ush-
MAY-nu ka-RA-ta bish-ME-kha

We lend power to the holiness of this
day. For it is tremendous and awe
filled, and on it Your kingship will be
exalted, Your throne will be
established in loving-kindness, and
You will sit on that throne in truth.
It is true that You are the one who
judges, and reproves, who knows
all, and bears witness, who
inscribes, and seals, who reckons
and enumerates. You remember all
that is forgotten. You open the book
of records, and from it, all shall be
read. In it lies each person's insignia.
And with a great shofar it is

sounded, and a thin silent voice shall be heard. And the angels shall be alarmed, and dread and fear shall seize them as they proclaim: behold! the Day of Judgment on which the hosts of heaven shall be judged, for they too shall not be judged blameless by You, and all creatures shall parade before You as a herd of sheep. As a shepherd herds his flock, directing his sheep to pass under his staff, so too You shall pass, count, and record the souls of all living, and decree a limit to each persons days, and inscribe their final judgment.

On *Rosh Hashanah* (Jewish New Year) it is inscribed, and on *Yom Kippur* (Day of Atonement) it is sealed - how many shall pass away and how many shall be born, who shall live and who shall die, who in good time, and who by an untimely death, who by water and who by fire, who by sword and who by wild beast, who by famine and who by thirst, who by earthquake and who by plague, who by strangulation and who by lapidation, who shall have rest and who wander, who shall be at peace and who pursued, who shall be serene and who tormented, who shall become impoverished

and who wealthy, who shall be
debased, and who exalted.
But repentance, prayer and
righteousness avert the severity of
the decree.
For Your praise is just as your name. You
are slow to anger and quick to be
appeased. For You do not desire the
death of the condemned, rather,
that they turn from their path and
live and you wait for them until the
day of their death, and if they
repent, you receive them
immediately. It is true - [For] You
are their Creator and You
understand their inclination, for
they are but flesh and blood. We
come from dust, and return to dust.
We labour by our lives for bread, we
are like broken shards, like dry
grass, and like a withered flower;
like a passing shadow and a
vanishing cloud, like a breeze that
passes, like dust that scatters, like a
fleeting dream.
But You are the King who lives eternal.
There is no end to Your years and there
is no limit to the length of Your days.
Immeasurable are the chariots of
angels who glorify You, and there is
no way to describe Your
imperceptable Name. Your Name is
fitting for You, and You are worthy

of Your Name; and our name, You
have called by Your Name.

Three Extra Blessings

Three themes define the holiday of *Rosh Hashanah*: kingship, remembrance, and the blowing of the ram's horn (*shofar*). These themes come alive in the *Musaf* service, which includes three special blessings added to the regular prayers. These blessings are called *Malchuyot* (Kingship), *Zichronot* (Remembrance), and *Shofarot* (Shofar). Each one draws from ten biblical verses that illuminate its theme, creating a rich blend of passages from throughout Scripture that capture what *Rosh Hashanah* is all about.

Malchuyot: The Day God Became King

Rosh Hashanah commemorates far more than the beginning of a new year. It marks the day Adam was created and, through his creation, the day God was crowned King of the universe. While God had already brought forth angels, animals, and the entire natural world, true kingship requires willing subjects, not merely commanded servants or instinctual creatures.

When Adam first opened his eyes and recognized God as Master and King of all creation, something extraordinary occurred. For the first time in history, a being endowed with free will consciously chose to acknowledge God's sovereignty. Thus, the day marking humanity's creation became the day of God's coronation.

In the *Malchuyot* blessing, we express gratitude for the special relationship God established with the Jewish people while acknowledging His rule over all existence. We conclude with earnest hope that the day will arrive when all nations recognize God's sovereignty, fulfilling the vision that began with humanity's first conscious moment in the Garden of Eden; a time when all creation will unite in acknowledging the one true King.

Malchuyot

It is our obligation to praise the Master of all, to ascribe greatness to the Creator of [the world in] the beginning: that He has not made us like the nations of the lands, and has not positioned us like the families of the earth; that He has not assigned our portion like theirs, nor our lot like that of all their multitudes. For they prostrate themselves to vanity and nothingness, and pray to a god that cannot deliver. But we bow, prostrate ourselves, and offer thanks before the Supreme King of kings, the Holy One blessed is He, Who spreads the heavens, and establishes the earth, and the seat of His glory is in the heaven above, and the abode of His invincible might is in the loftier heights. He is our God, there is nothing else. Our King is true, all else is insignificant, as it is written in His Torah: "And You shall know this day and take into your heart that the Lord is God in the

heavens above and upon the earth
below; there is nothing else."
We therefore put our hope in You, the
Lord our God, to soon behold the
glory of Your might in banishing
idolatry from the earth; and the
false gods will be utterly
exterminated to perfect the world as
the kingdom of Shadai. And all
mankind will invoke Your Name, to
turn back to You, all the wicked of
the earth. They will realize, and
know, all the inhabitants of the
world, that to You every knee must
bend, every tongue must swear
allegiance to You. Before You, O
Lord, our God, they will bow and
prostrate themselves, and to the
glory of Your Name give honor. And
they will accept upon themselves
the yoke of Your kingdom, and You
will reign over them, soon, forever
and ever. For the kingdom is Yours,
and to all eternity You will reign in
glory, as it is written in Your Torah:
"the Lord will reign forever and
ever."
And it is said: "He beheld no iniquity in
Jacob, nor did He see wrongdoing in
Israel; the Lord, His God is with him,
and the love of the king is among
them." And it is said: "And He was
King in Jeshurun, with the gathering

of the heads of the people, the tribes
of Iisrael were united."

And in Your holy words it is written:
"For the kingship is the Lord's, and
He rules over nations." And it is said:
"The Lord has begun His reign, He
has clothed Himself in majesty; the
Lord has clothed Himself, He has
girded Himself with strength. He
has also firmly established the
world so that it cannot be moved."
And it is said: "Lift up your heads,—
gates, and be uplifted entranceways
to eternity, so that the King of Glory
may enter. Who is this King of
Glory? the Lord, strong and mighty;
the Lord, the Mighty One in battle.
Lift up your heads,—gates, and lift
up entranceways to eternity, so that
the King of Glory may enter. Who is
He, this King of Glory? the Lord of
Hosts, He is the King of Glory,
Selah."

And by the hand of Your servants, the
Prophets it is written: "Thus said the
Lord, King of Israel and its
Redeemer, the Lord of Hosts: 'I am
the first and I am the last; and
beside Me, there is no God'." And it
is said: "And deliverers will go up to
Mount Tziyon to judge the mount of
Esav, and the kingdom will be the
Lord's." And it is said: "And the Lord

will be King over the whole earth;
on that day the Lord will be One and
His Name One."

And in Your Torah it is written: "Hear,
Israel: the Lord is our God the Lord
is One!"

Our God and God of our fathers, reign
over the entire world with Your
glory, and be uplifted over all the
earth with Your honor, and appear
in the splendor of Your majestic
might over all who dwell in the
inhabited world of Your earth; so
everything that has been made will
know that You have made it, and it
will be understood by everything
that was formed that You have
formed it. And they will say
everyone who has breath in his
nostrils, "the Lord, God of Israel is
King and His Kingship rules over all.

(*On Shabbat, add:* Our God and God of
our fathers, be pleased with our
rest) Sanctify us with Your
commandments and give our share
in Your Torah; satisfy us from Your
goodness and gladden us with Your
deliverance, (*On Shabbos, add:* And
give us as our inheritance the Lord
our God with love and with
pleasure Your holy Shabbat; and
may Israel rest thereon— they who
are sanctifiers of Your Name) and

purify our hearts to serve You in
truth, for You are the true God, and
Your word is true and enduring
forever. Blessed are You the Lord,
King over all the earth, Sanctifier
(*On Shabbos, add:* of Shabbos and) of
Yisrael and the Day of
Remembrance.

Zichronot (Remembrance): The God Who Remembers Everything

Standing before God as King on *Rosh Hashanah*, we recognize that nothing escapes His divine awareness. The *Zichronot* blessing emphasizes that God remembers every action, every word, every moment of our lives throughout the year. According to tradition, this is the day when God opens the Book of Life, reviewing the deeds of every individual as He determines what will be inscribed for the year ahead. While this comprehensive remembrance and divine accounting might initially seem daunting, it contains profound comfort. God's memory serves our benefit. He recalls not only our failures but also our good deeds, our spiritual struggles, and our sincere efforts toward improvement.

More significantly, God remembers the accumulated merit of our ancestors and His eternal covenant with the Jewish people. The righteous acts of Abraham, Isaac, and Jacob continue to resonate through history, creating a treasury of merit that benefits us today. When we conclude with "Who remembers His covenant," we acknowledge that God's memory encompasses all of history, linking us to every act of faith and devotion performed by those who came before us, and affirming that His covenant relationship with us endures beyond any single year's accounting.

Zichronot

> You remember the dealings of [men in]
> today's world, and You [also]
> consider the behavior of all those
> who lived in earlier times. In Your
> Presence are revealed all hidden
> things and the multitude of secrets
> from the beginning of creation; for
> there is no forgetfulness before the
> throne of Your Glory, and there is
> nothing hidden from Your eyes. You
> remember all that has been done,
> and even all that which is formed is
> not concealed from You. All is
> revealed and known before You, the
> Lord, our God Who observes and
> looks until the end of all
> generations. For You set an
> appointed time of remembrance, to
> consider every soul and being; to
> cause numerous deeds to be
> remembered and the multitude of
> creatures without end. From the
> beginning of creation, You have
> made this known, and from before
> time You have revealed it. This day
> [Rosh Hashana] is the beginning of
> Your work a memorial of the first
> day. For it is a statute for Israel a

[day of] judgment of the God of
Jacob. And over countries
[judgment] is pronounced, which of
them is destined for the sword [war]
and which for peace, which for
famine and which for abundance.
And on it, creatures are brought to
mind, to be remembered for life or
for death. Who is not considered on
this day? For the remembrance of all
that is formed comes before You: the
dealings of man, and the decree of
his fate, and the misdeeds of man's
actions, the thoughts of man and his
schemes, and the motives for the
deeds of man. Fortunate is the man
who does not forget You, the son of
man who gains strength in You. For
those who seek You will never
stumble, and never will they be
disgraced— all who trust in You. For
the remembrance of all their deeds
come before You, and You examine
the deeds of all of them.

And Noah too, You remembered with
love, and [therefore] decreed for him
a promise of deliverance and
compassion, when You brought the
flood-waters to destroy all flesh
because of the wickedness of their
deeds. Therefore, his remembrance
came before You, the Lord, our God,
to multiply his seed like the dust of

the earth, and his descendants as
the sand of the sea; as it is written in
Your Torah; "And God remembered
Noah and all the beasts and all the
cattle that were with him in the Ark,
and God caused a wind to pass over
the earth, and the waters were
calmed."

And it is said: "And God heard their
groaning cry, and God remembered
His covenant with Abraham, with
Isaac, and with Jacob." And it is said:
"I will remember My covenant with
Jacob, and also My covenant with
Isaac, and also My covenant with
Abraham, will I remember; and the
land [of Israel] I will remember."

And in Your holy words it is written: "He
made a memorial for His wonders,
gracious and merciful is the Lord."
And it is said: "He gave food to those
who fear Him; He is ever mindful of
His covenant." And it is said: "And
He remembered His covenant for
them, and He relented in accordance
with His abundant kindness."

And by the hand of Your servants, the
Prophets it is written: "Go and
proclaim it in the ears of
Yerushalayim, saying: thus said the
Lord, I remembered for you the
kindness of your youth, the love of
your bridal days, how you followed

Me into the wilderness, in a land
that was not cultivated." And it is
said: "I will remember My covenant
[which I made] with you in the days
of your youth, and I will fulfill it for
you as an everlasting covenant."
And it is said: "Is Ephraim not My
precious son, is he not a child of
delight? For whenever I speak of
him, I recall him even more;
Therefore, My innermost being is
aroused for him, I will surely have
compassion on him, says the Lord."

Our God and God of our fathers
remember us favorably before You
and be mindful of us for deliverance
and compassion from the eternal
high heavens. Remember in our
behalf, the Lord, our God, the
covenant, the kindness and the oath
which You swore to our father
Abraham on Mount Moriah, and let
there appear before You the binding
with which our father Abraham
bound his son Isaac upon the altar,
and how he suppressed his
compassion to do Your will with a
whole heart; so may Your
compassion suppress Your anger
against us, and in Your great
goodness turn Your fierce anger
away from Your people, and from
Your city, from Your land, and from

Your territorial heritage. And fulfill
for us the Lord, our God the promise
You made in Your Torah, through
Your servant, Moses, from the
mouth of Your glory, as it is said: "I
will remember for them the
covenant with their forefathers
whom I took out of the land of
Egypt, before the eyes of the
nations, to be their God; I am the
Lord." For He Who remembers all
forgotten things from eternity, are
You, and there is no forgetfulness
before the Throne of Your Glory; and
the binding of Isaac— in behalf of
his descendants— may You
remember it today with
compassion. Blessed are You the
Lord, Who remembers the covenant.

Shofarot: The Sound That Transforms

The Bible describes *Rosh Hashanah* as "a day when the horn is
sounded" (Numbers 29:1). Blowing the *shofar* on this day
fulfills a dual function that perfectly embodies the essence of
Rosh Hashanah. Its piercing blasts simultaneously announce
the coronation of our King (*Malchuyot*) and summon us to
stand before His throne in judgment (*Zichronot*). The Talmud
teaches that God instructs us: "And recite before Me on *Rosh
HaShana* verses that mention Kingships, Remembrances, and
Shofar: Kingships so that you will crown Me as King over you;

Remembrances so that your remembrance will rise before Me for good; and with what? With the *shofar*."[9]

The *shofar*'s significance extends beyond this sacred day. Its call connects us to Mount Sinai, where the Torah was revealed accompanied by thunder and an intensifying *shofar* blast, as Scripture records: "The sound of the *shofar* grew louder and louder" (Exodus 19:19). It also directs our vision toward the future, when the great *shofar* will herald the final redemption, as Isaiah prophesies: "And it shall come to pass on that day, that a great *shofar* shall be blown, and those who were lost in the land of Assyria and those who were banished to the land of Egypt shall come and worship the Lord on the holy mountain in Jerusalem" (Isaiah 27:13). Thus, through the simple blast of a ram's horn, we traverse the entire scope of history, from divine revelation to annual judgment to the ultimate redemption of all creation.

Shofarot

> You were revealed in Your cloud of glory
>   to Your holy people to speak to
>   them. From the heavens, You let
>   them hear Your voice, and revealed
>   Yourself to them in pure clouds. So
>   too, the entire world quivered before
>   You, and the works of creation
>   trembled before You, when You, our
>   King revealed Yourself upon Mount
>   Sinai to teach Your people Torah and
>   commandments. You let them hear
>   the majestic splendor of Your voice,

---

9. Babylonian Talmud, Rosh Hashanah 16a

and Your holy words from flames of
fire; amidst thunder and lightning
You revealed Yourself to them, and
with the sound of a *shofar*, You
appeared to them,

as it is written in Your Torah: "And it
was on the third day, as morning
dawned there was thunder and
lightning, and a dense cloud over
the mountain, and the sound of a
shofar was exceedingly loud; and all
the people in the camp trembled."
And it is said: "And the sound of the
shofar became increasingly louder;
Moses spoke and God answered him
by voice." And it is said: "And all the
people saw the sounds and the
flames, and the sound of the *shofar*,
and the mountain in smoke; and the
people saw and were shaken, and
stood from afar."

And in Your holy words it is written:
"God has ascended with a blast, the
Lord, with the sound of a *shofar*."
And it is said: "With trumpets and
the sound of a *shofar* raise your
voices before the King, the Lord."
And it is said: "Blow a *shofar* on the
New Moon, as the appointed time
for our festive-day. For it is a statute
for Israel, a day of judgment of the
God of Jacob." And it is said: "Praise
God. Praise the Almighty in His

Sanctuary Praise God in the firmament of His might. Praise Him for His mighty deeds, Praise Him according to the abundance of His greatness. Praise Him with the blowing of a *shofar*, Praise Him with lyre and harp. Praise Him with drum and dance, Praise Him with stringed instruments and flute. Praise Him with resounding cymbals, Praise Him with clanging cymbals. Let every soul praise God, Praise God."

And by the hand of Your servants, the Prophets it is written: "All who inhabit the world of man and who dwell on earth— when the banner is raised on the mountains you will see it; and when a *shofar* will be sounded, you will hear it." And it is said: "And it will be on that day, that a great *shofar* will be sounded, and they will come— those who were lost in the land of Assyria, and those who were outcasts in the land of Egypt, and they will prostrate themselves to the Lord, on the holy mountain in Jerusalem." And it is said: "And the Lord will appear over them, and His arrow will go forth like lightning; and my Master, the Lord, will sound the *shofar* and go forth in the whirlwinds of the south. The Lord of Hosts will protect them." So may You be a shield over Your people, Israel, with Your peace. **Our God** and God of our fathers, sound a great Zion for our liberty and raise a banner to gather our exiles. And bring near our scattered people from among the nations, and gather our dispersed from the ends of [the] earth. Bring us to Zion, Your city, with joyous song,— to Jerusalem, house of Your Sanctuary, with eternal joy. And there we will offer before You our obligatory sacrifices, as we were commanded in Your Torah, through the hands of Moses, Your servant, from the mouth of Your glory, as it is said: "And on the day of your rejoicing, and on your appointed festivals, and on your New Moons, you will sound the trumpets over your burnt-offerings and over the sacrifices of your peace offerings, and they will be a memorial for you before your God; I am the Lord, your God." For You hear the sound of the *shofar*, and listen to the *teruah*; and there is none like You. Blessed are You, the Lord, Who hears the sound of the *teruah* of His people, Israel, with compassion.

The medieval philosopher Rabbi Joseph Albo[10] observed that these three blessings added to the *Musaf* service of *Rosh Hashanah* express three fundamental principles of Jewish belief. These three blessings work together to express the core of Jewish faith. *Malchuyot* proclaims that God rules over all creation. *Zichronot* affirms that God is actively involved in our world and knows every detail of our lives. *Shofarot* celebrates the Torah as God's eternal gift to humanity. Together, they transform *Rosh Hashanah* from a simple calendar observance into a profound encounter with the very foundations of faith.

The Heart of Prayer

The prayers of *Rosh Hashanah*, with their ancient Hebrew and complex theological concepts, might seem daunting to those unfamiliar with Jewish liturgy. Yet the tradition teaches that God desires not eloquence but sincerity, not perfection but genuine intention.

A beloved parable captures the heart of this day. In a small village, a young shepherd boy found himself in a synagogue on *Rosh Hashanah* for the very first time. He could not read the Hebrew prayers, nor did he understand the formal words spoken by the congregation. Overwhelmed by the sincerity in the room, he closed his eyes and began to recite the only thing he knew: the Hebrew alphabet. "Dear God," he whispered with tears in his eyes, "I don't know the words of the prayers, but You can take these letters and form the words that are in my heart." The congregants were at first disturbed by the interruption. But the rabbi stopped them, his face radiant with emotion. "His simple offering," the rabbi said, "has pierced the heavens more directly than all our eloquent prayers."

---

10. Rabbi Yosef Albo, *Sefer Ha'Ikrim* 1:4.

This story serves as a reminder that *Rosh Hashanah* is not about polished expressions, but about the honest outpouring of the soul.

The *Shofar* Service

Integral to the observance of *Rosh Hashanah* is the sounding of the *shofar*, a ram's horn, which produces one of the most stirring sounds in all of Jewish ritual. As mentioned above, the Torah itself describes *Rosh Hashanah* as a "day of sounding the *shofar*" (Numbers 29:1), and the Psalms declare "blow the *shofar* at the new moon, at the full moon for our feast day" (Psalms 81:4), a verse traditionally understood to refer to *Rosh Hashanah*. This ancient instrument is central to the holiday's observance. Yet the *shofar* is far more than a ceremonial horn; its simple sound carries depths of meaning that have stirred Jewish hearts for millennia.

Why the *Shofar*?

On one level, the piercing call of the *shofar* mirrors the trumpet fanfares that herald a king's coronation, and on *Rosh Hashanah*, we are indeed crowning God as King. As David writes: "With trumpets and the sound of *shofar*, call out in the presence of the King, Almighty" (Psalms 98:6). Each blast cuts through the air like a royal proclamation, as the entire Jewish people participate in this cosmic coronation ceremony, proclaiming God's sovereignty over all creation.

The *shofar* also connects us to pivotal moments in Jewish history: it reminds us of the ram sacrificed in place of Isaac at the binding (Genesis 22:13), a story we read on *Rosh Hashanah* to recall how Abraham's ultimate devotion earned merit for his descendants. It echoes the thunderous *shofar* blast that accompanied the giving of the Torah at Mount Sinai (Exodus

19:16, 19), reminding us that *Rosh Hashanah* is when we accept God's kingship just as our ancestors accepted His Torah. And it anticipates the *shofar* that will sound with the coming of the redemption (Isaiah 27:13), for *Rosh Hashanah* begins the process that will culminate in God's kingdom being fully revealed to the world.

Perhaps most powerfully, as Maimonides teaches, the *shofar* serves as a wake-up call for repentance. Its message resonates clearly: "Sleeping ones! Awaken from your sleep! Slumbering ones! Awaken from your slumber! Examine your deeds. Remember your Creator and return to your true self."[11] The piercing sound cuts through our daily routines and forces us to confront the essential questions: Who are we? Where have we been? Where are we headed?

But the *shofar* operates on an even deeper level as well. Similar to the story of the boy who didn't know how to articulate his prayers above, the sound of the *shofar* serves as a wordless prayer, expressing what lies deepest in our hearts but cannot be captured in language. It functions as a silent plea that conveys profound messages and spiritual content even in the absence of words. When we are too overwhelmed to formulate proper prayers, too moved to voice our deepest longings, or too broken to articulate our failures, the *shofar* speaks for us. Its ancient voice carries our unspoken hopes, our fears, and our desperate desire for connection with God directly to the throne of judgment.

The Three Sacred Sounds

The *shofar* produces three distinct types of blasts, each carrying its own spiritual message. The *tekiah* is a long, straight blast,

---

11. Laws of Repentance 3:4

clear and unwavering. The *shevarim* consists of three shorter, broken sounds that resemble sighs or sobs. The *teruah* is a series of nine rapid, staccato notes that are meant to sound like short, piercing cries. It also sounds like an urgent alarm.

These sounds represent different cries of the human soul. The *tekiah* proclaims God's kingship with clarity and strength. The *shevarim* expresses broken-hearted yearning, our deep desire to connect, to grow, to achieve our potential. The *teruah* sounds like short, piercing cries. Together, they also serve as our spiritual alarm clock, jolting us from complacency and demanding honest self-examination.

The Mystery of One Hundred Blasts

While the Torah requires only a basic pattern of *shofar* sounds, Jewish custom calls for one hundred blasts to be heard on each of the two days of *Rosh Hashanah*. This tradition traces back to a remarkable teaching in the Talmud[12] connecting the *shofar* to the cries of Sisera's mother. Sisera was a Canaanite general who oppressed the Israelites for twenty years before being defeated and killed (Judges 4). The Book of Judges describes his mother waiting anxiously at her window for him to return: "Through the window she looked forth and cried, the mother of Sisera cried through the lattice: 'Why is his chariot so long in coming? Why tarry the wheels of his chariots?'" (Judges 5:28). According to tradition, she uttered one hundred cries of anguish when she realized her son would never return home.

Why would the Jewish people model the sacred sounds of *Rosh Hashanah* after the laments of a pagan mother mourning her barbaric son? Rabbi Joseph B. Soloveitchik offers an insightful

---

12. Babylonian Talmud Rosh Hashanah 33b

explanation.[13] The *shofar*'s purpose, he teaches, is to awaken us from spiritual slumber through a sudden, jarring recognition that our comfortable assumptions about life are fundamentally flawed. Like Sisera's mother, who waited confidently for her son's triumphant return only to face the devastating reality of his defeat, we too must confront the painful truth that our actions have separated us from God. In that moment of recognition, we find ourselves without our usual defenses, overwhelmed by how far we've fallen spiritually, and struggling to find the right words for prayer or promises to change. The *shofar*'s sharp blast forces us to feel this same kind of shock—the collapse of our false sense of security and the frightening awareness of where we really stand spiritually. Just as Sisera's mother could only cry out without words, we too must let the *shofar* strip away our pretenses and bring us to our most honest, exposed state before God.

A Horn That Demands Response

The shape of the *shofar* itself embodies the spiritual journey it calls us to undertake. Beginning with a narrow mouthpiece and widening toward its opening, it symbolizes our progression from narrow, limited consciousness to expanded awareness of God's presence in our lives. Its bent shape symbolizes the humility we feel as we stand before God in judgment.

We are commanded to hear the sound of the *shofar*, not merely to blow it. We must listen actively, asking ourselves: When the *shofar* sounds, what do I want to hear? What do I want to change? Am I ready to respond to its call?

---

13. *Before Hashem You Shall Be Purified*, p. 10

The *shofar*'s piercing call echoes through the synagogue on *Rosh Hashanah*, cutting through our defenses and reaching directly into our hearts. The prophet Amos said, "Shall a trumpet be blown in the city, and the people not be afraid?" (Amos 3:6). In those moments of raw sound, we stand before the Almighty without barriers, ready to begin the sacred work of examining our lives and choosing the path forward into the new year.

Before blowing the *shofar* in synagogue, it is customary to recite Psalm 47 seven times:

> la-m'-na-TZAY-akh liv-nay KO-rakh
>   miz-MOR
> kol ha-a-MEEM tik-u KHAF ha-REE-u
>   lay-lo-HEEM b'-KOL ri-NAH
> kee a-do-NAI el-YON no-RA ME-lekh
>   ga-DOL al kol ha-A-retz
> yad-BAYR a-MEEM takh-TAY-nu ul-u-
>   MEEM TA-khat rag-LAY-nu
> yiv-khar LA-nu et na-kha-la-TAY-nu et
>   g'-ON ya-a-KOV a-sher a-HAYV SE-
>   lah
> a-LAH e-lo-HEEM bit-ru-AH a-do-NAI
>   b'-KOL sho-FAR
> za-m'-RU e-lo-HEEM za-MAY-ru za-m'-
>   RU l'-mal-KAY-nu za-MAY-ru
> kee ME-lekh kol ha-A-retz e-lo-HEEM
>   za-m'-RU mas-KEEL
> ma-LAKH e-lo-HEEM al go-YEEM e-lo-
>   HEEM ya-SHAV al ki-SAY kod-SHO
> n'-dee-VAY a-MEEM ne-e-SA-fu am e-

lo-HAY av-ra-HAM kee lay-lo-HEEM
ma-gi-nay E-retz m'-OD na-a-LAH

To the Chief Musician, A psalm of the
sons of Korach. All peoples, clap
hands! shout to God with the voice
of joyous song. For the Lord is Most
High, awesome; a great King [is He]
over all the earth. He subdues
peoples under us, and nations under
our feet. He chose for us our
inheritance, the pride of Jacob
which He loves forever. God has
ascended with a blast— the Lord,
with the sound of the *shofar*. Sing
praises to God, sing praises; sing
praises to our King, sing praises. For
King of all the earth is God, sing
praises [you who are] skillful. God
has reigned over all nations, God is
seated upon His holy throne. The
nobles of the nations gathered the
nation of the God of Avraham; for
God has the power to shield the
earth, He is greatly exalted.

The following verses are then said responsively:

מִן הַמֵּצַר קָרֶאתִי יָהּ עָנָנִי בַמֶּרְחַב יָהּ:

min ha-may-TZAR ka-RA-ti YAH a-NA-
nee ba-mer-KHAV YAH

"From the narrowness [of distress] I
    called [to God,] He answered me
    with the breath of Divine relief."
    Psalms 118:5

*The first letters of the following six verses in the Hebrew text form the
words* קְרַע שָׂטָן, *which means cut off the accuser.*

קוֹלִי שָׁמָעְתָּ אַל תַּעְלֵם אָזְנְךָ לְרַוְחָתִי
לְשַׁוְעָתִי:

ko-LEE sha-MA-ta al ta-LAYM oz-n'-
    KHA l'-rav-kha-TEE l'-shav-a-TEE

"You have heard my voice; do not shut
    Your ear to my [prayer for] relief, to
    my cry." Lamentations 3:56

רֹאשׁ דְּבָרְךָ אֱמֶת וּלְעוֹלָם כָּל מִשְׁפַּט
צִדְקֶךָ:

ROSH d'-va-r'-KHA e-MET ul-o-LAM
    kol mish-PAT tzid-KE-kha

"The beginning of Your word is truth
    and forever are all Your righteous
    mandates." Psalms 119:160

עֲרֹב עַבְדְּךָ לְטוֹב אַל יַעַשְׁקֻנִי זֵדִים:

a-ROV av-d'-KHA l'-TOV al ya-ash-KU-
    nee zay-DEEM

"Be surety for Your servant for good let
me not be oppressed by insolent
sinners." Psalms 119:122

שָׂשׂ אָנֹכִי עַל אִמְרָתֶךָ כְּמוֹצֵא שָׁלָל רָב:

SAS a-no-KHEE al im-ra-TE-kha k'-mo-
TZAY sha-LAL RAV

"I am happy with Your word like one
who finds great gain." Psalms
119:162

טוֹב טַעַם וָדַעַת לַמְּדֵנִי כִּי בְמִצְוֹתֶיךָ
הֶאֱמָנְתִּי:

TUV TA-am va-DA-at la-m'-DAY-nee
kee v'-mitz-vo-TE-kha he-e-MAN-
tee

"Good Torah reasoning and knowledge
teach me for in Your
commandments I have believed."
Psalms 119:66

נִדְבוֹת פִּי רְצֵה נָא יְהוָֹה וּמִשְׁפָּטֶיךָ לַמְּדֵנִי:

nid-VOT PEE r'-tzay NA a-do-NAI u-
mish-pa-TE-kha la-m'-DAY-nee

"[With] the offerings of my mouth be
pleased, I beseech You, O Lord; and
Your mandates, teach me."

Psalms 119:108

The one who sounds the shofar says:

עָלָה אֱלֹהִים בִּתְרוּעָה יְהֹוָה בְּקוֹל שׁוֹפָר:

a-LAH e-lo-HEEM bit-ru-AH a-do-NAI
b'-KOL sho-FAR

"God has ascended with a blast— the
Lord, with the sound of the *shofar*."
Psalms 47:6

The *shofar*'s call transcends even the most dire circumstances. Perhaps no stories illustrate this more powerfully than those from one of the darkest chapters of Jewish history. In the shadows of the Holocaust, when stripped of synagogues, prayer books, and basic human dignity, the essence of the *shofar*'s call revealed itself with startling clarity.

Even amid unimaginable suffering, the Jewish spirit clung to the sanctity of *Rosh Hashanah*. In one documented account, a group of prisoners in a concentration camp risked their lives to hide a *shofar*. On *Rosh Hashanah*, they gathered in secret and blew a single, trembling blast. That sound, brief and raw, was enough to move grown men to tears. It was a moment of divine connection in a place of unimaginable darkness. The *shofar*'s voice broke through the silence of despair and reminded those who heard it that their souls still belonged to Heaven.

This story illuminates how the ancient traditions of *Rosh Hashanah* continue to speak to the human soul across millennia. In moments when everything earthly fails, when comfort, security, and even hope seem lost, the call to stand before our Creator, to crown Him as King, and to seek renewal remains unshakeable. The *shofar*'s blast, whether sounded in magnificent synagogues or whispered in hidden corners, carries the same eternal message: that our deepest identity lies not in our circumstances but in our relationship with the Divine. This is the enduring gift of *Rosh Hashanah*—a reminder that no matter how dark the hour, the gates of heaven remain open to any human heart that seeks to enter.

Second Meal

After the morning prayers are recited, we return home for the second festive meal of the holiday. Though it is one of the Days of Awe, *Rosh Hashanah* is also a festival. Once again, families gather around the table for meals filled with delicious food, traditional songs, and conversations about Torah and Jewish values. It is a time to connect with loved ones, reflect on the past year, and set intentions for growth in the year ahead. Parents often use this time to share stories and lessons with their children, ensuring the transmission of the holiday's meaning and traditions to the next generation.

Tashlich: Casting Away Sins

On the afternoon of the first day of *Rosh Hashanah*, many Jewish families and communities have the custom to make their way to a nearby body of water for the *Tashlich* ceremony. The ritual involves reciting biblical passages near a body of water while symbolically casting away our sins into the water. The Hebrew word *tashlich* means "to cast off," and the ritual is a way to symbolically leave our wrongdoings behind as the new year begins. When the first day falls on *Shabbat*, the ceremony is typically postponed to the second day.

The practice draws its inspiration from the prophet Micah's powerful promise: "You will cast all their sins into the depths of the sea" (Micah 7:19). Some see a reference to the *Tashlich* ceremony in the biblical scene in Nehemiah 8:1, where "all the people gathered as one in the street that is in front of the gate of water" on *Rosh Hashanah*.

The ceremony is ideally performed near water containing fish, which carry their own symbolic meaning. Just as fish are protected by the water that surrounds them, we pray for God's protection. Yet like fish that can suddenly be caught in a net despite swimming freely, we too can unexpectedly fall into sin's trap. And as fish keep their eyes constantly open, we hope that God maintains watchful care over His people.

The *Tashlich* ceremony does not grant us forgiveness. But when approached with a sincere intention to repair our relationship with God, *Tashlich* becomes a meaningful part of the repentance process, helping us internalize the very real possibility of spiritual renewal.

From the first candle lit to welcome the holiday to the final notes of the *shofar* echoing through the sanctuary, *Rosh Hashanah* weaves together the most fundamental questions of human existence. Who are we? To whom do we belong? How shall we live? The holiday's answer resonates through every prayer, every symbol, every moment of reflection: we are children of the Most High, created in His image, called to lives of purpose and meaning.

The round *challah* dipped in honey speaks to our hopes. The *shofar*'s piercing call awakens our souls. The waters of *Tashlich* symbolically carry away what we wish to leave behind. And through it all, we stand not as isolated individuals but as part of an eternal covenant, linked to Abraham's faith, Moses' revelation, and countless generations who have answered the same divine summons to return, to renew, to begin again.

This is the enduring gift of *Rosh Hashanah*, a reminder that no matter how far we may have wandered, the gates of heaven remain open to the human heart that seeks to enter. In crowning God as King, we discover our own truest selves. In accepting His judgment, we find His mercy. And in the promise of a new year, we glimpse the eternal possibility of redemption that lies at the very heart of faith itself.

This redemptive vision encompasses all humanity, reflecting the hope that all nations will soon recognize God's sovereignty, anticipating the day when "the great *shofar* will sound" (Isaiah 27:13) and all peoples will worship together on God's holy mountain (Isaiah 2:3).

COLLECTED INSIGHTS

The Fragility of Life and the Power of Repentance

Sara Lamm

There's a moment during *Rosh Hashanah* and *Yom Kippur* services when everything feels more vivid, more intense—when the words of the prayer, *Unetaneh Tokef*, draw us in. It's a prayer that stirs our souls, awakening an acute awareness of both our mortality and the greatness of God's judgment. It's a prayer where the language brings both comfort and urgency, reminding us that while life is fleeting, there is always an opportunity to change, to grow, and to draw nearer to God.

The prayer, recited on both *Rosh Hashanah* and *Yom Kippur*, vividly paints a picture of the Day of Judgment, contrasting the temporary nature of human life with the eternal reign of God. It stirs a deep recognition of how fragile we truly are. But rather than leaving us in despair, it emphasizes the transformative power of repentance (*teshuvah*), prayer (*tefillah*), and righteousness (*tzedakah*) to reshape our destinies.

This theme of human frailty and divine compassion resonates deeply within the Bible. Over and over, we find the interplay between the limitations of human existence and the boundless grace of God, which calls us to respond with a heart open to change.

In *Unetaneh Tokef*, the fragility of human life is emphasized with striking imagery: "We come from dust and return to dust." This echoes the words of Genesis 3:19, when God speaks to Adam after the Fall, declaring:

"By the sweat of your brow shall you get bread to eat, until you return to the ground— For from it you were taken. For dust you are, And to dust you shall return." Genesis 3:19

This is a humbling reminder of the transitory nature of human life. Like Adam, we are part of creation, finite beings bound by time.

King Solomon expresses this same sentiment in the book of Ecclesiastes. He writes:

"Both go to the same place; both came from dust and both return to dust." Ecclesiastes 3:20

We cannot escape our inherent mortality despite our achievements, wealth, or power. Yet, this realization is not meant to instill fear but rather to inspire a deeper connection to the One who gave us life. Knowing that our time is limited encourages us to seek out what truly matters—our relationship with God and how we live in accordance with His will.

As the prayer continues, it likens God's judgment to a shepherd counting his flock, "As a shepherd herds his flock, directing his sheep to pass under his staff... You shall pass, count, and record the souls of all living." This tender imagery reminds us of Psalm 23, where David declares, "The Lord is my shepherd; I shall not want. He makes me lie down in green pastures... Even though I walk through the valley of the shadow of death, I will fear no evil, for You are with me."

The role of God as a shepherd is a recurring metaphor in the Bible, symbolizing His care, guidance, and protection. The shepherd's staff represents both authority and gentleness, a symbol of God's watchful eye over His people. As we stand in judgment, it's not as strangers, but as beloved sheep who are known and cared for by their Shepherd. This offers great comfort in a prayer that speaks of judgment. Even in our weakest moments, God's guiding presence remains.

The climax of *Unetaneh Tokef* offers a lifeline: "But repentance, prayer, and righteousness avert the severity of the decree." This triumphant call reminds us that while our fate may be inscribed on *Rosh Hashanah* and sealed on *Yom Kippur*, it is not necessarily final. We are given the tools to change, to repent, to seek forgiveness, and to engage in acts of righteousness.

The Hebrew Bible overflows with examples of repentance leading to God's mercy. In the story of Jonah, the people of Nineveh are given a dire prophecy of destruction. But they repent, accompanied by fasting and wearing sackcloth, and they are forgiven. This shows us the power of sincere repentance.

Prayer too, holds immense power. When King Hezekiah fell deathly ill, the prophet Isaiah told him to put his house in order, for he would not recover. Yet Hezekiah turned to God in prayer, and God added fifteen years to his life. This illustrates how prayer can change what seems like an inevitable outcome. As we approach the Day of Judgment, we must remember that we are never powerless; we can always turn to God through prayer.

And finally, righteousness, acts of kindness and charity, are integral to our spiritual life. Proverbs 10:2 teaches, "Righteousness delivers from death," a clear affirmation that our good deeds have the power to save us. In fact, Jewish tradition holds that acts of *tzedakah* (charity) can annul a harsh decree, emphasizing the importance of living a life filled with kindness and compassion.

Rosh Hashanah and *Yom Kippur*, often called the Days of Awe, bring us face to face with the reality of our mortality. Yet, the message is not one of despair. Instead, it's a call to action, a reminder that we have the power to shape our destinies through our choices. Life may be fleeting, but within that short time, we can do so much to repair the world and our relationship with God.

Unetaneh Tokef reminds us of both our fragility and our incredible capacity for growth and change. It challenges us to embrace repentance, prayer, and righteousness as pathways to renewal. As we stand in judgment, we are also standing in grace, shepherded by a God who desires life and goodness for us all.

So as we hear the *shofar* blast and the silent cry of the heart, may we find the strength to turn back to God, knowing that every prayer, every act of kindness, and every moment of repentance brings us closer to Him, and closer to life.

Echoes of Liberty: The Message of the Shofar

Rabbi Yaakov Wolff

When I was ten years old, we took a drive from New Jersey to Baltimore. Along the way, we made a short stop in Philadelphia where we decided to explore Independence Hall, the US Mint, and, finally, the Liberty Bell. As we approached the iconic, cracked bell, I couldn't help but notice the inscription: Proclaim Liberty Throughout All the Land Unto All the Inhabitants thereof.

The words "Proclaim liberty throughout the land" are taken from Leviticus 25:10:

"and you shall hallow the fiftieth year. You shall proclaim liberty throughout the land for all its inhabitants. It shall be a jubilee for you: each of you shall return to his holding and each of you shall return to his family." Leviticus 25:10

This verse seemed like a fitting connection between the Hebrew Bible's idea of liberty and that of the Founding Fathers. Surprisingly, this verse also holds a central place in understanding the Jewish holiday of *Rosh Hashanah* (Jewish New Year).

The highlight of *Rosh Hashanah* is the blowing of the *shofar*, the ram's horn. The verse instructs us:

"In the seventh month, on the first day of the month, you shall observe a sacred occasion: you shall not work at your occupations. You shall observe it as a day when the *shofar* is sounded." Numbers 29:1

Though the English translation explains the verse to mean that it is a day when the *shofar* is sounded, the word *shofar* does not actually appear in the verse. The verse actually says that it should be a day of *teruah*, referring to a sound or blast, but does not specify which instrument to use to make that sound. It is the Jewish sages who deduced that a *shofar* is needed, based on a verse about the Jubilee year, which specifies that a *shofar* should be sounded to make the teruah sound:

"Then you shall sound the *shofar* loud; in the seventh month, on the tenth day of the month—the Day of Atonement—you shall have the *shofar* sounded throughout your land." Leviticus 25:9

This verse immediately precedes the verse above inscribed on the Liberty Bell.

On *Yom Kippur* (Day of Atonement) of the Jubilee year, the *shofar* was sounded, slaves were set free, and liberty was declared throughout the land.

The sages understood that just as the *teruah* blasts emanate from a *shofar* on the Jubliee year, a *shofar* must be used to make the *teruah* sound on *Rosh Hashanah* as well. But is this connection merely a textual inference, or is there a deeper link between the Jubilee and *Rosh Hashanah*?

According to Jewish tradition, *Rosh Hashanah* serves as a day of judgment. Since we are undergoing judgment, it is essential to repent for our sins and commit to self-improvement. Maimonides explains that this system of judgment and repentance hinges on a fundamental concept: free will.[14] Only if we have the freedom to choose between right and wrong can we be held accountable for our mistakes and rewarded for our successes. Only when we possess agency can we be expected to repent and grow.

---

14. Laws of Repentance chapter 5

This is the connection between *Rosh Hashanah* and the Jubilee year. On the Jubilee, a time when we blow a *shofar*, our slaves go free. Similarly, on *Rosh Hashanah*, the *shofar* reminds us that we are free to choose lives of good over evil, right over wrong, and life over death.

Some individuals tend to view their shortcomings with a deterministic outlook, thinking, "This is who I am." This perspective can be convenient because it absolves us of responsibility. However, when standing in judgment on *Rosh Hashanah,* this viewpoint is not an option. We hear the resounding blast of the *shofar* and it seems to scream at us, "You are free! You are not bound by any predetermined fate!"

Liberty is a beautiful concept, but it comes with its share of responsibilities. Being free means shouldering the weight of responsibility, embracing agency, and being held accountable. At times, these burdens may seem heavy, but in the long run, they infuse our lives with meaning. They empower us to take ownership of our lives, celebrate our achievements, and inspire others.

On *Rosh Hashanah,* let's strive to internalize the call of the *shofar*: we are free!

The High Holidays: Everyone's Holiday

Adam Eliyahu Berkowitz

When I think about the High Holidays, I picture synagogues full of Jews—the men wrapped in snow-white prayer shawls swaying silently, the women praying fervently. These are intensely Jewish experiences, the pinnacle of the Hebrew calendar. Yet here's what strikes me as remarkable: at the very moment when Jews are most focused on their relationship with God, the prayers themselves envision something universal. A verse from Zechariah, repeated throughout the *Rosh Hashanah* and *Yom Kippur* liturgy, captures this perfectly: And the Lord shall become King over all the earth; on that day shall the Lord be one, and His name one." (Zechariah 14:9).

This isn't coincidental. Every Jewish child knows that *Rosh Hashanah* begins the ten-day period when Jews stand in divine judgment. But the Talmud[15] reveals something broader: on *Rosh Hashanah*, the anniversary of humanity's creation, every single human being passes before God individually.

The *Torah* reading reinforces this universal scope. On *Rosh Hashanah*, we read about God hearing the prayers of Hagar and Ishmael: "The Lord heard the cry of the boy, and an angel of the Lord called to Hagar from heaven and said to her, 'What troubles you, Hagar? Fear not, for the Lord has heeded the cry of the boy where he is'" (Genesis 21:17-18). Neither Hagar nor Ishmael was part of the covenant with Abraham, yet their story takes center stage on this holiest day.

This pattern continues on *Yom Kippur*. The *Haftarah* reading— the selection from the Prophets—is the Book of Jonah. On the

---

15. Babylonian Talmud, Rosh Hashanah 18a

very day when Jews fast in repentance, we read about the successful repentance of Nineveh, a metropolis of non-Jews. The message couldn't be clearer: God's mercy extends to all who seek it.

And it reaches its climax during *Sukkot*. Directly after *Yom Kippur*, Jews enter their *sukkot*, temporary dwellings that commemorate Israel's forty years in the desert. Yet *Sukkot* is actually the most international Jewish holiday of the year. When the Temple stood in Jerusalem, seventy bulls were offered during the seven-day festival corresponding to the seventy nations of the world. According to Zechariah, this will be intensified in the end times: "All who survive of all those nations that came up against Jerusalem shall make a pilgrimage year by year to bow low to the King Lord of Hosts and to observe the festival of *Sukkot*" (Zechariah 14:16).

Rabbi Jonathan Sacks captured this idea beautifully when he noted that three biblical figures blessed God's name using the Hebrew phrase *baruch Hashem* (blessed is God's name)—Noah, Eliezer, and Jethro—yet none belonged to the Abrahamic covenant. "The Torah is signaling its most subtle and least understood idea," he wrote, "that the God of Israel is the God of all humankind, even though the religion of Israel is not the religion of all humankind."[16]

Rabbi Sacks cited the *Talmudic* sage Rabbi Akiva, who said: "Beloved is humanity, for it was created in the image of God. Beloved is Israel, for they are called children of God."[17] Though the Jewish people were chosen to represent God on earth, everyone is a child of God.

---

16. Rabbi Jonathan Sacks, "The Universal and the Particular," *Covenant & Conversation*, Parashat Yitro, available at https://www.rabbisacks.org
17. Ethics of Our Fathers 3:14

This is the profound paradox of Jewish particularism. The more deeply Jews embrace their unique calling, the more they point toward humanity's shared destiny. When we stand in judgment on the anniversary of creation, all of God's creations stand with us. When we pray for rain during *Sukkot*, all of mankind joins in thanksgiving and hope. Our most intensely Jewish moments become windows into God's universal kingdom, anticipating the day when all nations will recognize the One who rules over all the earth.

Our Father, Our King

Shira Schechter

One year during the High Holidays, a young man new to religious observance found himself struggling to keep up with the prayers in the synagogue. With his Hebrew still shaky, he decided to save time by skipping the opening phrase of each line in the *Avinu Malkeinu* (Our Father, Our King) prayer, one of the most central prayers of the season. This prayer, a series of 44 requests, begins each line with the words *Avinu Malkeinu*, "Our Father, Our King," followed by pleas for healing, sustenance, forgiveness, and peace. As the congregation fervently recited the prayer, he whispered only the requests, believing they were the essence of the prayer. But later, he came to a profound realization: the true power of *Avinu Malkeinu* isn't found in the requests themselves, but in the words he had been skipping.

What is the significance of these two Hebrew words?

The prayer "Our Father, Our King" can be traced back to a famous story in the Talmud.[18] During a severe drought in ancient Israel, Rabbi Elazar led the community in prayer, reciting 24 blessings for rain, but the skies remained dry. Then, Rabbi Akiva stepped forward with a much simpler plea: "Our Father, our King! We have no one else but You! Our Father, our King! For Your sake, have mercy upon us." Immediately, rain began to fall. Why did Rabbi Akiva's brief, straightforward prayer succeed where the lengthy prayers of Rabbi Elazar did not?

The answer lies in the profound meaning behind the phrase

---

18. Babylonian Talmud, Ta'anit 25b

"Our Father, Our King." On the surface, the words seem simple, but they encapsulate the dual nature of our relationship with God, a duality that resonates throughout the High Holidays. God is both a loving parent, as described in Psalm 103:13: "As a father has compassion for his children, so Hashem has compassion for those who fear Him," and a sovereign ruler, as stated in Isaiah 33:22: "For Hashem shall be our ruler, Hashem shall be our prince, Hashem shall be our king; He shall deliver us."

As a father, He shows us compassion and mercy, guiding us and forgiving our transgressions. As a king, He exercises authority and power, establishing justice and setting expectations, while also having the ability to fulfill our deepest needs and grant our requests. This balance between God's roles as both Father and King is at the heart of the prayer.

By invoking God as both "Father" and "King," Rabbi Akiva recognized and tapped into these two fundamental aspects of our relationship with the Divine. This dual invocation gives the prayer its emotional and spiritual depth, transforming each petition into more than just a request but also a statement of faith, trust and love.

During the High Holidays, this duality is deeply felt. As we stand before God, we experience a mixture of hope and anxiety. We are aware that our actions are being weighed and that our fate for the coming year hangs in the balance. Yet, we are also reassured that the One who judges us is not a distant ruler but a loving Father who understands our struggles, seeks our ultimate good, and also has the power to grant our petitions and change our destiny.

As we repeat *Avinu Malkeinu* throughout the High Holidays, especially in the final moments of *Yom Kippur* (Day of

Atonement), we are reminded of this dual perspective. As the gates of heaven begin to close, we stand before a Judge who is also our Father, and we know that the opportunity for mercy is still within reach. Each repetition of "Our Father, Our King" serves to reinforce the idea that while we are accountable for our actions, we remain embraced by divine love and compassion.

For the young man in the synagogue, realizing that "Our Father, Our King" was the heart of the prayer transformed his spiritual life. It reminded him that we are not just petitioners before a distant sovereign; we are children turning to a loving parent who also reigns over the world.

As we recite *Avinu Malkeinu*, let us do so with an awareness of the dual relationship we invoke—appealing both to a King who holds power and to a Father who loves. And may we all be inscribed and sealed for a year of goodness, peace, and blessings.

The Call of the *Shofar*: From Creation to Redemption

Rabbi Pesach Wolicki

Rosh Hashanah, the Jewish New Year, is considered a day for introspection and repentance. It is one of the High Holy Days, the most sacred days on the Jewish calendar. But strangely, the Bible tells us very little about this day. Here is the full description of this festival, mentioned only twice in the Torah:

The Lord spoke to Moshe, saying: "Speak to the Children of Israel thus. In the seventh month, on the first day of the month, you shall observe complete rest, a sacred occasion commemorated with loud blasts. You shall not work at your occupations; and you shall bring an offering by fire to Hashem." Leviticus 23:23-25

"In the seventh month, on the first day of the month, you shall observe a sacred occasion: you shall not work at your occupations. You shall observe it as a day when the *shofar* is sounded." Numbers 29:1

Despite the English translations, the word trumpet – *shofar* – never appears in these verses. The Hebrew word used, *teru'ah*, only means "blast." In other words, *teru'ah* is not the name of the instrument, the horn or *shofar*. It is the word for the act of blowing or of the sound made by the blowing. The only thing the Bible tells us about this festival is that it is a day of *teru'ah* – trumpet blasts. No other information is given. So how did we come to see this as a sacred day of introspection, repentance, and judgement before God? Why do we call it the New Year?

The blowing of the *shofar* is the central ritual of the *Rosh Hashanah* synagogue service. During the service, one hundred sounds are blown which are divided into sets of three different sounds. These sets are repeated numerous times during the course of the service.

The three sounds are:

Tekiah – a long straight blast, usually lasting 3 or 4 seconds.

Shevarim – a three-part broken blast; a kind of "toot-toot-toot"

Teru'ah – a rapid-fire broken blast of at least 9 very short sounds in quick succession; almost like machine gun fire.

The sets that make up the 100 *shofar* blasts are arranged in three different ways.

1. *Tekiah – Shevarim – Teru'ah – Tekiah* (4 *shofar* sounds)
2. *Tekiah – Shevarim – Tekiah* (3 *shofar* sounds)
3. *Tekiah – Teru'ah – Tekiah* (3 *shofar* sounds)

Every set begins and ends with the longer straight sound, *tekiah*. The "broken" sounds are in between. This setup contains a deep message for any person of faith. To understand this message, we must turn to the Bible and read very carefully.

The Day of Broken Sounds

The Hebrew word *teru'ah*, the word the Bible uses to describe this festival, actually means "broken trumpet blasts." The root of this Hebrew word means "broken into pieces" or "unsteady." The Jewish sages living over 2000 years ago were not sure whether these blasts should be broken into very short rapid-fire sounds or should be slightly longer, like the sound of a person sobbing. They decided that both sounds should be made to cover the two possible meanings of this word. The *shevarim* sound and the *teru'ah* sound are these two sounds.

Put simply, *shevarim* and *teru'ah* are two different types of *teru'ah* – broken blasts.

The word *tekiah* also means "trumpet blast," but it refers to a long, unbroken blast. Both these words appear in the Bible, as we will see in detail soon.

To sum up, *Rosh Hashanah* is referred to in the Bible as a day for sounding the *shofar* with *teru'ah* – "broken blasts." To understand what this means, we must look carefully at another Biblical passage.

Sounds of crisis & Sounds of peace

In Numbers 10, God commanded Moses to make two silver trumpets. These trumpets were not *shofar*s – ram's horns. But in the instructions for their use both Hebrew words for "trumpet blast," *tekiah* and *teru'ah* are used. To make it easier to follow, I will translate *tekiah* as "long blast" and *teru'ah* as "broken blast."

When a broken blast is sounded, the tribes camping on the east are to set out. At the sounding of a second broken blast, the camps on the south are to set out. The broken blast will be the signal for setting out. To gather the assembly, blow a long blast, but not a broken blast. The sons of Aaron, the priests, are to blow the trumpets. This is to be a lasting ordinance for you and the generations to come. When you go into battle in your own land against an enemy who is oppressing you, sound a broken blast on the trumpets. Then you will be remembered by the Lord your God and rescued from your enemies. Also, at your times of rejoicing—your appointed festivals and New Moon feasts—you are to sound a long blast over your burnt offerings and fellowship offerings, and they will be a memorial

177 177

479788

for you before your God. I am the Lord your God. – Numbers 10:5-10

Notice how each type of blast is used. The broken blasts signaled that the people were setting out to travel or going into battle. The long blasts were to gather the assembly and for times of rejoicing and festivals.

We see from this that the *teru'ah* – the broken blast – signifies times of struggle and transition. It is a sound of brokenness, crying, and instability. *Tekiah*, on the other hand, is a solid and steady sound. This is the sound of gathering, of peace, of festivities. But why then, would a festival be called a day of *teru'ah*. Didn't we just read in Numbers 10 that the festivals are a time for *tekiah* – the long blasts?

The answer to this question reveals the deepest meaning of *Rosh Hashanah*. I mentioned earlier every *shofar* "set" on *Rosh Hashanah* begins and ends with *tekiah*. The *shevarim* and *teru'ah* – the broken blasts – are always in between the *tekiah*s.

Tekiah, Teruah, Tekiah: From Adam to the End

God created humanity in a state of perfection. He created a pure and perfect world. *Tekiah*. Humanity then fell into sin. Tragedies and evil entered the world. Much was broken. It is this broken world that we live in. *Teru'ah*. As faithful servants of God, it is our mission to fix the world. As people of faith, we know that one day, humanity will return to a state of purity and perfection. The perfect Kingdom of God awaits us. *Tekiah*.

It is not surprising that *tekiah*, the symbol of the perfect world, is used by Isaiah to describe the great day of redemption in the End Times:

And in that day, a great *shofar* shall be sounded; and the strayed who are in the land of Assyria and the expelled who are in the land of Egypt shall come and worship Hashem on the holy mount, in Yerushalayim. Isaiah 27:13

Tekiah, teru'ah, teki'ah – perfection, brokenness, perfection again. This is the story of humanity and the story of each of us as individuals. We enter the world pure and free of sin. As we mature, we have plans and dreams. Our deepest desire is to be the best version of ourselves. *Tekiah.* But life brings struggle. We go through seasons when we feel shaky and broken. *Teru'ah.* But God gives us the opportunity to draw close to Him, to repent, and to start over. We begin again with new hope and new dreams. *Tekiah.*

Rosh Hashanah is the New Year because it is a day when we are called to reconnect with our original purpose, the original purpose of creation. The *shofar* reminds us of the perfect world that God created, the brokenness we are called to repair, and the perfect end that awaits in the future. *Tekiah, teru'ah, tekiah.*

Divine Attendance: The Power of Being Seen

Rabbi Yaakov Wolff

If you take a look at the curriculum for a degree in education, you will see lots of courses about teaching methods, classroom management and imparting values. But there is one ritual, that repeats itself hundreds of thousands of times, that is usually overlooked.

A seasoned teacher was once asked what she thought was the most vital element in a class. Her response was unexpectedly simple: attendance.

The reply was surprising. How could taking attendance overshadow the profound knowledge imparted, the intricate skills honed, and the deep-seated values instilled throughout the class? And how does this anecdote connect to *Rosh Hashanah*, the Jewish New Year?

The parallel might not be apparent at first glance, but delving into the significance of this sacred celebration can offer us a profound understanding.

Rosh Hashanah has multiple roles. It marks the start of a new year, but it is also the birthday of creation and a day of reckoning. These roles bring with them mixed emotions. On the one hand, it's a happy occasion welcoming a new year and a fresh start. On the other hand, it's a solemn day where God assesses and judges every person.

How can we make sense of all of these different feelings packed into one day?

To answer this question let's go back to the verses in Genesis 1. A recurring theme in the creation story is God seeing that things He created are good. The first time it occurs is after the creation of light at the very beginning of creation:

Hashem saw that the light was good, and Hashem separated the light from the darkness. Genesis 1:4

This repeats for all the various parts of creation until the climax at the end of the sixth day:

And Hashem saw all that He had made, and found it very good. And there was evening and there was morning, the sixth day. Genesis 1:31

These verses are puzzling. As a human, I have to inspect everything that I make to ensure that it comes out right. If I were making soup, for example, I'd chop vegetables, add seasoning, cook them together and then taste the broth. Then I would adjust the seasoning and cook it some more until I was satisfied with the final product. Only once I have gone through all of those steps and determined that it is to my liking would I declare that the soup is good.

But when God made the world, it was a precise, divine, and perfect creation. So what does it mean that after each thing He created "He saw that it was good"?

The answer to this question is that seeing isn't just about gathering information, it is also a way of communicating. That's why eye contact during a conversation is so important; it makes both people feel acknowledged and valued.

Now, let's apply this to the classroom. When the teacher takes attendance it is not just about noting who's present and who's absent. It's a silent but powerful message to each student: "I see you, you matter to me, you have value."

Returning to the creation story, when God looked at each part ofcreation He wasn't inspecting it for quality control. Instead, by gazing upon His creations He was making them good! Anything, or anyone, that God looks at gains divine importance and value. That is why God looked at each creation after its completion and declared them all to be good.

This idea also finds expression in the judgment of *Rosh Hashanah*. Being judged by God might seem frightening, but it's also uplifting. The fact that God is watching us and judging us means that He cares about us and values us. While we might feel the weight of judgment, we also bask in the comfort of God's unwavering attention and care, and the fact that we are being "seen" by Him. This is why the day can encompass both fear and joy, celebration along with trepidation.

3

THE TEN DAYS OF REPENTANCE

You've prepared for the most important meeting of your life. You've spent an entire month getting ready, examining yourself, making amends, and preparing to stand before the ultimate Judge. The day arrives—*Rosh Hashanah*—and you feel the weight of divine attention as your name is called and your year is reviewed.

But then something remarkable happens.

Instead of receiving an immediate verdict, you're told: "The decision isn't final yet. You have ten days."

Ten days to plead your case. Ten days to demonstrate change. Ten days when the courtroom of heaven remains in session and the final decree hangs in the balance.

This is the extraordinary gift of the Ten Days of Repentance.

Most legal systems operate on the principle of finality. Once the judge's gavel falls, the verdict is sealed. Appeals may be possible, but they're lengthy, complicated processes with no guarantee of success. But the divine courtroom operates by different rules entirely—rules of mercy that transcend human logic.

Jewish tradition teaches that on *Rosh Hashanah*, God opens the books and begins reviewing each person's year. Initial judgments are written, but they remain unsealed. The cosmic court stays in session for a total of ten days, from *Rosh Hashanah* through *Yom Kippur* (Day of Atonement), creating a window of opportunity that exists nowhere else in the calendar.

It's as if you're taking the most important exam of your life, one that determines your entire future. Just as you're about to hand in your paper, the professor says, "Actually, I'm going to give you ten more days to review your answers, add anything you missed, and submit a better version." Who wouldn't seize that opportunity?

The Ten Days of Repentance offer something even more precious than a second chance—they offer the possibility of complete transformation. During these days, the rules of time itself seem suspended. Past mistakes can be transformed into stepping stones for growth. Broken relationships can be mended. Hearts hardened by months or years of spiritual neglect can be softened and renewed.

The Hebrew phrase "*Aseret Yemei Teshuvah*," the Ten Days of Repentance, contains within it the secret of this period's power. The Hebrew word *teshuvah* doesn't just mean "repentance"; it means "return." These days offer us the chance to return to who we were always meant to be, to come home to our truest selves.

Yet for all their spiritual intensity, the Ten Days of Repentance aren't meant to be a period of despair or self-flagellation. They're infused with hope because they're based on a radical premise: that change is always possible, that no one is ever beyond redemption, that the human capacity for growth can overcome any past failure.

The Ten Days of Repentance ask us to live with unusual intensity and focus. Every prayer carries extra weight. Every act of kindness matters more. Every moment of self-reflection has heightened significance. It's like turning up the spiritual volume of life to levels we rarely sustain, creating conditions where profound change becomes not just possible, but inevitable.

As we enter these sacred days, we carry with us all the preparation of *Elul* and all the spiritual awakening of *Rosh Hashanah*. But we also carry something else: the knowledge that the story isn't over yet, that the final chapter of this year's spiritual journey is still being written.

The courtroom remains in session. The door to transformation stands open.

The question isn't whether change is possible—it's whether we're ready to embrace it.

THE TEN DAYS OF REPENTANCE – THE BRIDGE TO FORGIVENESS

Biblical and Traditional Sources

The source for this period lies in both biblical and rabbinic teachings. While the Torah emphasizes *Yom Kippur* as the Day of Atonement, as it says: "For on this day He will forgive you, to purify you, that you may be clean from all your sins before the Lord" (Leviticus 16:30), Jewish tradition developed the understanding that the preceding ten days serve as preparation for this ultimate day of forgiveness.

The Sages expand on this concept, teaching that during these ten days, God is particularly accessible and eager to forgive those who genuinely turn toward Him. This is based on the verse in Isaiah: "Seek the Lord while He may be found, call upon Him while He is near" (Isaiah 55:6). According to the Talmud, this refers specifically to the Ten Days of Repentance, when God is closest to humanity and most receptive to sincere repentance.[1]

The Process of Divine Judgment

On *Rosh Hashanah*, God opens the Book of Life and begins the process of divine judgment, carefully reviewing each person's deeds from the past year and writing down the initial verdict for each soul. Yet this initial inscription represents only the beginning of the process, not its conclusion. The judgment remains unsealed, creating a precious ten-day window when the gates of divine mercy stand wide open. These ten days from *Rosh Hashanah* through *Yom Kippur* become a sacred opportunity for spiritual repair and growth, during which we

---

1. Babylonian Talmud, Rosh Hashanah 18a

can still influence the final decree that will be sealed on the Day of Atonement.

But to understand why these days hold such extraordinary transformative power, we need to explore the mystical foundations that make this period unique in the Jewish calendar. According to Jewish mystical tradition, *teshuvah* (repentance) was created before the world itself. As the Talmud teaches: "Seven things were created before the world was created: Torah, repentance, the Garden of Eden, hell, the Throne of Glory, the Temple, and the name of the Messiah." This isn't merely a chronological statement; it reveals that *teshuvah* operates according to spiritual laws that transcend the physical world.

The great sage Rabbi Judah Lowe, known as the Maharal of Prague, explains[2] that the Torah was given to human beings living in the physical world, so it operates according to the rules of justice that govern earthly existence. If someone commits a crime, even genuine remorse doesn't erase the need for justice in a human court. But *teshuvah* operates according to different laws—divine laws that can actually transform the past.

This explains why *Rosh Hashanah*, with its themes of divine judgment, comes before the period of *teshuvah*. On *Rosh Hashanah*, we face judgment according to divine justice, a true and honest accounting of our deeds. But the ten days that follow introduce us to something beyond justice: divine mercy that can transform even our failures into stepping stones toward growth.

This sacred period teaches us about the delicate balance

---

2. *Netivot Olam*, section on Teshuvah, chapter 2.

between divine justice and divine mercy. While *Rosh Hashanah* emphasizes God's role as Judge, the following days reveal God's even deeper desire to forgive and embrace those who return to Him. The liturgy of these days constantly references the Thirteen Attributes of Mercy. But it's important to understand that these attributes don't negate divine justice; they transcend it. God remains completely just, but His mercy creates new possibilities for those who genuinely seek to return.

During these days, God examines not just our actions but our hearts. The divine gaze penetrates beyond external behaviors to see our deepest intentions, our struggles, our moments of genuine longing for goodness. This isn't a harsh scrutiny meant to condemn, but a loving examination that seeks every possible reason to grant forgiveness.

The Three Transformative Practices

Jewish tradition[3] teaches that during this crucial period, three powerful acts can transform a harsh divine decree and change our spiritual fate: *teshuvah*, *tefillah*, and *tzedakah*, generally translated as "repentance, prayer, and charity." This is based on the verse in 2 Chronicles 7:14, which says: "If My people, who are called by My name, will humble themselves and pray and seek My presence and turn from their wicked ways, then I will hear from heaven, and I will forgive their sin and will heal their land."

The sages identified within this single verse all three redemptive actions: "will humble themselves and pray" refers directly to the power of sincere prayer; "seek My presence"

---

3. Jerusalem Talmud, Ta'anit 2:1

refers to charity;[4] and "turn from their wicked ways" describes the process of repentance and spiritual return. What makes this verse particularly significant is God's emphatic response, "then I will hear from heaven," indicating that these three practices compel God's attention and activate His compassion. The verse concludes with the promise of forgiveness of sin and healing of the land, suggesting that sincere engagement in repentance, prayer, and charity can reverse even the most dire circumstances.

The Ten Days of Repentance are more than just a waiting period; they represent an active time of transformation and spiritual growth. During these days, people engage in deep self-reflection, honestly examining their actions and working to strengthen their relationship with God. This inner work extends naturally to repairing damaged relationships with family and friends, increasing charitable giving, and dedicating more time to prayer and study. Prayer takes on special importance, with additional prayers that focus our hearts on repentance and return.

Rather than passive waiting, this time calls for active spiritual effort, the hopeful work of becoming who we were meant to be. The great medieval Jewish philosopher Maimonides captured the opportunity and the call to action of these ten days: "Even though repentance and crying out to God are always timely, during the ten days from *Rosh Hashanah* to *Yom Kippur* it is exceedingly appropriate, and accepted immediately [on high]...[5] Therefore, it is customary for all of Israel to give profusely to charity, perform many good deeds, and be

---

4. The Talmud connects "seek My presence" to charity through the verse "I will see Your presence in righteousness (*tzedek*)" (Psalms 17:15), linking seeing God's presence with acts of charity (*tzedakah*).

5. Laws of Repentance 2:6

occupied with observance of God's commandments from *Rosh Hashanah* until *Yom Kippur* to a greater extent than during the remainder of the year."[6]

Teshuvah: Return, Not Just Repentance

Most people hear the word "repentance" and think of feeling guilty, beating themselves up, maybe shedding a few tears of regret. But the Hebrew word *teshuvah* tells a different story. It literally means "return," and that single word changes everything. *Teshuvah* implies something far more transformative: a complete turning around, a return to our truest selves and to God.

The great medieval philosopher Maimonides describes the essence of *teshuvah*: "What constitutes complete repentance? When one is confronted with the identical situation in which he previously sinned, and it lies within his power to commit the sin again, but he refrains and does not commit it because of his repentance, not because of fear or lack of strength."[7] Maimonides understood that real change isn't about good intentions, it's about making different choices.

Judaism teaches that *teshuvah* has the remarkable power to transform the past itself. As the Sages wrote, "Great is repentance, for intentional sins are transformed into merits."[8] The very actions that once created distance from God become stepping stones that bring us closer to Him. This idea transcends ordinary human understanding and suggests that a sincere return to God can actually rewrite our spiritual history.

A beautiful parable illustrates this paradox: If you take a rope

---

6. Laws of Repentance 3:4
7. Laws of Repentance 2:1
8. Babylonian Talmud, Yoma 86b

and cut it in two, the ends become separated. But when you tie those ends back together, the knot actually makes that point stronger than the original rope ever was. In addition, the distance between the ends of the rope becomes closer. This is the power of *teshuvah*. Not only does it repair the relationship between us and God, but it creates a bond even stronger and closer than the one that existed before we sinned.

We see this principle in human relationships all the time. Think about a couple who says their marriage became stronger after working through a major crisis, or friendships that deepened after surviving a serious conflict. The process of breaking and healing, when done with genuine care, can create bonds that are more resilient than relationships that never faced any challenges.

This extraordinary potential of *teshuvah* leads to one of the most remarkable statements in all of Jewish literature. The Talmud declares: "In the place where *ba'alei teshuvah* (those who have returned to God through repentance) stand, even the completely righteous cannot stand."[9] This doesn't diminish the greatness of those who have never sinned, but rather reveals that the spiritual heights achieved through genuine *teshuvah* can surpass even lifelong righteousness. The struggle to return, the pain of recognizing one's failures, and the joy of divine forgiveness create a depth of relationship with God that may not be accessible through any other path.

The prophet Hosea captured this ultimate destination of *teshuvah* when God called through him in a verse that opens the reading from the Prophets during these ten days: "Return, O Israel, all the way to (*ad*) the Lord your God" (Hosea 14:2).

---

9. Babylonian Talmud, Berachot 34b

The Hebrew word *ad* means "until" or "all the way to," and the commentators explain that true *teshuvah* brings a person *ad*, all the way up to the very Throne of Glory itself.[10] Through genuine return, the human soul can achieve the closest possible proximity to the Divine.

This explains why these ten days are so precious. During this period, God is waiting to accept our return with open arms, and our capacity for genuine transformation is heightened. The question isn't whether we deserve forgiveness, but whether we're ready to embrace the profound change that *teshuvah* demands.

This transformative understanding of *teshuvah* helps explain a remarkable insight about the structure of these days themselves. The Lubavitcher Rebbe, Rabbi Menachem Mendel Schneerson, noticed something significant about how the Ten Days of Repentance are arranged. These days, he taught, serve as the inauguration period for the new year. Between the bookends of *Rosh Hashanah* and *Yom Kippur* are seven days, a full week—one Sunday, one Monday, one Tuesday, and so forth. This is no coincidence.

The Rebbe explained that this complete week provides us with a unique opportunity for comprehensive spiritual repair. Each day of this special week corresponds to all the days of that type from the previous year. The Sunday that falls during the Ten Days of Repentance becomes our chance to atone for mistakes made on all the Sundays of the past year. Monday offers the same opportunity for all the Mondays that came before, and so on through the entire week.

---

10. Rabbi David Kimchi on Hosea 14:2, based on the Babylonian Talmud, Yoma 86a

But true *teshuvah* involves more than just regret for past failures; it requires genuine resolution for the future. Therefore, this seven-day period also serves as spiritual preparation for the year ahead. On the Sunday of this week, we should plan specifically for better Sundays in the coming year, drawing strength and clarity for future obligations. The same applies to each day of the week during this sacred time.

Prayer as Transformation

Prayer during the Ten Days of Repentance becomes something far more powerful than our regular conversations with God. The Hebrew word *lehitpalel*, meaning "to pray," reveals something profound about the nature of authentic prayer. The root *palal* means "to judge," so the reflexive verb *lehitpalel* literally means "to judge oneself"—revealing that prayer is fundamentally about self-evaluation and self-judgment.

Rabbi Jonathan Sacks captured this beautifully: "The Hebrew verb *lehitpalel*, meaning 'to pray,' is reflexive, implying an action done to one's self. Literally, it means 'to judge oneself.' It means, to escape from the prison of the self and see the world, including ourselves, from the outside. Prayer is where the relentless first person singular, the 'I,' falls silent for a moment and we become aware that we are not the centre of the universe."[11]

Rabbi Samson Raphael Hirsch[12] understood this transformation in concrete terms. He explained that authentic prayer means taking God's truth and allowing it to penetrate every aspect of our lives, creating harmony between our

---

11. Rabbi Jonathan Sacks, "When the 'I' is Silent" (Vayetse), *Covenant & Conversation* commentary series.

12. Samson Raphael Hirsch, *The Pentateuch: Translation and Commentary*, trans. Isaac Levy (Gateshead: Judaica Press, 1982), commentary on Genesis 20:7

existence and God's will. Prayer involves working on ourselves internally, elevating our understanding of divine truth and strengthening our commitment to serve God. The root *palal*, he taught, refers to what a judge does—bringing justice and divine truth into any situation.

Think about what this means: authentic prayer isn't just quiet self-reflection. It's an active process of stepping outside our limited perspective and inviting God's truth to reshape us from within. When we truly pray, we're not merely examining ourselves; we're allowing God's perspective on reality to penetrate our lives and transform how we see everything.

During the Ten Days of Repentance, this process of stepping outside ourselves and drawing in divine truth becomes especially powerful. We're praying during a time when the cosmic court is in session, when divine judgment is being rendered. This knowledge transforms how we pray. When the stakes are this high, the "relentless first person singular, the 'I,'" naturally falls silent, creating space for genuine transformation.

The urgency of these sacred days strips away our usual self-centeredness and distractions, creating conditions where we can truly "escape from the prison of the self." We're no longer going through the motions of prayer; we're actively stepping outside our limited perspective and inviting God to reshape who we are.

This is why prayer during the Ten Days of Repentance has the power to avert the evil decree. We're not just asking God to change our circumstances—we're actually becoming different people by allowing God's truth to transform us. The person who emerges from authentic *tefillah* during these days is someone for whom the old harsh judgment no longer applies, because they have learned to see reality from God's perspective rather than being trapped in the prison of their own limited viewpoint.

Tzedakah: Not Just Charity

Tzedakah, generally translated as charity, represents the third practice that can transform divine judgment, but the Hebrew word reveals something crucial: *tzedakah* comes from *tzedek*, meaning justice or righteousness. This completely changes how we understand giving during these days. We're not being generous benefactors graciously sharing our wealth—we're simply doing what justice requires.

Why does this matter? Because it changes everything about how we understand giving. When we practice *tzedakah*, we're recognizing that our resources come from God and were meant to be shared with those who need them. It's less about our kindness and more about setting the world right.

The Lubavitcher Rebbe explained why *tzedakah* represents justice rather than mere generosity. His teaching rests on a fundamental principle: everything we possess ultimately belongs to God. We are entrusted with resources, not as owners but as stewards, with the clear expectation that we will share with those in need.

There's also a profound reciprocity at work. We regularly appeal to God for blessings - health, sustenance, success - despite having no claim on His generosity. If we expect God to give freely to us, justice demands that we give freely to others, even when they have no claim on us either.

The Transformative Power of Giving

188 | BEFORE THE KING

This understanding reveals why *tzedakah* becomes so significant during the Ten Days of Repentance. When we give meaningfully during this period, we are demonstrating that we are just servants of God entrusted with divine resources. True *tzedakah* requires a recognition that anything extra that we have was intended by God for those in need, and we are simply the conduits through which His providence flows. This recognition transforms charity from an act of personal generosity into an acknowledgment of God's sovereignty, one of the essential messages of this period.

Furthermore, by giving charity we demonstrate internal transformation. Maimonides taught that genuine repentance requires giving "according to one's capacity,"[13] which has been understood to mean that we are required to give to the point of real sacrifice. This kind of giving forces us to confront our true priorities. When we choose to give sacrificially, we prove that spiritual values have become more compelling than material comfort. This shift in values is precisely what authentic *teshuvah* demands; not just changing our behavior, but fundamentally reshaping our understanding of what matters most.[14]

Rabbi Jonathan Sacks[15] described *tzedakah* as fundamentally shifting our life question from "what does the world give us?" to "what do we give the world?" This transformation of perspective is precisely why *tzedakah* has the power to change divine judgment—when we become people who lift others, we discover that "in truth you lift yourself."

---

13. Laws of Repentance 2:4
14. Rabbi Bernie Fox, "Tzedakah's Role in the Teshuvah Process"
15. Jonathan Sacks, "U'teshuvah, u'tefillah, u'tzedakah, ma'avirin et roah' hagezerah," Rabbi Sacks Legacy Facebook page, September 22, 2020, https://www.facebook.com/rabbisacks/posts/3504407379610392/

Tzedakah, along with prayer and repentance, has the power to transform even harsh divine decrees. This isn't simply because charitable giving earns divine favor, but because meaningful *tzedakah* also represents the emergence of a fundamentally changed person. When we give, we demonstrate that our values have been clarified and our priorities realigned with divine will. The person who once prioritized material concerns over spiritual obligations no longer exists, replaced by someone who truly understands what matters most.

Having explored the profound spiritual foundations of *teshuvah*, *tefillah*, and *tzedakah*, we now turn to the practical question: How do we actually live these transformative practices during the Ten Days of Repentance? Understanding the theory prepares us for the essential work of implementation.

THE SACRED WORK OF RETURN: A PRACTICAL GUIDE TO THE TEN DAYS OF REPENTANCE

The Process of Personal *Teshuvah*

True *teshuvah* begins with honest self-examination. During these ten days, many people set aside time for what is called *cheshbon hanefesh*, an accounting of the soul. This involves reviewing the past year's actions, identifying patterns of behavior that distance us from God and others, and recognizing areas where growth is needed. This isn't meant to be an exercise in self-criticism, but rather a loving assessment aimed at spiritual improvement; a process designed to help us answer the fundamental questions: "Who am I, and who do I aspire to be?"

The practice of *teshuvah* involves carefully defined steps. Maimonides[16] outlines the essential components based on biblical verses that illuminate each stage of the process: abandoning the sin, resolving not to repeat it again, feeling genuine remorse and confession before God.

Deciding to abandon the sin completely and never repeat it is based on the verse in Isaiah in which he declares: "May the wicked abandon his ways and the man of iniquity his thoughts, and let him return to the Lord" (Isaiah 55:7). The sinner must not only stop the harmful behavior but remove it entirely from his thoughts and resolve never to commit it again.

Next comes genuine remorse for past actions. Jeremiah captures this when he writes: "After I returned, I regretted" (Jeremiah 31:19). This isn't mere regret at being caught or

---

16. Laws of Repentance 2:2

facing consequences, but sincere sorrow over having violated God's will and damaged one's relationship with the Divine.

Finally, there must be a verbal confession before God, stating aloud these matters that have been resolved in the heart. This is based on Numbers 5:7: "They shall confess their sin which they have done." This oral acknowledgment transforms private resolution into a declaration before the Divine, giving voice to the inner transformation and completing the process of *teshuvah*.

A Word About Verbal Confession

Unlike confession in other religious traditions, Jewish confession is a private matter between the individual and God. If that is so, why is it necessary at all? Doesn't God know what is in our hearts? Why must we express it verbally?

Rabbi Joseph B. Soloveitchik explains[17] that confession is not merely an add-on to repentance; it is the act that brings it to life. Without confession, the process of repentance remains unfinished. Speaking one's sins aloud transforms our internal feelings of regret into something tangible and concrete, holding us accountable in a way that silent reflection cannot.

A person may feel remorse or regret, but it is only through confession, by putting emotions into words, that they truly understand the depth of their feelings. Thoughts and emotions do not fully crystallize until they are expressed verbally. As Rabbi Soloveitchik notes, a person himself does not know what stirs even in his own heart until he shapes his emotions and thoughts into verbal expression. Before this verbal acknowledgment, a person may only have a vague sense of

---

17. Joseph B. Soloveitchik, *Al HaTeshuvah* (New York: World Zionist Organization, 1980), 4045, 61-65.

their failings, but by articulating their transgressions, they bring them into sharp focus. Words have the power to illuminate the seriousness of our actions, and the spoken confession forces us to confront the truth directly.

But there is another benefit to verbal confession. Rabbi Soloveitchik acknowledges that verbal expression of sin is not easy. It requires breaking through layers of pride, fear, and self-deception. Rabbi Soloveitchik likens verbal confession to a form of self-sacrifice, a personal offering to God. When we confess our sins, we sacrifice our ego, our carefully guarded defenses, and our sense of control. In his words, "Confession forces a person, with great suffering, to recognize the facts as they are and to express the truth clearly." This admission of guilt is not just an acknowledgment of wrongdoing; it is a deeply humbling experience in which one strips away all the excuses and defenses built up to protect one's self-image.

The act of confessing one's sins aloud is transformative because it forces us to confront our failings with honesty and humility. This process, though painful, is necessary for true spiritual renewal. As Rabbi Soloveitchik teaches, it is only through this struggle, through the act of speaking the truth about ourselves and the shame that comes with it, that we burn away our pride and our illusions, and in doing so, we find purification and forgiveness.

Seeking Forgiveness from Others

One of the most significant aspects of the Ten Days of Repentance involves interpersonal reconciliation. Jewish law is clear that *teshuvah* for sins against other people requires seeking their forgiveness directly. As Maimonides writes: "sins between man and man; for example, someone who injures a colleague, curses a colleague, steals from him, or the like will never be forgiven until he gives his colleague what he owes him and appeases him."[18]

This process requires humility and courage. The person who has caused harm must approach the injured party, acknowledge the wrongdoing specifically, express genuine remorse, and ask for forgiveness. If the request is initially refused, Jewish law requires making the attempt up to three times. However, the injured party is also obligated to be receptive to sincere requests for forgiveness.

Rabbi Soloveitchik's ideas about confessing our wrongs before God can be applied to our human relationships as well. When we set aside our ego and admit that we have wronged another person, we open the door to healing. Just as with verbal confession, true healing in relationships begins when we are willing to confront the reality of our actions. A relationship damaged by hurt and anger cannot heal until one acknowledges their role in causing the harm. By verbalizing our regret and offering sincere apologies, we not only validate the other person's pain but also begin to rebuild trust. This is the moment when reconciliation becomes possible, just as confession is the starting point for our spiritual renewal.

Many people use the Ten Days of Repentance to reach out to family members, friends, colleagues, or neighbors with whom relationships have been strained. Phone calls, letters, or personal visits become opportunities for healing long-standing wounds. The goal isn't merely to clear one's conscience, but to genuinely repair relationships and restore harmony.

---

18. Laws of Repentance 2:9

Daily Prayers and Additions

As we mentioned above, prayer during the Ten Days of Repentance is especially significant, since it is one of the three essential practices, along with repentance and charity, that can transform a harsh divine decree. During the Ten Days of Repentance, the regular prayer services are enhanced with special additions that focus on themes of *teshuvah*, divine mercy, and spiritual renewal.

Selichot - Penitential Prayers

During this time, Jewish communities recite *Selichot*, penitential prayers, late at night or early in the morning, continuing the practice that began during the month of *Elul* (see chapter on *Elul*). These prayers, with their haunting melodies and profound poetry, create an atmosphere of spiritual intensity that prepares the heart for genuine repentance.

The *Selichot* prayers include the *Thirteen Attributes of Mercy*, based on God's revelation to Moses after the sin of the Golden Calf: "The Lord, the Lord God, merciful and gracious, slow to anger, and abundant in loving-kindness and truth, keeping mercy for thousands, forgiving iniquity and transgression and sin" (Exodus 34:6-7). These attributes become a central focus during the Ten Days, as we appeal to God's merciful nature.

Psalm 130: The Cry from the Depths

One of the most moving additions to the daily prayers during the Ten Days of Repentance is the recitation of Psalm 130, added into the morning prayers. The psalm's relevance to the High Holiday season is obvious, as it speaks directly to the heart of the Ten Days of Repentance: "If You keep account of sins, O LORD, Lord, who will survive? Yours is the power to forgive so that You may be held in awe" (Psalm 130:3-4). These verses acknowledge both human frailty and divine mercy, recognizing that if God were to judge us strictly by our failures, none could survive such scrutiny. Yet the psalm offers hope: "O Israel, wait for the LORD; for with the LORD is steadfast love and great power to redeem. It is He who will redeem Israel from all their iniquities." (Psalm 130:7-8). God's nature includes forgiveness, making repentance and renewal possible.

But perhaps the most moving part of the Psalm is the beginning. This psalm opens with words that seem to emerge from the very soul of these sacred days: "A song of ascents. Out of the depths I call You, O LORD. O Lord, listen to my cry; let Your ears be attentive to my plea for mercy." (Psalm 130:1-2). The Hebrew phrase *mima'amakim*, "out of the depths" perfectly captures the spiritual journey of repentance, a cry that rises from the deepest places of human experience, seeking God's attention and mercy.

Rabbi Joseph B. Soloveitchik[19] offered a profound interpretation of this phrase, understanding *mima'amakim* in two complementary ways. First, it can mean calling out from the depths of despair, agony, and distress—from life's most challenging circumstances. The mystical work known as the Zohar describes ten levels of *mima'amakim*, including experiences like poverty and old age, that can bring a person to their lowest point.

But Rabbi Soloveitchik saw a second, deeper meaning of the word: calling out from the depths of one's true personality. Beneath the public face we show the world lies our private,

---

19. *Rosh Hashanah Machzor*, commentary adapted from the teachings of Rabbi Joseph B. Soloveitchik (New York: K'hal Publishing in conjunction with the Orthodox Union), 245-246.

authentic self—mysterious, hidden, sometimes unknown even to ourselves. This innermost core represents our truest identity, the part of us that remains untouched by sin and failure. It is from this sacred depth that genuine prayer and repentance can emerge, for it is here that we encounter who we really are before God.

The power of both interpretations of this psalm was witnessed in one of history's darkest moments. A Jewish doctor and atheist, imprisoned in a Latvian concentration camp during the Holocaust, wrote of the daily horror. Inmates were awakened at 4:30 AM for fourteen hours of back-breaking labor in sub-zero temperatures, wearing threadbare clothing. Upon their return each evening, they faced a terrifying inspection at the camp gates, where doctors examined each prisoner. Those deemed too weak to continue working were sent immediately to the gas chambers.

In his memoir, this doctor described a group of religious students and their rabbi who were imprisoned alongside him. Each night, after surviving another day of this nightmare, these students would sit on the barracks floor with their teacher and recite psalms, including the words "*Mima'amakim keratikha Hashem*," "Out of the depths I call to You, O Lord." Witnessing this scene, the atheist doctor wrote that he would have given his very life to possess the faith necessary to recite psalms under such unimaginable circumstances.

This story illuminates both dimensions of *mima'amakim*—the students called out from the depths of unimaginable suffering while simultaneously accessing the deepest, most authentic parts of their souls that remained connected to God despite everything.

This is why Psalm 130 resonates so powerfully during the Ten Days of Repentance. Whether we call out from the depths of despair or from the hidden depths of our souls, these ancient words give voice to our deepest longing for connection with the Divine. The psalm reminds us that no matter how far we may feel from God, whether due to our failures, our circumstances, or our doubts, the path of prayer and repentance remains open, leading from the deepest valleys back toward the light.

Psalm 130

> SHEER ha-ma-a-LOT mi-ma-a-ma-
> KEEM k'-ra-TEE-kha a-do-NAI. a-
> do-NAI shim-AH v'-ko-LEE tih-YE-
> nah az-NE-kha ka-shu-VOT l'-KOL
> ta-kha-nu-NAI. im a-vo-NOT tish-
> mor YAH a-do-NAI mee ya-a-MOD.
> kee i-m'-KHA ha-s'-lee-KHAH l'-MA-
> an ti-va-RAY. ki-VEE-tee a-do-NAI
> ki-v'-TAH naf-SHEE v'-lid-va-RO
> ho-KHA-l'-tee. naf-SHEE la-do-NAI
> mi-sho-m'-REEM la-BO-ker sho-m'-
> REEM la-BO-ker. ya-KHAYL yis-ra-
> AYL el a-do-NAI kee im a-do-NAI
> ha-KHE-sed v'-har-BAY i-MO f'-
> DUT. v'-HU yif-DEH et yis-ra-AYL
> mi-KOL a-vo-no-TAV.

> A song of ascents. Out of the depths I
> call You, O LORD. O Lord, listen to
> my cry; let Your ears be attentive to
> my plea for mercy. If You keep

account of sins, O LORD, Lord, who
will survive? Yours is the power to
forgive so that You may be held in
awe. I look to the LORD; I look to
Him; I await His word. I am more
eager for the Lord than watchmen
for the morning, watchmen for the
morning. O Israel, wait for the
LORD; for with the LORD is
steadfast love and great power to
redeem. It is He who will redeem
Israel from all their iniquities

Our Father, Our King

On weekdays during this period, the prayer *Avinu Malkeinu*
("Our Father, Our King") is recited with special intensity. This
ancient prayer, traditionally attributed to the great sage Rabbi
Akiva, perfectly captures the dual relationship we have with
God, as our loving Father and our sovereign King. Each line
begins with the words "Our Father, our King" and continues
with a declaration or supplication: "Our Father, our King, we
have sinned before You... Our Father, our King, have mercy
upon us... Our Father, our King, inscribe us in the Book of Life."
(For a lengthier description, see chapter on *Rosh Hashanah*).

Additions to the *Amidah* Prayer

The regular *Amidah* (standing prayer) also receives special
additions and changes during these days. We continue to say
the insertions that began on *Rosh Hashanah*, such as
"Remember us for life, O King who desires life," and "Inscribe
us in the Book of Life for Your sake, O God of life," which
implore God to remember us favorably and Inscribe us in the

Book of Life. We also change the ending of the third blessing from "the holy God" to "the holy King" as we do on *Rosh Hashanah*, a reflection of the fact that during this time we acknowledge God's sovereignty and corronate Him as our King.

During the weekdays of the Ten Days of Repentance, we make an additional change to the *Amidah* and replace the ending of the eleventh blessing, "King who loves righteousness and justice," with the words "the King of judgment." This change reflects the heightened awareness of divine judgment during this period. While God always embodies both justice and mercy, during these days we emphasize His role as Judge, acknowledging that we stand before Him for evaluation and verdict. The shift in language reminds us that this is a time of spiritual accounting, when our deeds are being weighed and our fate for the coming year is being determined. By calling God "the King of judgment," we recognize the gravity of these days while simultaneously expressing our trust in His fair and righteous judgment.

Psalm 27

Recitation of Psalm 27, which has been said daily since the beginning of the month of *Elul*, continues throughout the Ten Days of Repentance. This psalm, with its themes of seeking God's presence and trusting in divine protection, provides daily encouragement during this intense spiritual period. The psalm's central plea captures the essence of what we hope to achieve during these days of repentance: "One thing I ask of the Lord, this I seek: that I may dwell in the house of the Lord all the days of my life, to gaze upon the beauty of the Lord and to seek Him in His temple" (Psalm 27:4). This verse expresses the ultimate goal of *teshuvah*; not just forgiveness, but renewed closeness with God and the privilege of dwelling in His presence. (For a lengthier description of this psalm, see the chapter on *Elul*)

Increased Charity and Good Deeds

Tzedakah, along with prayer and repentance, has the power to transform even harsh divine decrees. This isn't simply because charitable giving earns divine favor, but because meaningful *tzedakah* represents the emergence of a fundamentally changed person. When we give sacrificially, we demonstrate that our values have been clarified and our priorities realigned with divine will. The person who once prioritized material concerns over spiritual obligations no longer exists, replaced by someone who truly understands what matters most.

This understanding of *tzedakah's* transformative power translates into concrete practices during these days. Many people increase their charitable giving significantly. Some calculate their annual charitable obligation and make sure it's fulfilled before *Yom Kippur*. Others take on additional charitable commitments for the coming year.

Beyond monetary charity, the Ten Days of Repentance are a time for increased acts of loving-kindness (*chesed*) and good deeds, as Maimonides writes: "it is customary for all of Israel to give profusely to charity, perform many good deeds, and be occupied with *mitzvot* (divine commandments) from *Rosh Hashanah* until *Yom Kippur* to a greater extent than during the remainder of the year."[20] This might involve visiting the sick, comforting mourners, helping neighbors with practical needs, or volunteering for community organizations.

---

20. Laws of Repentance 3:4

Rabbi Joseph B. Soloveitchik[21] taught that the connection between giving and atonement traces back to the Bible, to the incident of the Golden Calf. After Moses secured divine forgiveness for the Jewish people, the immediate response wasn't celebration but action: God commanded the building of the Tabernacle through voluntary donations. From the earliest moments of Jewish history, giving became the pathway to atonement and the prescribed response to serious transgression. We implement this during the month of *Elul* and the Ten Days or Repentance.

The Cosmic Significance of Our Actions

This intensified focus on good deeds stems from Maimonides' teaching about the cosmic significance of every individual action.[22] He taught that throughout the year, a person should view themselves as equally balanced between merit and sin, and similarly, the world itself stands equally balanced.

What does this mean in practice? If someone performs one sin, they tip both their personal balance and that of the entire world toward guilt and potential destruction. Conversely, if they perform one good deed, they tip both scales toward merit, bringing deliverance and salvation to themselves and to all of creation.

This extraordinary responsibility is reflected in the verse from Proverbs: "A righteous person is the foundation of the world" (Proverbs 10:25). The righteous individual literally becomes a supporting pillar for all of existence, because through their positive actions, they can tip the balance of the entire world

---

21. Quoted in Rabbi Bernie Fox, "Tzedakah's Role in the Teshuvah Process"
22. Laws of Repentance 3:4

toward merit. Each act of righteousness becomes part of the very foundation that upholds all of creation.

During the Ten Days of Repentance, when divine judgment hangs in the balance, this cosmic responsibility becomes even more urgent. Every act of kindness, every moment of Torah study, every expression of compassion carries the potential not only to transform our own spiritual standing but to tip the scales of divine judgment for the entire world toward mercy and blessing.

Enhanced Torah Study

Many people increase their Torah study during the Ten Days of Repentance, recognizing that spiritual growth requires deeper engagement with God's wisdom and values. This might involve attending additional classes, studying texts related to *teshuvah* and the High Holidays, or simply spending more time in personal study and reflection.

The *Shabbat* of Return

The *Shabbat* that falls between *Rosh Hashanah* and *Yom Kippur* is known as the "Shabbat of Return," or, in Hebrew, *Shabbat Shuvah*. This unique *Shabbat* takes its name from the prophetic reading, known as the *Haftarah*, recited in the synagogue, which begins with the words of the prophet Hosea: "Return (*shuvah*), O Israel, to the Lord your God, for you have stumbled in your iniquity" (Hosea 14:2).

This *Haftarah* is actually a compilation of verses from three different prophets, Hosea, Micah, and Joel, all focusing on the theme of return and God's boundless mercy. It includes one of the most beautiful expressions of divine forgiveness in all of Scripture: "Who is a God like You, who pardons iniquity and forgives the transgression of the remnant of His heritage? He does not retain His anger forever, because He delights in mercy" (Micah 7:18).

Traditionally, this *Shabbat* features special sermons focused on *teshuvah*. In many communities, the rabbi has the custom to deliver his most important sermon of the year on this day, addressing the themes of repentance, spiritual growth, and preparation for *Yom Kippur*. These sermons often explore the deeper meanings of the High Holiday period and offer practical guidance for the spiritual work ahead. It's a time when the joy of *Shabbat* merges with the solemnity of the Days of Awe, creating a unique atmosphere of hopeful introspection.

Notably, the prayer *Avinu Malkeinu* is not recited on *Shabbat Shuvah*, as the pleading nature of this prayer is considered incompatible with the joy and rest of *Shabbat*. This reminds us that even during the Days of Awe, *Shabbat* maintains its character as a day of delight and spiritual refreshment.

Preparing for *Yom Kippur*

As the Ten Days of Repentance progress and the preparation for *Yom Kippur* intensifies, we complete the process of seeking forgiveness from others, making additional charitable donations and cultivating the proper mindset for this holiest day of the Jewish year.

These final days are a time for intensive self-reflection and prayer. While *teshuvah* is always available to us throughout the year, the knowledge that the "Book of Life" will soon be sealed creates special urgency and tremendous hope. During this extraordinary period when divine mercy is most accessible, we have heightened opportunities to influence the coming year through *teshuvah*, prayer, and charity.

The specific customs and preparations for *Yom Kippur* eve, including the pre-fast meal, traditional blessings, and special ceremonies, mark the sacred transition into Judaism's most solemn day, when all the spiritual work of these ten days reaches its climax.

The Gates of Return

The Ten Days of Repentance offer us one of Judaism's most precious gifts: the promise that no matter how far we may have strayed, the path of return always remains open. These days remind us that human beings are not prisoners of their past mistakes, but rather possess the capacity for genuine transformation.

The Hebrew prophets understood this profound truth. Hosea's call to "return" isn't just addressed to ancient Israel, it echoes across the centuries to every human heart that longs for renewal: "Return, O Israel, to the Lord your God, for you have stumbled in your iniquity. Take with you words, and return to the Lord" (Hosea 14:2-3).

This period teaches us that *teshuvah* isn't primarily about perfection; it's about direction. God doesn't demand that we achieve spiritual perfection before He accepts our return. Instead, He looks for sincere effort, genuine remorse, and authentic commitment to growth. The very fact that we're reaching toward Him is itself a form of return.

Through prayer, charity, and genuine *teshuvah*, these sacred days prepare us for the ultimate expression of divine mercy that awaits us on *Yom Kippur*. As we've learned during these days of intensive spiritual work, we are more than the sum of our mistakes. We are beings created in the divine image, with an infinite capacity for return, renewal, and growth. The gates of return stand open, and *Yom Kippur* awaits to seal our spiritual renewal.

As *Yom Kippur* approaches, we carry with us everything we've learned about return, transformation, and the infinite capacity of the human heart to change.

These haven't been easy days. Real *teshuvah* never is. But they've been days filled with possibility—the kind of possibility that can fundamentally reshape both soul and destiny.

COLLECTED INSIGHTS

Forget Your Past - For Now

Rabbi Elie Mischel

When I was working as a corporate attorney in New Jersey, I joined a volunteer program in which lawyers helped Holocaust survivors fill out incredibly long and detailed applications for Holocaust reparations from Germany. Though this was more than sixty years after the Holocaust had ended, Germany had only recently introduced a new reparations program for survivors who had been in certain ghettos. The application for these funds was incredibly long and complex, and so my job was to sit with the survivors, listen to their stories, and then help them fill out the application.

It was a powerful experience, sitting with each of these survivors and hearing them tell their painful stories at length. I had to ask many specific questions and do my best to get the survivors to say the right things so that they would qualify for the reparations payments. I would ask questions like "Are you sure you never spent time in the Łódź ghetto? You must have spent at least a night or two there..." If we had to slightly stretch the truth to get them money from the Germans, so be it!

I remember meeting a survivor, Helen, who came to the clinic with her daughter. Her daughter explained to me that though she had always known her mother was a survivor, her mother never spoke about her experiences. It was only now – this was 2008! – that Helen was finally opening up about her story. Helen's daughter came to the clinic with pages and pages of notes she had written over the last few weeks – stories her mother had shared for the first time, more than 60 years after the Holocaust!

I was very curious as to why Helen had only now decided to speak about her story, but I felt it was inappropriate to ask. But then Helen herself explained. I think she felt, for some reason, that she had to justify her silence for all those years. She said: "After the war, I didn't know what to do; I didn't know where I would go. There was so much uncertainty! And even when I came to America, and met my husband and had children – still, we had very little. We were trying to make a life for ourselves here. Who could think about the past? The present was hard enough! But now, things are different; life is mostly behind me now. Now I can finally talk about what happened…"

Helen, of course, was not alone. So many survivors remained silent for decades – they didn't even speak to their spouses and children about what happened! – before finally opening up about their stories. A flood of new Holocaust memoirs came out in the 1980s and 90s; finally, after years of silence, many survivors were ready to talk.

The reason it took them so long to open up has much to teach us about the holiday of *Rosh Hashanah*, the Hebrew New Year.

Many survivors intuitively understood that their first priority, before anything else, was to secure a future for themselves. They were alone and had very little. Who had the luxury of looking back? The danger of being paralyzed by grief was too great! And so they put the past into a box, and looked forward.

It was only once they had built new lives for themselves, when they finally felt secure, that they could begin to grapple with their past. Only after they built new lives could they permit themselves to remember the terror and destruction of their experiences in the Holocaust.

Rosh Hashanah is the first day of the Ten Days of Repentance that culminates with the holiday of *Yom Kippur* (Day of Atonement). But even though Jews spend most of this day praying in synagogue, the prayers make almost no mention of our sins. On *Rosh Hashanah*, we don't talk about or confess our sins and we don't apologize.

Why do we begin the Ten Days of Repentance by completely ignoring our past mistakes?

As Helen and other survivors understood, to mend the past, you must first ignore the past and create a new future. On the first day of the new year, we are not yet ready to look backwards, to grapple with our brokenness and with all that we did not accomplish. Before we can look backwards, we must first look forward and remember that it's possible to begin again. This is why the Ten Days of Repentance begin not with confession, but with renewal - preparing us for the deeper work of *teshuvah* that follows.

In the book of Deuteronomy, Moses commands the people of Israel:

"Take to heart these instructions with which I charge you this day." Deuteronomy 6:6

Why does Moses say that the Bible's commandments are being given to the people "this day"? This was 38 years after the people received the Bible at Mount Sinai!

The commentators explain that Moses is sharing a critically important teaching – that those who wish to serve God must always be willing to start anew. Don't think about who you were yesterday; ignore the way you lived in the past. Set your past aside for now and begin again.

There is, of course, a time and place for reflection and repentance. But on the Hebrew New Year, on the first of the Ten Days of Repentance, we must turn the page on our past and begin anew. Only after we establish this foundation of renewal can we begin the sacred work of examining our past that the remaining days will demand.

May God strengthen and exalt us on this holy day, and may He help each and every one of us, wherever we are on life's journey, believe that we can begin again.

The Depths of Repentance

Shira Schechter

Every morning during the Ten Days of Repentance, Jewish communities around the world add a single psalm to their prayers. Psalm 130 begins with just five Hebrew words: *Shir hama'alot mima'amakim keratikha Adonai* - "A song of ascents. Out of the depths I call You, O Lord." These words, recited by millions, capture the essence of what these sacred days demand from us.

The Hebrew phrase *mima'amakim* - "from the depths" - immediately establishes the emotional landscape of this prayer. We recognize this place. The depths of despair when we face our failures. The depths of exhaustion after struggling with the same weaknesses year after year. The depths of uncertainty about whether change is even possible. From this place of vulnerability, the psalmist teaches us to call out to God.

Yet Rabbi Joseph B. Soloveitchik revealed that these "depths" contain a profound secret. The word appears in plural form - not "from the depth" but "from the depths" - suggesting multiple levels of meaning. Beyond the obvious interpretation of calling from life's low points, Rabbi Soloveitchik taught that *mima'amakim* refers to the deepest recesses of the human soul itself.

This insight transforms our understanding of the entire psalm. When we call to God from the depths, we're not just crying out from our pain and disappointment. We're calling from the innermost core of who we are - the part of us that remains untouched by sin and failure, the part that still yearns for connection with the Divine. Even when our actions have created distance from God, something within us remains pure and seeking.

This dual meaning illuminates the psalm's most striking verses: "If You keep account of sins, O Lord, Lord, who will survive? Yours is the power to forgive so that You may be held in awe" (Psalm 130:3-4). The psalmist acknowledges a stark reality - measured by strict justice, none of us would survive divine scrutiny. But the verse doesn't end in despair. Instead, it pivots to hope: God's very nature includes the power to forgive.

During the Ten Days of Repentance, this message becomes urgently personal. We stand before the divine court knowing our failures, yet we're not calling from a place of complete brokenness. We're calling from that authentic core within us that recognizes what we could become. The psalm teaches us that repentance isn't about drowning in guilt, it's about accessing the deepest part of ourselves that still believes transformation is possible.

The psalm's conclusion captures this perfectly: "It is He who will redeem Israel from all their iniquities" (Psalm 130:8). The promise isn't just forgiveness, but redemption; a complete restoration to who we were meant to be. This isn't merely wiping the slate clean, it's about returning to our truest selves.

When we recite Psalm 130 during these days of repentance, something profound occurs. We begin by acknowledging our depths - both our lowest moments and our deepest spiritual core. But we don't remain there. The act of calling out, of giving voice to both our pain and our hope, begins to transform us. We discover that even in acknowledging our failures, we're simultaneously connecting with the part of us that transcends those failures.

This is why Psalm 130 appears daily during the Ten Days of Repentance. Each morning, it reminds us that the work of these days isn't just about confronting our sins - it's about remembering who we really are beneath all our mistakes. From that place of authentic recognition, genuine transformation becomes not just possible, but inevitable.

Judaism's Secret for Time Travel

Adam Eliyahu Berkowitz

As a child, I was fascinated by science fiction. I remember sitting in front of a black and white television set when I was eight years old as I watched Neil Armstrong take his first "small step" onto the moon. I always knew that this was only the beginning.

To me, though, the most fascinating sci-fi novels involved time travel. But I instinctively knew that time travel would prove to be far more challenging to science than travel through space.

So when I began to delve into Jewish studies, I was thrilled to discover that the Torah had unlocked the secret to time travel.

Allow me to explain.

In Judaism, there is a concept of repentance. We generally think of repentance as a feeling of regret; feeling bad for what we did wrong. But even if I am very sorry for sinning, I cannot go back in time and repeal the action. What's done is done.

Or is it?

The word for "repentance" in Hebrew is *teshuva*, which literally means "return". In the final chapter of the Talmud tractate known as Yoma, Reish Lakish, a former highwayman, explains that *teshuva* done out of love turns sins into meritorious deeds.[23] It is as if the penitent has gone back in time and changed the events and redefined his role in them!

The ten-day period between *Rosh Hashanah* (Hebrew New Year) and *Yom Kippur* (Day of Atonement) is known as the Ten

---

23. Babylonian Talmud, Yoma 86b

Days of Repentance. According to Maimonides, "even though repentance and crying out to God are always timely, during the ten days from *Rosh Hashanah* to *Yom Kippur* it is exceedingly appropriate, and accepted immediately [on high]."[24]

Therefore, the Ten Days of Repentance is the most appropriate time to do *teshuva*, and we add special prayers of repentance during this time. *Yom Kippur,* the Day of Atonement, is the culmination of this period. The day is spent fasting and praying, pouring out our hearts to God and confessing our past sins.

In fact, *Yom Kippur* is called the Day of Atonement, because, in the words of Maimonides,[25] "the essence of *Yom Kippur* [Day of Atonement] atones for those who repent as it states: "For on this day atonement shall be made for you to cleanse you of all your sins; you shall be clean before Hashem (Leviticus 16:30)."

The Bible describes sin as an affliction with life and death ramifications. Infants will die as a result of sin. Israel will lose wars because of sin. Repentance, achieved through verbal confession and not through animal sacrifices, will revive the land (Hosea 14:1-10).

"I will heal their affliction, Generously will I take them back in love; For My anger has turned away from them." Hosea 14:5

Micah emphasizes the time-traveling aspect of *teshuva* (Micah 7:18-20). While noting the necessity for repentance for past sins, the prophet also gives a glimpse into the future of the nation, describing how the Jews will merit forgiveness and God will fulfill the promises he made to Abraham, Isaac and Jacob:

---

24. Laws of Repentance 2:6
25. Laws of Repentance 1:3

Who is a God like You, forgiving iniquity and remitting transgression; Who has not maintained His wrath forever against the remnant of His own people, because He loves graciousness! He will take us back in love; He will cover up our iniquities, You will hurl all our sins Into the depths of the sea. You will keep faith with Jacob, Loyalty to Abraham, as You promised on oath to our fathers in days gone by. Micah 7:18-20

The Sages state that "Great is *teshuva*, for it predates the creation of the world." Implicit in this teaching is that *teshuva* can transcend nature and even reason. *Teshuva* was created before the laws of nature. It is instilled in every aspect of creation. There is no reason to despair. The entire world stands ready to facilitate your *teshuva*.

As a child, I dreamed of traveling to distant galaxies. As an adult, I discovered something far more extraordinary - the ability to travel back in time and transform my past through *teshuva*.

4

YOM KIPPUR – THE DAY OF ATONEMENT

The journey is almost complete.

Through thirty days of *Elul*, we awakened to the possibility of change. On *Rosh Hashanah*, we coronated God as King and stood before the divine throne as He reviewed our lives and began the process of judgment. During the Ten Days of Repentance, we pleaded our case, sought forgiveness, and opened our hearts to transformation.

Now we arrive at the destination toward which everything has been leading: *Yom Kippur*, the Day of Atonement.

This is the day when the books are finally sealed. When divine mercy reaches its peak and the gates of heaven stand widest open. When we fast from sunset through nightfall, becoming like angels for twenty-five hours, stripped of physical distractions so our souls can soar directly to God.

Yom Kippur stands alone in the Jewish calendar—and perhaps in all of human experience—as a day when ordinary time stops and extraordinary transformation becomes possible. On this day, the High Priest once entered the Holy of Holies, the only human being permitted to stand in the very presence of God on earth. Today, each of us can achieve that same intimacy through prayer, repentance, and the mysterious alchemy of divine forgiveness.

The day promises what seems impossible: that our sins can be completely erased, that we can emerge as pure as we were on the day we were born, that the gap between who we are and who we were meant to be can be closed entirely.

How can twenty-five hours contain such power? How can fasting and prayer accomplish what months or years of struggle cannot? How does a single day hold the key to spiritual rebirth?

The answer lies in understanding that *Yom Kippur* is not just another day on the calendar. It is a gift from beyond time itself, a divine invitation to transcend our human limitations and touch the infinite.

The service is about to begin. The last shofar blast awaits.

Are we ready for the ultimate return?

YOM KIPPUR – THE DAY OF ULTIMATE RETURN

Rabbi Joseph B. Soloveitchik once recalled a moment that captured the essence of *Yom Kippur's* transformative power. Standing in the synagogue courtyard with his father, Rabbi Moshe Soloveitchik, just before the final *Yom Kippur* service, he witnessed an exquisite autumn sunset painting the sky in purple and gold. It had been a fresh, clear day filled with sunshine and light, one of those delicate days of summer's end. As evening approached and the sun sank beyond the trees, his father turned to him and said: "This sunset differs from ordinary sunsets for with it forgiveness is bestowed upon us for our sins." Rabbi Soloveitchik reflected: "The Day of Atonement and the forgiveness of sins merged and blended here with the splendor and beauty of the world and with the hidden lawfulness of the order of creation and the whole was transformed into one living, holy, cosmic phenomenon."[1]

This profound moment illuminates something essential about *Yom Kippur*: it is a day when the ordinary world becomes infused with extraordinary possibility for spiritual transformation, when even a sunset carries the power of divine forgiveness.

The Architecture of Forgiveness

Yom Kippur means the Day of Atonement. Jewish tradition understands atonement as far more than simply pardoning our sins. True atonement involves a fundamental transformation of the soul, a process that doesn't merely forgive our failures but actually purifies us from them entirely.

---

1. Joseph B. Soloveitchik, *Halakhic Man* (Philadelphia: Jewish Publication Society, 1983), 38.

The Sages teach that the day itself carries an inherent power to cleanse that exists nowhere else in the calendar. As the Torah declares: "For on this day atonement shall be made for you to purify you of all your sins; you shall be pure before the Lord" (Leviticus 16:30). The Hebrew phrase "*lifnei Hashem*," "before the Lord," suggests that on this day we achieve a level of purity that allows us to stand directly in God's presence, like the High Priest entering the Holy of Holies.

The Torah emphasizes this day's unique status repeatedly: "The tenth day of this seventh month is the Day of Atonement. It shall be a sacred occasion for you: you shall afflict yourselves" (Leviticus 23:27). This divine command to "afflict" ourselves creates the space necessary for spiritual transformation, removing the distractions of physical pleasure so we can focus entirely on our relationship with God.

While sincere human repentance is necessary, the power of purification ultimately comes from God's mercy alone. While sincere regret can help us improve our future actions, only divine grace can actually erase the stain of past transgressions. God, in His abundant kindness, established both the Day of Atonement and the commandment of repentance to allow us to achieve what would otherwise be impossible: the complete removal of our sins.

Rabbi Akiva captured this divine gift beautifully when he proclaimed: "Fortunate are you, Israel – for before Whom do you purify yourselves and Who purifies you? Your Father in heaven, as we read: 'I will sprinkle pure water upon you, and you shall be pure' (Ezekiel 36:25), and 'God is the hope (*mikveh*) of Israel' (Jeremiah 17:13). Just as a *mikveh* (ritual bath) purifies the impure, so too, God purifies Israel."[2]

Rabbi Eliezer Melamed explains that this metaphor of the ritual bath reveals something profound about *Yom Kippur*'s unique spiritual dynamics. Throughout the year, various barriers can obscure our connection to the Divine. But on *Yom Kippur*, those barriers dissolve. The gates of heaven open wide, and divine light shines directly into the depths of our souls. Our elevated souls can immerse themselves in this light as if entering a cosmic *mikveh*, emerging purified from the spiritual residue of sin and failure.[3]

The Crescendo of the High Holidays

Yom Kippur serves as the climactic finale of a carefully orchestrated spiritual journey that began forty days earlier on the first of *Elul*. Each stage of this process builds toward this ultimate day of transformation.

Elul provided the time for honest self-examination and gradual awakening to our spiritual condition. *Rosh Hashanah* established God's kingship and opened the divine court for judgment. The Ten Days of Repentance offered intensive opportunities for repair through *teshuvah*, prayer, and charity. Now, on *Yom Kippur,* all this preparation reaches its fulfillment as divine judgment is finalized and sealed.

The progression follows a profound spiritual logic rooted in the biblical understanding of repentance. As the prophet Isaiah declares: "Seek the Lord while He may be found, call upon Him while He is near. Let the wicked abandon his ways and the

---

2. Babylonian Talmud, Yoma 85b

3. Rabbi Eliezer Melamed, "06 – Yom Kippur," *Peninei Halakha*, Yeshivat Har Bracha website, https://ph.yhb.org.il/en/category/15/15-06/.

man of iniquity his thoughts, and let him return to the Lord, and He will have mercy on him, and to our God, for He will abundantly pardon" (Isaiah 55:6-7). We needed *Elul*'s extended preparation to develop the honesty required for genuine repentance. We needed Rosh *Hashanah's* emphasis on divine sovereignty to understand that we stand before the ultimate Judge. We needed the Ten Days of Repentance's focus on transformation to begin the hard work of change. Only then are we ready for *Yom Kippur*'s culminating gift: the divine promise of complete atonement for those who approach with sincere hearts.

Beyond Human Limitations

What makes *Yom Kippur* unique among all Jewish observances is its invitation to transcend ordinary human existence and access a fundamentally different mode of being. On *Yom Kippur*, we are like angels. This transformation isn't merely symbolic; it represents a profound theological shift in our relationship with the physical and spiritual worlds.

Angels, in Jewish thought, exist in a state of pure spiritual focus. They have no physical needs or desires, and they serve God with complete devotion. Their existence is entirely aligned with divine will. On *Yom Kippur*, we temporarily enter this angelic realm, stepping outside the normal boundaries of human experience to achieve a level of spiritual clarity impossible during ordinary time.

Yet this elevation serves a distinctly human purpose that even angels cannot achieve. Angels were created perfect and remain unchanging. But human beings possess something remarkable: the capacity for *teshuvah*, the ability to transform our past and recreate ourselves through return to God.

222 | BEFORE THE KING

The prophet Isaiah captures this transformative potential: "Though your sins be as scarlet, they shall be white as snow; though they be red like crimson, they shall become like wool" (Isaiah 1:18).

On *Yom Kippur*, we temporarily adopt angelic purity not to escape our humanity, but to access the highest spiritual potential that lies within it. By setting aside physical concerns, we create space for the soul to encounter God directly. We achieve a level of closeness that bridges the gap between human and Divine.

In this elevated state, genuine transformation becomes not just possible but natural.

The Sacred Drama of the Temple Service

Central to understanding *Yom Kippur*'s meaning is the elaborate Temple service that represented the spiritual heart of this day. When the Temple stood in Jerusalem, *Yom Kippur* was the only day of the year when the High Priest could enter the Holy of Holies, the innermost sanctuary where God's presence dwelt on earth.

The Torah provides detailed instructions for this sacred service: "Aaron shall bring the bull of his sin offering, to make atonement for himself and for his household; he shall slaughter his bull of sin offering. And he shall take a panful of glowing coals scooped from the altar before the Lord, and two handfuls of finely ground aromatic incense, and bring this behind the curtain. He shall put the incense on the fire before the Lord, so that the cloud from the incense screens the cover that is over the Ark of the Covenant, lest he die" (Leviticus 16:11-13).

This service was a cosmic drama. The High Priest, representing all of Israel, would enter the most sacred space in the universe to achieve atonement for himself, his fellow priests, and the entire Jewish people. The Sages describe this elaborate service in further detail: the special white linen garments that replaced his usual golden vestments, the clouds of incense, the sprinkling of blood on the golden cover of the Ark of the Covenant, and the awesome moment when he would pronounce God's ineffable name.[4]

The Sages also describe the great joy that would accompany the moment when the High Priest emerged safely from the Holy of Holies. His successful completion of the service meant that atonement had been achieved, forgiveness granted, and God's favor secured for the coming year.

Even though we no longer have the Temple, the *avodah* (Temple service) remains central to *Yom Kippur* observance. Through prayers that relive this ancient service, we participate in that sacred drama of atonement, experiencing the same essential process of purification and renewal that once unfolded in Jerusalem.

The Promise of Transformation

Perhaps most remarkably, *Yom Kippur* promises not just forgiveness but genuine transformation. The day doesn't simply wipe our slate clean; it offers the possibility of becoming fundamentally different. Through its unique combination of fasting, prayer, confession, and repentance, *Yom Kippur* creates the ideal conditions for authentic transformation.

---

4. Mishnah Yoma, chapters 3-7

This promise finds its foundation in Moses' words to the people: "and you shall return to the Lord, your God, and you and your children shall heed God's command with all your heart and soul, just as I enjoin upon you this day... Then the Lord, your God, will open up your heart and the hearts of your offspring—to love the Lord your God with all your heart and soul, in order that you may live." (Deuteronomy 30:2,6). Genuine repentance leads us back to our truest selves and to God.

The Sages declared that *Yom Kippur* itself brings atonement.[5] The day itself carries a spiritual energy that can purify the soul, clarify our values, and reconnect us to our deepest purpose. When we engage sincerely with *Yom Kippur*'s demands—the physical challenges of fasting, the emotional difficulty of honest confession, the spiritual effort of sustained prayer—we emerge as people who have been fundamentally renewed.

This transformation extends beyond the individual to the entire community. *Yom Kippur* is both a deeply personal day of soul-searching and a collective experience of purification. As we confess together, fast together, and pray together, we create a sacred community bound by shared vulnerability and common hope for forgiveness.

---

5. Baylonian Talmud, Yoma 85b

THE PATH TO PURIFICATION: A JOURNEY THROUGH *YOM KIPPUR*

Preparing for the Holiest Day

Now that we understand the extraordinary spiritual opportunity that Yom Kippur represents, we can turn to how we prepare for and observe this holiest day.

The preparation for such a momentous day began on the first day of the Hebrew month of *Elul*, but reaches its culmination on the day before the fast. This day carries its own spiritual intensity as we make our last preparations to enter the sacred Day of Atonement. Every custom and practice observed on this day is designed to ensure we approach *Yom Kippur* with the proper spiritual mindset, having removed every possible barrier between ourselves and divine forgiveness.

Selichot: The Final Call

On the morning before *Yom Kippur*, communities recite a brief set of penitential prayers called *Selichot*. Unlike the lengthy *Selichot* recited throughout the month of *Elul* and the rest of the Ten Days of Repentance, these final prayers are notably shorter. Why this change in length at such a crucial moment?

According to tradition, by this point, the intensive spiritual work should already be complete. The month of *Elul* and the Ten Days of Repentance have provided ample opportunity for thorough self-examination and repentance. These final *Selichot* serve not as an extended plea for forgiveness, but as a focused, concentrated appeal, like a final, brief conversation before a momentous meeting. The brevity reflects confidence that the real work has been done; now we simply present ourselves, prepared and ready, before the divine throne of judgment.

Acts of Charity and Merit

It is customary to give charity generously before *Yom Kippur*, with the belief that charity helps secure atonement for sins. As we explored in previous chapters, the Sages teach that "repentance, prayer, and charity can annul the harsh decree." This final opportunity to perform charity before the Day of Atonement serves as both spiritual preparation and a practical demonstration of our transformed values. The act of giving charity before *Yom Kippur* is thought to bring special merit for the year ahead, as we enter the fast having just demonstrated our commitment to justice and compassion.

Kaparot: Symbolic Transfer

One of the most distinctive customs of *Yom Kippur* eve is the ritual of *Kaparot*. For those who follow this custom, it is traditionally performed by gently waving a live chicken over one's head while reciting specific prayers. This ceremony symbolically transfers one's sins onto the bird as we ask that whatever negative divine judgments were supposed to befall us in the coming year should befall the chicken instead. The bird is then donated to people who are in need in a final act of charity.

In modern times, many people substitute money for the chicken, which is then given to charity as a merit for the person to be granted a good and peaceful new year. The Hebrew word *kaparot* means "atonements," and the ritual represents our hope to begin anew, free of the spiritual burden of past transgressions, as we approach the sacred day of *Yom Kippur*.

Spiritual Purification

Another custom observed by many, especially men, before *Yom Kippur* is immersion in a ritual bath called a *mikveh*. This purification ritual represents spiritual renewal and rebirth. Just as the *mikveh* transforms the ritual status of those who immerse, emerging from its waters before *Yom Kippur* symbolizes our readiness to enter the day of repentance with a spiritually cleansed soul, prepared for the sacred encounter with the Divine.

Blessing the Children

Before *Yom Kippur* begins, it is customary for parents to bless their children with the traditional priestly blessing, in addition to offering prayers which ask for God's protection and guidance toward a life of moral integrity and spiritual purpose. This tender moment acknowledges that while *Yom Kippur* is a day of judgment, it is also a day of blessing and renewal. Parents pray that their children will be inscribed and sealed for a good year.

In invoking Sarah, Rebecca, Rachel, and Leah for daughters, and Ephraim and Manasseh for sons, parents connect their children to an unbroken chain of faith, offering not just parental love but a complete vision of the good life, guided by Torah, sustained by honest work, and surrounded by generations of righteousness.

Blessing of the Children

> *For a son:*
> **May** God make you like Ephraim and
>   Manasseh.
> May the Lord bless you and guard you.
> May the Lord shine His countenance
>   upon you, and be gracious unto you.
> May the Lord turn His countenance
>   toward you and grant you peace.

Continue "And may it be the will" below

For a daughter:
May God make you like Sarah, Rebecca,
Rachel and Leah.
May the Lord bless you and guard you.
May the Lord shine His countenance
upon you, and be gracious unto you.
May the Lord turn His countenance
toward you and grant you peace.

(Continue:)
And may it be the will of our Father in
heaven, to place in your heart love
and fear of Him. May the fear of the
Lord be upon your face all the days
of your life, so that you will not sin.
May your desire be for Torah and
Mitzvot (commandments), may
your eyes look straightforward, may
your mouth speak [with] wisdom,
may your heart meditate [with]
reverence, may your hands be
engaged in mitzvos, and may your
feet hasten to do the will of our
Father in heaven. May the Almighty
grant you children who will [grow
up to] be righteous, occupying
themselves with Torah and mitzvot
(commandments) all their days.
May your source be blessed, and
may He grant that your livelihood
come with honesty, ease and

abundance, from His generous
hand, and not from the gifts of men;
a livelihood that will free you to
serve God. May you be inscribed and
sealed for good, long life together
with all the righteous of Israel.
Amen.

The Pre-Fast Feast

Perhaps most surprisingly, the day of fasting is preceded by a day of eating. The Sages derive this practice from Leviticus 23:32: "You shall afflict your souls on the ninth day of the month in the evening." Since the verse mentions afflicting ourselves on the ninth day of the Hebrew month of *Tishrei*, while *Yom Kippur* is the tenth of the month, the sages interpret this as a commandment to eat and drink on the ninth day in preparation for the fast.[6]

Several reasons are offered for this pre-fast command to eat. The most practical reason is to prepare for the fast and provide strength to pray properly on *Yom Kippur*.[7] Because the day is spent fasting and praying, one should eat heartily the day before, giving the body sufficient nourishment to endure the full day of fasting without compromising one's ability to concentrate on prayer and repentance.

This commandment also reveals something deeper about divine compassion. While God asks us to abstain from food and drink for a single day each year as part of our atonement, He simultaneously provides for our physical needs by

---

6. Babylonian Talmud, Yoma 81b
7. Rashi, Yoma 81b; *Sha'arei Teshuva* 4:10

requiring us to nourish ourselves beforehand, ensuring we can complete the fast safely and successfully.[8]

Some authorities offer a different perspective on the pre-fast meal. They suggest that eating heartily the day before actually intensifies the affliction of fasting, fulfilling the verse "You shall afflict your souls on the ninth day of the month." According to this view, a day of abundant food and drink makes the following day's fast even more challenging.[9]

Perhaps most beautifully, the pre-fast feast addresses a fundamental tension in the nature of *Yom Kippur* itself. All Torah commandments are meant to be fulfilled with wholehearted joy, including physical enjoyment. The command to repent certainly deserves joyful celebration, since through it we are purged of our sins. *Yom Kippur* is indeed a festival that deserves celebration with food and drink. However, during the actual process of repentance, open joy would be inappropriate, as genuine *teshuvah* requires sorrow and regret over past failures. We are therefore commanded to give physical expression to the joy of repentance on the eve of *Yom Kippur*.[10]

Rabbi Abraham Issac HaKohen Kook offers another profound insight into why we eat before *Yom Kippur*. He explains that genuine repentance operates on two distinct levels, both hinted at in the Torah's description of *teshuvah* in Deuteronomy.

"And it shall come to pass when all these things come upon you, the blessing and the curse that I have set before you, and

8. Rosh, Yoma 8:22; *Tur* OḤ 604
9. Shibolei Ha-leket; *Arukh Ha-Shulḥan* 604:4
10. *Sha'arei Teshuva* 4:8

you will take it to your heart among all the nations where the Lord your God has driven you. And you will return unto the Lord your God and hearken to His voice, according to all that I command you this day, you and your children, with all your heart and with all your soul... And the Lord your God will circumcise your heart and the heart of your children to love the Lord your God with all your heart and with all your soul, so that you may live" (Deuteronomy 30:1-2, 6).

These verses speak of both our "return" to God and God's need to "circumcise our hearts" to restore love for Him, suggesting that sin damages us in two ways: it violates divine will and creates emotional distance from God.

Repairing each type of damage requires a different approach. Rebuilding our intimate connection with God happens best when we step away from worldly distractions and focus purely on the spiritual, exactly what *Yom Kippur*'s fasting and prayers accomplish. However, proving that we've truly changed our behavior can only happen while we're fully engaged with the world and its temptations.

This creates an apparent problem: if *Yom Kippur*'s otherworldly atmosphere is necessary for spiritual reconnection but insufficient for complete behavioral change, how can the day achieve full repentance? Rabbi Kook's answer is elegant: the ninth and tenth days work together as one complete experience. On *Yom Kippur* eve, we engage with the physical world, eating, drinking, conducting business, while remaining carefully mindful of God's presence and avoiding all prohibitions. This demonstrates that we can navigate worldly pleasures without stumbling spiritually. Only after proving our capacity for practical *teshuvah* in the material realm do we ascend to the heightened spiritual *teshuvah* of *Yom Kippur* itself. Together, the ninth and tenth create the complete arc of repentance, moving from active engagement with the world to pure spiritual transcendence.[11]

Verbal Confession

Before sitting down to the final meal on *Yom Kippur* eve, called the *seudah ha-mafseket* or "separating meal," observant Jews recite the verbal confession (*viduy*) as part of the afternoon prayer service. *Viduy*, meaning "confession" in Hebrew, is a verbal acknowledgment before God of our moral failures and shortcomings, accompanied by genuine regret and resolve to change. While *viduy* is what we do throughout *Yom Kippur* itself, the Sages teach that this confession must also be said before eating the final meal before *Yom Kippur*, lest one's mind become confused during the meal from the abundance of food and drink, making meaningful confession impossible afterward.[12] Others provide an even more sobering reason: we confess before the meal in case we should choke while eating and never have the chance to recite *viduy* on *Yom Kippur* itself.

The practice of reciting *Viduy* forces us to confront our failures while we are still clear-minded and capable of sincere repentance. This confession serves as a bridge between the everyday world we're leaving behind and the sacred territory of *Yom Kippur* we're about to enter, ensuring that we cross that threshold already having begun the process of sincere repentance and return to God.

Like Angels for a Day

Yom Kippur stands alone in the Jewish calendar as a day that

---

11. Rabbi Abraham Isaac HaCohen Kook, *Ein Ayah* on *Ein Yaakov*, commentary on *Berakhot*, volume I, section 38.
12. Babylonian Talmud, Yoma 87b

elevates us beyond ordinary human experience. Through its distinctive commandments and practices, the Day of Atonement temporarily strips away the ordinary concerns of physical existence, revealing the pure spiritual core that lies at the heart of our identity.

Jewish tradition teaches that on *Yom Kippur*, we transcend our ordinary human limitations and become, in a profound sense, like the angels in heaven. As Rabbi Judah Loew, known as the Maharal of Prague, explains, "All of the *mitzvot* (commandments) that God commanded us on [*Yom Kippur*] are designed to remove, as much as possible, a person's relationship to physicality, until he is completely like an angel."[13] This transformation is not merely metaphorical but manifests in concrete ways throughout the holy day.

Like angels, we abstain from eating and drinking, devoting ourselves entirely to praising God and prayer, rather than attending to bodily needs. We dress in white, echoing the pure radiance associated with celestial beings. We spend the day in prayer with our feet together, emulating the angels' "straight leg" from Ezekiel's vision: "Their leg was a straight leg" (Ezekiel 1:7), a posture that suggests unwavering spiritual focus like that of the angels.

Even our liturgy reflects this angelic status. The phrase "Blessed be the name of His glorious kingdom forever and ever" is recited daily after the first verse of the *Shema* prayer. According to the Sages, when Moses ascended to heaven, he heard the angels singing these very words to God and brought this prayer down to Israel. Since this verse belongs to the angels, it is normally recited in an undertone throughout the

---

13. Maharal of Prague (Rabbi Judah Loew), *Derush Le-Shabbat Teshuvah*, in *Derashot Maharal*.

year; only on *Yom Kippur*, when we are compared to heavenly angels, is this verse recited aloud.

By temporarily setting aside our physical needs and desires, we can approach God with the same single-minded devotion that characterizes the angels, making ourselves worthy of divine forgiveness and renewal.

How to Observe the Day

Like other biblical festivals, *Yom Kippur* requires us to make it a sacred occasion, designating the day for holy purposes and honoring it with dignity. As the Torah declares: "The tenth day of this seventh month is the Day of Atonement. It shall be a sacred occasion for you" (Leviticus 23:27). This means preparing our homes, wearing our finest clothes, and setting the day apart from ordinary weekdays.

The day also requires complete rest from work, elevated even beyond regular *Sabbath* observance. The Torah emphasizes this repeatedly: "You shall do no work throughout that day. For it is a Day of Atonement, on which atonement is made on your behalf before the Lord your God... And whoever does any work throughout that day, I will cause that person to perish from among his people. Do no work whatsoever; it is a law for all time, throughout the ages, in all your settlements" (Leviticus 23:28-31). This isn't merely rest, it's a complete withdrawal from the creative activities that define ordinary life.

The Unique Commands of Atonement

Beyond these shared obligations, *Yom Kippur* introduces three commandments that are unique to this holiday, creating its distinctive spiritual landscape.

The Fast of Affliction

Yom Kippur is a day of affliction, as God commanded: "The tenth day of this seventh month is the Day of Atonement. It shall be a sacred occasion for you: you shall afflict yourselves, and you shall bring an offering by fire to the Lord... Indeed, any person who does not afflict himself throughout that day shall be cut off from his kin... It shall be a *Shabbat* of complete rest for you, and you shall afflict yourselves; on the ninth day of the month at evening, from evening to evening, you shall observe this your Sabbath" (Leviticus 23:26-32).

The sages understood this "affliction" to refer to five specific forms of self-denial, each designed to elevate the soul above physical needs: refraining from eating and drinking, abstaining from bathing, not wearing leather shoes, refraining from applying oils or lotions, and abstaining from marital relations. These restrictions are meant to be transformative, creating space for pure spiritual focus by temporarily setting aside the body's ordinary demands.

When we remove the distractions of eating, drinking, and other physical pleasures, we can focus entirely on prayer, repentance, and spiritual reflection. The hunger we feel reminds us of our dependence on God for everything, fostering the humility essential for genuine repentance.

Repentance and Confession

The second unique commandment is active repentance and confession of sins. The Torah establishes this obligation clearly: "For on this day, atonement shall be made for you to purify you of all your sins; you shall purify yourselves before the Lord" (Leviticus 16:30). Maimonides explains that since it is a time of forgiveness and pardon, *teshuvah* becomes an obligation on this day.[14]

For sins committed against God, we turn directly to Him in prayer and confession. However, for wrongs committed against other people, we must first seek forgiveness from those we've harmed before approaching God. *Yom Kippur* cannot cleanse interpersonal wounds until we've done the difficult work of repair and reconciliation with our fellow human beings.

The Sacred Service

The third unique element was the elaborate Temple service performed on *Yom Kippur* as described in Leviticus 16:1-34, which culminated with the High Priest entering the Holy of Holies. *Yom Kippur* was the only time anyone entered that sacred space throughout the entire year. This service included special sin offerings: a bull for the priests, two goats (one sacrificed, one sent to the wilderness carrying the people's sins), and the dramatic moment when the High Priest spoke God's ineffable name and sprinkled blood before the divine presence.

Today, without the Temple, the day itself provides atonement, supported by our fasting and repentance. The prayers, especially the *Musaf* (additional) service, take the place of the ancient sacrifices, allowing us to experience spiritual elevation through words and intention rather than ritual offerings.

Customs That Transform the Day

Beyond the biblical commandments, Jewish tradition has developed customs that deepen *Yom Kippur*'s transformative

---

14. Laws of Repentance 2:7

power. Many wear white clothing, as this color powerfully symbolizes the spiritual transformation we seek on this holiest day, reflecting the promise in Isaiah: "Though your sins be as scarlet, they shall be white as snow" (Isaiah 1:18). This verse expresses the fundamental hope of *Yom Kippur*, that our sins become purified through divine forgiveness.

The Sages capture the remarkable feeling of confidence behind this custom: "What nation is like this nation! Generally, when a person must appear before the court, he wears black clothing... But not so Israel, who wear white [clothing]... knowing that God performs miracles for them."[15] While the world expects defendants to dress in mourning, Jews approach divine judgment with hope and trust in God's mercy.

This tradition also connects us to the ancient Temple service, where the High Priest donned special white linen garments worn only during the *Yom Kippur* ritual. Yet the *kittel*, a white garment worn by married men on *Yom Kippur*, carries a sobering reminder as well. It resembles a burial shroud, confronting us with our mortality and the urgency of repentance. Through this simple garment, we embody both our highest spiritual aspirations and our humblest acknowledgment of human frailty.

In addition to wearing white, on *Yom Kippur* we recite five distinct prayer services, adding an additional prayer to the usual four recited on Jewish festivals. From the first prayer recited at sunset on *Yom Kippur* eve, through the *Ne'ilah* service recited at the day's close, these prayers immerse us completely in the work of repentance and renewal, ensuring that virtually every waking moment helps us reach the goal of genuine

---

15. *Yolkut Shimoni* 825:2

repentance and renewed closeness with God that *Yom Kippur* is meant to achieve.

A Day Unlike Any Other

Through this unique combination of biblical commandments and traditional practices, *Yom Kippur* creates an experience unmatched anywhere else in Jewish life. The physical afflictions clear space for spiritual focus, the obligation of repentance demands honest self-confrontation, and the customs elevate the entire community into a realm where forgiveness and renewal become possible. On this day, the ordinary rules of life are suspended, and we discover what it means to stand, pure and unencumbered, before the Divine.

The Sacred Night Begins

As the sun sets on the eve of *Yom Kippur*, Jewish homes and synagogues transform to welcome the holiest night of the year. Even though no meals will be eaten for the next twenty-five hours, it is customary to set the table with a white tablecloth, reflecting the purity and sanctity of the day ahead.

Before the fast begins, candles are lit just as they are before every *Shabbat* and Jewish holiday, marking the transition from the ordinary world into sacred time. The flickering flames illuminate homes as families head to the synagogue for the evening service that will carry them into the Day of Atonement.

The *Yom Kippur* service begins with *Kol Nidrei*, the haunting declaration that opens the *Yom Kippur* liturgy. This ancient Aramaic formula annuls vows and pledges that we may have made rashly, or we will be unable to fulfill in the coming year. More than a legal technicality, *Kol Nidrei* represents our desire to approach God with complete honesty, free from the entanglements of unfulfilled promises. The melody, passed down through generations, fills the synagogue with an otherworldly quality that immediately signals we have entered something beyond ordinary time.

Following *Kol Nidrei* comes the evening prayer service, the first of five services recited over this holy day. This isn't just another ordinary evening prayer. It marks the beginning of an intense spiritual journey, setting the stage for the soul-searching and repentance that define *Yom Kippur*. As the congregation settles into prayer, the ordinary concerns of daily life fade away, replaced by the urgent call to return to our truest selves before God. The evening service launches the intensive spiritual journey of *Yom Kippur*, establishing our aspiration to angelic purity and divine forgiveness that will carry us through the transformative day ahead. Special melodies used only on the nights of *Rosh Hashanah* and *Yom Kippur* weave through the prayers, creating an otherworldly atmosphere that immediately signals the transition into sacred time.

One of the service's most distinctive features occurs during the *Shema* prayer, Judaism's central declaration of faith. After reciting "Hear O Israel, the Lord is our God, the Lord is One," the line "Blessed be the name of His glorious kingdom forever and ever," normally whispered because it is a pronouncement that really belongs to angels, is proclaimed aloud for all to hear. Since on *Yom Kippur* we are like angels, we can boldly speak these celestial words. This small change in volume makes a big statement: for these 25 hours, we have transcended our ordinary human limitations. In that moment, the boundary between earth and heaven grows thin.

The evening service also introduces the intensive process of confession that will define the next twenty-five hours. While we already recited confessions on *Yom Kippur* eve as a precaution, this marks the beginning of confessions on the holy day itself.

Every *Amidah* (standing prayer) on *Yom Kippur* concludes with extensive confessions, recited with heads bent in contrition. These confessions methodically list our sins according to the Hebrew alphabet, ensuring we acknowledge failures across the entire spectrum of human behavior.

The full *Yom Kippur* confession prayers:

> e-lo-HAY-nu vay-lo-HAY a-vo-TAY-nu
> ta-VO l'-fa-NE-kha t'-fi-la-TAY-nu,
> v'-al tit-a-LAM mi-t'-khi-na-TAY-nu
> she-AYN a-NAKH-nu a-zay fa-
> NEEM uk-shay O-ref lo-MAR l'-fa-
> NE-kha
> a-do-NAI e-lo-HAY-nu vay-lo-HAY a-
> vo-TAY-nu tza-dee-KEEM a-NAKH-
> nu v'-lo kha-TA-nu a-VAL a-NAKH-
> nu va-a-vo-TAY-nu kha-TA-nu:
> a-SHAM-nu. ba-GAD-nu. ga-ZAL-nu.
> di-BAR-nu DO-fee. he-e-VEE-nu. v'-
> hir-SHA-nu. ZAD-nu. kha-MAS-nu.
> ta-FAL-nu SHE-ker. ya-ATZ-nu RA.
> ki-ZAV-nu. LATZ-nu. ma-RAD-nu.
> ni-ATZ-nu. sa-RAR-nu. a-VEE-nu.
> pa-SHA-nu. tza-RAR-nu. ki-SHEE-
> nu O-ref. ra-SHA-nu. shi-KHAT-nu.
> ti-AV-nu. ta-EE-nu. ti-ta-NU:
> SAR-nu mi-mitz-vo-TE-kha u-mi-
> mish-pa-TE-kha ha-to-VEEM v'-lo
> SHA-vah LA-nu. v'-a-TAH tza-DEEK

al kol ha-BA a-LAY-nu. kee e-MET
a-SEE-ta va-a-NAKH-nu hir-SHA-
nu:

mah no-MAR l'-fa-NE-kha yo-SHAYV
ma-ROM. u-mah n'-sa-PAYR l'-fa-
NE-kha sho-KHAYN sh'-kha-KEEM.
ha-LO kol ha-nis-ta-ROT v'-ha-nig-
LOT a-TAH yo-DAY-a:

a-TAH yo-DAY-a ra-ZAY o-LAM. v'-ta-a-
lu-MOT sit-RAY khol KHAI: a-TAH
kho-FAYS kol khad-RAY VA-ten u-
vo-KHAYN k'-la-YOT va-LAYV: AYN
da-VAR ne-e-LAM mi-ME-kha. v'-
AYN nis-TAR mi-NE-ged ay-NEY-
kha: uv-KHAYN y'-hee ra-TZON mil-
fa-NE-kha a-do-NAI e-lo-HAY-nu
vay-lo-HAY a-vo-TAY-nu. she-t'-
kha-PAYR LA-nu al kol kha-to-tay-
NU. v'-tis-LAKH LA-nu al kol a-vo-
no-TAY-nu. u-tim-KHAL LA-nu al
kol p'-sha-AY-nu:

al KHAYT she-kha-TA-nu l'-fa-NE-kha
b'-O-nes uv-ra-TZON:

v'-al KHAYT she-kha-TA-nu l'-fa-NE-
kha b'-i-MUTZ ha-LAYV:

al KHAYT she-kha-TA-nu l'-fa-NE-kha
bi-v'-LEE DA-at:

v'-al KHAYT she-kha-TA-nu l'-fa-NE-
kha b'-vi-TUY s'-fa-TA-yim:

al KHAYT she-kha-TA-nu l'-fa-NE-kha
b'-ga-LUY u-va-SA-ter:

v'-al KHAYT she-kha-TA-nu l'-fa-NE-
kha b'-gi-LUY a-ra-YOT:

al KHAYT she-kha-TA-nu l'-fa-NE-kha
b'-di-BUR PEH:
v'-al KHAYT she-kha-TA-nu l'-fa-NE-
kha b'-DA-at uv-mir-MAH:
al KHAYT she-kha-TA-nu l'-fa-NE-kha
b'-har-HOR ha-LAYV:
v'-al KHAYT she-kha-TA-nu l'-fa-NE-
kha b'-ho-na-AT RAY-a:
al KHAYT she-kha-TA-nu l'-fa-NE-kha
b'-vi-DUY PEH:
v'-al KHAYT she-kha-TA-nu l'-fa-NE-
kha bi-v'-ee-DAT z'-NUT:
al KHAYT she-kha-TA-nu l'-fa-NE-kha
b'-za-DON u-vish-ga-GAH:
v'-al KHAYT she-kha-TA-nu l'-fa-NE-kha
b'-zil-ZUL ho-REEM u-mo-REEM:
al KHAYT she-kha-TA-nu l'-fa-NE-kha
b'-KHO-zek YAD:
v'-al KHAYT she-kha-TA-nu l'-fa-NE-
kha b'-khi-LUL ha-SHAYM:
al KHAYT she-kha-TA-nu l'-fa-NE-kha
b'-tif-SHUT PEH:
v'-al KHAYT she-kha-TA-nu l'-fa-NE-
kha b'-tum-AT s'-fa-TA-yim:
al KHAYT she-kha-TA-nu l'-fa-NE-kha
b'-YAY-tzer ha-RA:
v'-al KHAYT she-kha-TA-nu l'-fa-NE-
kha b'-yod-EEM uv-lo yod-EEM:
v'-al ku-LAM e-LO-ah s'-lee-KHOT. s'-
LAKH LA-nu. m'-KHAL LA-nu. ka-
PAYR LA-nu:
al KHAYT she-kha-TA-nu l'-fa-NE-kha

b'-kha-PAT SHO-khad:
v'-al KHAYT she-kha-TA-nu l'-fa-NE-
kha b'-KHA-khash uv-kha-ZAV:
al KHAYT she-kha-TA-nu l'-fa-NE-kha
b'-la-SHON ha-RA:
v'-al KHAYT she-kha-TA-nu l'-fa-NE-
kha b'-la-TZON:
al KHAYT she-kha-TA-nu l'-fa-NE-kha
b'-ma-SA uv-ma-TAN:
v'-al KHAYT she-kha-TA-nu l'-fa-NE-
kha b'-ma-a-KHAL uv-mish-TEH:
al KHAYT she-kha-TA-nu l'-fa-NE-kha
b'-NE-shekh uv-mar-BEET:
v'-al KHAYT she-kha-TA-nu l'-fa-NE-
kha bi-n'-tee-YAT ga-RON:
al KHAYT she-kha-TA-nu l'-fa-NE-kha
b'-si-KUR A-yin:
v'-al KHAYT she-kha-TA-nu l'-fa-NE-
kha b'-SEE-akh sif-to-TAY-nu:
al KHAYT she-kha-TA-nu l'-fa-NE-kha
b'-ay-NA-yim ra-MOT:
v'-al KHAYT she-kha-TA-nu l'-fa-NE-
kha b'-a-ZUT ME-tzakh:
v'-al ku-LAM e-LO-ah s'-lee-KHOT. s'-
LAKH LA-nu. m'-KHAL LA-nu. ka-
PAYR LA-nu:
al KHAYT she-kha-TA-nu l'-fa-NE-kha
bi-f'-ree-KAT OL:
v'-al KHAYT she-kha-TA-nu l'-fa-NE-
kha bi-f'-lee-LUT:
al KHAYT she-kha-TA-nu l'-fa-NE-kha
bi-tz'-dee-YAT RAY-a:

v'-al KHAYT she-kha-TA-nu l'-fa-NE-
kha b'-tza-RUT A-yin:

al KHAYT she-kha-TA-nu l'-fa-NE-kha
b'-ka-LUT ROSH:

v'-al KHAYT she-kha-TA-nu l'-fa-NE-
kha b'-kash-YUT O-ref:

al KHAYT she-kha-TA-nu l'-fa-NE-kha
b'-ree-TZAT rag-LA-yim l'-ha-RA:

v'-al KHAYT she-kha-TA-nu l'-fa-NE-
kha bir-khee-LUT:

al KHAYT she-kha-TA-nu l'-fa-NE-kha
bish-VU-at SHAV:

v'-al KHAYT she-kha-TA-nu l'-fa-NE-
kha b'-sin-AT khi-NAM:

al KHAYT she-kha-TA-nu l'-fa-NE-kha
bit-SU-met YAD:

v'-al KHAYT she-kha-TA-nu l'-fa-NE-
kha b'-tim-HON lay-VAV:

v'-al ku-LAM e-LO-ah s'-lee-KHOT. s'-
LAKH LA-nu. m'-KHAL LA-nu. ka-
PAYR LA-nu:

v'-al kha-ta-EEM she-A-nu kha-ya-
VEEM a-lay-HEM o-LAH:

v'-al kha-ta-EEM she-A-nu kha-ya-
VEEM a-lay-HEM kha-TAT:

v'-al kha-ta-EEM she-A-nu kha-ya-
VEEM a-lay-HEM kar-BAN o-LEH
v'-yo-RAYD:

v'-al kha-ta-EEM she-A-nu kha-ya-
VEEM a-lay-HEM a-SHAM va-DAI
v'-ta-LUY:

v'-al kha-ta-EEM she-A-nu kha-ya-

VEEM a-lay-HEM ma-KAT mar-
DUT:
v'-al kha-ta-EEM she-A-nu kha-ya-
VEEM a-lay-HEM mal-KUT ar-ba-
EEM:
v'-al kha-ta-EEM she-A-nu kha-ya-
VEEM a-lay-HEM mee-TAH bee-day
sha-MA-yim:
v'-al kha-ta-EEM she-A-nu kha-ya-
VEEM a-lay-HEM ka-RAYT va-a-
ree-REE:
v'-al kha-ta-EEM she-A-nu kha-ya-
VEEM a-lay-HEM ar-BA mee-TOT
bayt DEEN. s'-kee-LAH. s'-ray-FAH.
HE-reg. v'-KHE-nek.
al mitz-VAT a-SAY v'-al mitz-VAT lo ta-a-
SEH. BAYN she-YAYSH bah KUM a-
SAY. u-VAYN she-AYN bah KUM a-
SAY. et ha-g'-lu-YEEM LA-nu v'-et
she-ay-NAM g'-lu-YEEM LA-nu. et
ha-g'-lu-YEEM LA-nu k'-VAR a-mar-
NUM l'-fa-NE-kha. v'-ho-DEE-nu l'-
KHA a-lay-HEM. v'-et she-ay-NAM g'-
lu-YEEM LA-nu l'-fa-NE-kha HAYM
g'-lu-YEEM vi-du-EEM. ka-da-VAR
she-ne-e-MAR ha-nis-ta-ROT la-do-
NAI e-lo-HAY-nu. v'-ha-nig-LOT LA-
nu ul-va-NAY-nu ad o-LAM. la-a-SOT
et kol div-RAY ha-to-RAH ha-ZOT:
kee a-TAH sal-KHAN l'-yis-ra-AYL u-
ma-kho-LAN l'-shiv-TAY y'-shu-
RUN b'-khol DOR va-DOR u-mi-bal-

a-DE-kha AYN LA-nu ME-lekh mo-
KHAYL v'-so-LAY-akh e-LA A-tah:
e-lo-HAI. ad she-lo no-TZAR-tee AY-nee
kh'-DAI, v'-akh-SHAV she-no-TZAR-
tee k'-I-lu lo no-TZAR-tee. a-FAR a-
NEE b'-kha-YAI. kal va-KHO-mer b'-
mee-ta-TEE. ha-RAY a-NEE l'-fa-
NE-kha ki-kh'-LEE ma-LAY bu-
SHAH ukh-li-MAH. y'-hee ra-TZON
mil-fa-NE-kha a-do-NAI e-lo-HAI
vay-lo-HAY a-vo-TAI she-lo e-khe-
TA OD. u-mah she-kha-TA-tee l'-fa-
NE-kha ma-RAYK b'-ra-kha-ME-kha
ha-ra-BEEM. a-VAL lo al y'-DAY yi-
su-REEM va-kho-la-YEEM ra-EEM:

Our God and God of our fathers, let our
prayer come before you and do not
ignore our supplication. For we are
not so brazen-faced and stiff-necked
to say to you, O Lord, our God, and
God of our fathers, "We are
righteous and have not sinned." But,
indeed, we and our fathers have
sinned.

We have trespassed [against God and
man, and we are devastated by our
guilt]; We have betrayed [God and
man, we have been ungrateful for
the good done to us]; We have
stolen; We have slandered. We have
caused others to sin; We have
caused others to commit sins for

which they are called רְשָׁעִים,
wicked; We have sinned with
malicious intent; We have forcibly
taken others' possessions even
though we paid for them; We have
added falsehood upon falsehood;
We have joined with evil individuals
or groups; We have given harmful
advice; We have deceived; we have
mocked; We have rebelled against
God and His Torah; We have caused
God to be angry with us; We have
turned away from God's Torah; We
have sinned deliberately; We have
been negligent in our performance
of the commandments; We have
caused our friends grief; We have
been stiff-necked, refusing to admit
that our suffering is caused by our
own sins. We have committed sins
for which we are called רָשָׁע,
[raising a hand to hit someone]. We
have committed sins which are the
result of moral corruption; We have
committed sins which the Torah
refers to as abominations; We have
gone astray; We have led others
astray.

We have turned away from Your
commandments and from Your
good laws, and we have gained
nothing from it. And You are the
Righteous One in all [punishment]

that has come upon us; for You have
acted truthfully and we have acted
wickedly.

What shall we say before You, Who
dwells on high; and what shall we
relate to You Who dwells in the
heavens? For everything, both
hidden and revealed, You know. You
know the mysteries of the universe,
and the hidden secrets of every
individual. You search all our
innermost thoughts, and probe our
mind and heart. There is nothing
hidden from You, and there is
nothing concealed from Your sight.
And so may it be Your will O Lord our
God and God of our fathers, that You
pardon us for all our careless sins,
and that You forgive us for all our
deliberate sins, and that You grant us
atonement for all our rebellious sins:

For the sin we committed before You
under compulsion and willingly.

And for the sin we committed before
You by callously hardening the
heart.

For the sin we committed before You
inadvertently.

And for the sin we committed before
You with an utterance of the lips.

For the sin we committed before You
openly and secretly.

And for the sin we committed before
You in sexual immorality.
For the sin we committed before You
through [misuse of our power of]
speech.
And for the sin we committed before
You with knowledge and with
deceit.
For the sin we committed before You by
improper thoughts.
And for the sin we committed before
You by cheating a fellow-man.
For the sin we committed before You
with [mere] verbal confession.
And for the sin we committed before
You by joining in a lewd gathering.
For the sin we committed before You
intentionally and unintentionally.
And for the sin we committed before
You by insufficient respect for
parents and teachers.
For the sin we committed before You by
using coercion [to harm others].
And for the sin we committed before
You by desecrating the Divine
Name.
For the sin we committed before You
with foolish talk.
And for the sin we committed before
You with impurity of the lips.
For the sin we committed before You
with the Evil Inclination.

And for the sin we committed before
You knowingly and unknowingly.
And for all of these, God of pardon,
pardon us, forgive us, grant us
atonement.
For the sin we committed before You by
forcing someone to give or take
bribes.
And for the sin we committed before
You by false denial and false
promise.
For the sin we committed before You by
evil talk [slander].
And for the sin we committed before
You by scoffing.
For the sin we committed before You in
business dealings.
And for the sin we committed before
You in eating and drinking.
For the sin we committed before You by
[taking or giving] interest and by
usury.
And for the sin we committed before
You by haughtily stretching forth
the neck.
For the sin we committed before You
with gazing of the eyes.
And for the sin we committed before
You by the prattle of our lips.
For the sin we committed before You
with haughty eyes.
And for the sin we committed before
You with impudence.

And for all of these, God of pardon,
pardon us, forgive us, grant us
atonement.
For the sin we committed before You by
throwing off the yoke [of heaven].
And for the sin we committed before
You in passing judgment.
For the sin we committed before You by
entrapping a fellowman.
And for the sin we committed before
You by a begrudging eye.
For the sin we committed before You by
lightmindedness.
And for the sin we committed before
You by being stiff-necked
[stubborn].
For the sin we committed before You by
running to do evil.
And for the sin we committed before
You by talebearing.
For the sin we committed before You by
swearing in vain.
And for the sin we committed before
You by unwarranted hatred.
For the sin we committed before You by
breach of trust.
And for the sin we committed before
You by a confused heart.
And for all of these, God of pardon,
pardon us, forgive us, grant us
atonement.
And for sins for which we are obligated
to bring a burnt-offering.

And for sins for which we are obligated
to bring a sin-offering.

And for sins for which we are obligated
to bring a "fluctuating" offering.

And for sins for which we are obligated
to bring a guilt-offering for certain
or for doubtful trespasses.

And for sins for which we incur the
penalty of lashing for violations of
Rabbinic law.

And for sins for which we incur the
penalty of forty lashes.

And for sins for which we incur the
penalty of death at the hand of
Heaven.

And for sins for which we incur the
penalty of excision and
childlessness.

And for sins for which we are liable to
any of the four death penalties
inflicted by the [Rabbinic] Court
[which are]: stoning, burning,
beheading or strangulation.

For [transgressing] positive
commandments, and for
[transgressing] prohibitive
commandments, whether the
prohibition can be corrected by a
specifically prescribed act, or
whether it cannot be corrected by a
specifically prescribed act, for those
of which we are aware and for those
of which we are not aware. For

those of which we are aware, we
have already declared before You
and confessed them unto You; and
those of which we are not aware,
before You they are revealed and
known, as it is said, "The hidden
things belong to the Lord, our God,
but the revealed things are for us
and for our children forever, that we
might fulfill all the words of this
Torah."

For You are the Pardoner of Israel, and
the Forgiver of the tribes of Jeshurun
in every generation, and beside You,
we have no King Who forgives and
pardons—only You!

God, before I was formed, I was
unworthy [to be created]. And now
that I have been formed, it is as if I
had not been formed. I am like dust
while I live, how much more so
when I am dead. Here I am before
You like a vessel filled with shame.

May it be Your will, O Lord, my God, and
the God of my fathers, that I shall
sin no more, and the sins I have
committed before You, cleanse them
in Your abundant mercies; but not
through suffering and severe illness.

Following the recitation of the *Amidah* prayer and the verbal
confession, penitential prayers are recited. The congregation
recites these ancient liturgical poems with particular intensity,

knowing that the window for repentance is no longer measured in weeks or days, but in hours.

These prayers are followed by a communal recitation of the confession prayers, sung in a surprisingly upbeat melody for such a solemn day. This joyful tone reflects several profound theological insights: first, confession itself is a commandment, and all of God's commandments should be performed with happiness. Second, when we confess communally, we do so with confidence that our sins will be forgiven. Unlike individual confession, which may be done from a place of despair, communal confession expresses our trust in divine mercy since, according to Jewish tradition, God never rejects the prayers of a congregation.

The evening service concludes with the beloved prayer *Avinu Malkeinu* ("Our Father, Our King"), which takes on special urgency as we begin our earnest plea for divine mercy, followed by the *Aleinu* prayer that ends every prayer service. With these prayers complete, the framework for the day's intensive spiritual work has been established.

The Morning Service

As dawn breaks on *Yom Kippur*, the synagogue fills once again for the morning prayer service. Like the evening before, the *Shema* is recited with "Blessed be the name of His glorious kingdom forever and ever" proclaimed aloud, as we maintain our angelic status throughout the day. The *Amidah* maintains its additions for the Ten Days of Repentance as well as the extensive confessions, as we systematically acknowledge our failings and plead for divine mercy.

The morning service is followed by the Torah reading, which transports us back over two millennia to the ancient Temple in

Jerusalem. The Torah portion comes from Leviticus 16:1-34, which details the elaborate Temple service performed by the High Priest on *Yom Kippur*. This reading describes the only day of the year when the High Priest could enter the Holy of Holies, the innermost sanctuary where God's presence dwelt on earth. We hear about the intricate rituals: the special white linen garments, the offering of incense, the sprinkling of blood on the ark of the covenant, and the dramatic selection of two goats—one for sacrifice and one to be sent into the wilderness as the scapegoat, symbolically carrying away the sins of the entire nation.

This reading recalls the way that atonement was ideally achieved when the Temple stood, through the High Priest's service coupled with sincere repentance. Now that we no longer have a Temple, we rely entirely on our repentance and prayers to achieve forgiveness.

There is an additional reading from Numbers 29:7-11, which describes the other sacrificial offerings for *Yom Kippur*.

The *Haftarah*, the prophetic reading that follows the Torah reading, provides a stunning counterpoint to the Temple rituals. Taken from Isaiah 57:14-58:14, the prophet delivers a searing critique that challenges the very foundations of religious observance. In this section, God lambasts His people for their hypocrisy when fasting for Him, declaring that such fasting is worthless unless their society actively promotes the welfare of its most vulnerable. Isaiah thunders: "Is this the fast I desire? A day for people to starve their bodies?... No! This is the fast I want: unlock the chains of wickedness, untie the knots of servitude. Let the oppressed go free... Share your bread with the hungry, and welcome the homeless into your home."

It is noteworthy that the ancient rabbis chose this particular section of Isaiah for *Yom Kippur* morning. On the most important fast day of the Jewish year, the *haftarah* carries the message that fasting alone is not enough. God desires fasting only if there is a moral and ethical foundation to the ritual behavior. Isaiah reminds us that our spiritual purification on *Yom Kippur* must translate into concrete acts of justice and compassion in the world.

The juxtaposition is deliberate and profound: we read about the ancient Temple's elaborate sacrificial system, then immediately hear Isaiah's call for authentic righteousness. Together, these readings suggest that whether through ancient ritual or modern observance, true atonement requires both sincere repentance before God and genuine commitment to ethical behavior toward our fellow human beings.

The Additional Service: Reliving the Temple's Sacred Drama

Musaf, the additional prayer service unique to holidays, forms the emotional and liturgical centerpiece of *Yom Kippur*. The highlight of this prayer is the *avodah* recitation, where the congregation doesn't simply remember the Temple service—they relive it. This service invites us to transcend the boundaries of time and space, experiencing the most sacred moments in Jewish history as if we were present in the ancient Temple courtyard.

The recitation of the *avodah* begins with a selective review of biblical history, beginning with creation, reminding us that the Temple service was of cosmic importance. It then details the rituals of the Temple service in poetic form. The poem describes how, seven days before *Yom Kippur*, the High Priest was sequestered in a special chamber within the Temple complex, studying every detail of the sacred service with the elders. On the holiest day of the year, he alone could enter the Holy of Holies, the innermost sanctuary where God's presence dwelt on earth, and he must be well-versed in all of the details of the ritual.

It then takes us through each stage of this awesome responsibility: the High Priest's multiple immersions and purifications, his donning of simple white linen garments, his confession of sins—first for himself and his family, then for the priesthood, and finally for all Israel. Every time he uttered the holy name of God, the Tetragrammaton, which was spoken only on *Yom Kippur*, the people prostrated themselves and responded: "Blessed be His Name whose glorious kingdom is forever and ever".

When the prayer recalls the High Priest speaking God's most sacred name, the entire congregation falls prostrate, something extremely rare in Jewish worship.

The service also recounts the dramatic selection of the two goats by lottery, and the sending of the scapegoat into the wilderness, symbolically carrying away the sins of the nation. We read about the High Priest's careful entry into the Holy of Holies with clouds of incense, and his fervent prayer for the coming year's prosperity and peace. The *avodah* concludes with the magnificent poem called *Mareh Kohen*, often sung in a jubilant tone, describing the radiant splendor of the High Priest as he emerged successfully from the Holy of Holies, his face glowing with divine light.

During the times when the Temple in Jerusalem stood, this service of the High Priest in the Temple was the main focus of the day of *Yom Kippur*. Today, though the Temple lies in ruins, through this liturgical recreation we participate in the cosmic drama of atonement that once unfolded in Jerusalem. The service closes with ardent prayers for the rebuilding of the Temple and the restoration of its sacred service, expressing our deepest longing for the complete repair of the world and our relationship with God.

Other notable additions to the *Yom Kippur Musaf* service include the *Unetanneh Tokef* prayer (see chapter on *Rosh Hashanah*) and the Ten Martyrs poems. *Unetanneh Tokef* dramatically depicts the divine judgment occurring on this day: "On *Rosh Hashanah* it is written, and on *Yom Kippur* it is sealed, who will live and who will die...", while the Ten Martyrs poem recalls the courage of great Jewish rabbis who chose to die rather than abandon their faith during Roman persecution. Reading the Ten Martyrs poem immediately after the section of the *avodah* drives home the message that their deaths are seen as a form of sacrifice that atones for the Jewish people, similar to the *Yom Kippur* service in the Temple.[16]

The Afternoon Service: Confronting Our Most Human Struggles

As the long day progresses and our physical strength wanes, we begin the afternoon service. The *Amidah* prayer is preceded by another Torah reading and a reading from the Prophets, which work together to remind us that authentic repentance requires confronting our deepest human impulses and embracing the radical possibility of change.

The Torah Reading: Forbidden Relationships

The Torah reading is taken from Leviticus 18:1-30, and deals with forbidden sexual relationships, a topic that may seem

---

16. Babylonian Talmud, Moed Katan 28a

jarring on this holiest day. This tradition dates back at least to the second century, as evidenced by its mention in the Talmud. Several explanations have been offered for this seemingly incongruous choice.

Since everyone is present in the synagogue on *Yom Kippur*, some suggest that this provides an opportunity to address sins that are often private and secret. Others argue that it reminds us that despite our current spiritual elevation, we can fall to the worst transgressions in an instant. Still others suggest that on *Yom Kippur*, when our base desires are subdued, we are open and receptive to hearing about this important issue in an objective manner.[17]

Perhaps the deeper message is that authentic repentance requires acknowledging the full range of human temptation. As we stand before God seeking forgiveness, we cannot pretend that some aspects of human nature are beyond the need for moral reflection and divine guidance.

The Book of Jonah

Following this challenging Torah reading comes the complete Book of Jonah, one of the most beloved and perplexing stories in the Bible. The book explores themes of obedience, God's mercy extending to all nations, and the nature of divine compassion versus human desire for judgment.

God tells the prophet Jonah to go to Nineveh, the capital of Assyria, and warn the people that their city will be destroyed because of their wickedness. Instead of obeying, Jonah boards a ship heading in the opposite direction to Tarshish.

---

17. Rabbi Chaim Jachter, "A Frank Discussion of Yom Kippur's Torah Reading at Minchah," *Kol Torah* 32 (September 30, 2022).

During the voyage, God sends a violent storm. The sailors eventually realize Jonah is the cause and, at his own suggestion, throw him overboard. God provides a great fish that swallows Jonah, and he remains inside for three days and three nights. From inside the fish, Jonah prays a prayer of repentance, and the fish spits him onto dry land.

Jonah then goes to Nineveh and delivers God's message. Surprisingly, the entire city, from the king down to the common people, repents and turns from their evil ways. God sees their repentance and decides not to destroy the city.

This makes Jonah angry because he wanted to see Nineveh punished. He sits outside the city, sulking. God causes a plant to grow and provide shade for Jonah, then sends a worm to destroy it. When Jonah complains about losing the plant, God uses this as a teaching moment about compassion: if Jonah cares about a plant, shouldn't God care about the 120,000 people of Nineveh?

The story offers multiple lessons perfectly suited to *Yom Kippur*. Jewish sages have given a number of different reasons for reading Jonah on this day. First, it reminds us of God's infinite mercy; if God could forgive the wicked city of Nineveh, surely God can forgive us. Second, it demonstrates the power of sincere repentance to change divine decrees. Third, it shows that no one can escape God's reach or providence, and finally, it teaches that God's compassion extends to everyone.

The medieval commentator Rashi explains that Jonah fled his mission out of concern: if the non-Jewish Ninevites repented immediately while Israel continued to ignore prophetic calls, it would reflect poorly on God's chosen people. However, the story's deeper lesson is that divine mercy is limitless; God's compassion for others never diminishes the amount of forgiveness available to us.

By the time we reach the afternoon service, "we are all Jonah," tired, hungry, perhaps doubting whether our prayers matter, tempted to flee from the hard work of genuine change. We read Jonah to be reminded that this tumultuous, contradictory, difficult space is, in fact, the space of prayer and possibility.

The afternoon readings together present a complete picture of the human condition: our capacity for moral failure and our infinite potential for redemption. They remind us that *Yom Kippur* is not about achieving perfection, but about honest acknowledgment of our full humanity and trust in God's boundless capacity for forgiveness when we genuinely seek to change.

Neilah: The Final Hour

As the sun begins its descent toward the horizon and shadows lengthen across the synagogue floor, *Yom Kippur* enters its most dramatic and spiritually charged moment. The congregation, having fasted for nearly twenty-four hours, gathers for *Neilah*, short for *Ne'ilat She'arim*, which means the closing of the gates, the final prayer service before the gates of heaven close.

This is our last chance. For the entire day, we have stood before the divine court pleading our case, confessing our failures, and seeking forgiveness. Now, as God prepares to ascend from the seat of judgment and the heavenly gates begin to swing closed, we make our final appeal.

The Open Ark: Gates Wide Open

Throughout most of *Neilah*, the Holy Ark remains open. This powerful visual symbol reminds us that despite the approaching deadline, the Gates of Heaven remain wide open to our prayers and entreaties. The opened ark creates an atmosphere of accessibility; we can still reach through, our prayers can still ascend, our *teshuvah* can still be accepted.

The congregation stands for most of the service, mirroring the intensity of these final moments. Exhausted from fasting but spiritually energized by the approaching climax, worshippers pour their hearts out in these last precious minutes of direct access to divine mercy.

The Language of Finality

The liturgy of *Neilah* contains a crucial shift that reflects the urgency of the moment. Throughout the Ten Days of Repentance, our prayers have asked God to "inscribe us in the Book of Life," using the Hebrew word *kotveinu*, suggesting that our fate is still being written. But during *Neilah*, we change our plea to "seal us in the Book of Life," *chotmeinu*, acknowledging that the time for inscription has passed, and we now pray that God will seal our positive judgment with the divine stamp of approval.

This linguistic transformation captures the essence of *Neilah*: we are no longer asking for our names to be written; we are begging for the book to be closed with us safely inside.

Shortened Confessions

Even the confessional prayers that have punctuated every service throughout the day are shortened during *Neilah*. The time for lengthy self-examination has passed. As the day draws to a close and time is running out, we keep our confession short and focused.

The Climactic Verses

As *Neilah* reaches its crescendo and the *Avinu Malkeinu* prayer is recited for the final time, the congregation recites powerful affirmations that have echoed through the centuries. "Hear O Israel, the Lord our God, the Lord is One" is proclaimed once, declaring our faith in the One and Only God. This is followed by "Blessed be the name of His glorious kingdom forever and ever" recited three times, and finally "The Lord He is God" seven times. These declarations create a spiritual climax that lifts the entire congregation. As the gates of heaven close, we make sure our fundamental beliefs ring out clearly, that our core faith is proclaimed unmistakably before God and the assembled community.

Victory Celebration: The Final *Shofar*

Then comes a single, piercing blast of the *shofar* that marks the end of *Yom Kippur*. This is no ordinary shofar call; it carries multiple layers of meaning that have sustained the Jewish people through centuries of challenge.

Some traditions see this blast as a victory celebration. By the time *Yom Kippur* draws to a close, we trust that we have been granted a sweet year ahead. Like soldiers returning triumphant from battle, we blow the *shofar* to celebrate our victory over the prosecuting angel and the spiritual forces that would condemn us. We have faced judgment and emerged forgiven.

Others connect this moment to the giving of the Torah at Mount Sinai, when God's divine presence rested upon the mountain and a *shofar* blast announced the ascent of the *Shechinah* (divine presence). As the Psalmist writes, "God ascends with a blast; the Lord, with the sound of a shofar" (Psalms 47:6). Throughout *Yom Kippur*, we have experienced unprecedented closeness with God, and now the *shofar* blast symbolizes the ascent of the divine presence that has rested upon us throughout this holy day.

During the era of British control in Mandatory Palestine, a powerful tradition emerged at the Western Wall in Jerusalem. The British authorities had forbidden the sounding of the *shofar* at this sacred site, fearing it would stoke Jewish nationalism. But each year on *Yom Kippur*, brave young Jews would hide a *shofar* beneath their garments and slip it past the watchful eyes of British soldiers. At the close of the service, as the crowd held its breath, a single blast would ring out across the stones of the ancient Wall. Every year, those who sounded the shofar were arrested. Yet the act was repeated faithfully, year after year. These courageous Jews understood the risk, but for them, the *shofar's* call was a matter of spirit and identity. It was a declaration that no foreign power could silence the eternal bond between God and His people.

From Transcendence to Hope

The service concludes with the stirring cry of "Next year in rebuilt Jerusalem!"—*L'shanah haba'ah b'Yerushalayim hab'nuyah!* This ancient hope, traditionally associated with Passover, takes on special meaning at the end of *Yom Kippur*. Having experienced spiritual purification and divine forgiveness, we look forward not just to the coming year, but to the ultimate redemption when the Temple will be rebuilt and the *avodah* can once again be performed properly. We pray that our collective *teshuvah* and the forgiveness we have received will hasten the day when all humanity recognizes God's sovereignty and the ultimate redemption is fulfilled.

Neilah transforms exhaustion into exaltation, desperation into hope, and the fear of judgment into the joy of forgiveness. As the gates close and the holy day ends, we step back into ordinary time, but we do so as people who have been transformed, purified, and renewed for the year ahead.

The Return to Life

As the final shofar blast fades and the congregation erupts in joyful cries of "*Shanah tovah!*" - "A good year!" - the sacred day officially ends, but the transition back to ordinary time follows a careful ritual sequence.

The *Neilah* service is immediately followed by the regular weekday evening service. In many communities, it is then customary to perform the monthly *kiddush levanah*, "sanctification of the moon," under the open sky.

Back at home, the *Havdalah* ceremony marks our formal departure from the holy day. Unlike the regular *Havdalah* for *Shabbat*, the *Yom Kippur* version has unique features. The blessing over spices is omitted (unless *Yom Kippur* falls on Saturday), but the blessing over fire is included, because for the past day we were forbidden to use fire. The blessing is recited specifically over a flame that has been burning since before *Yom Kippur* began - a fire that "rested" through the holy day and that we can now once again use.

Only after *Havdalah* do we break our fast. The night following *Yom Kippur* is pervaded by festive joy. Confident that God has forgiven our sins, we celebrate our spiritual renewal as we enjoy a light meal.

Without delay, many begin looking toward the next holiday. It's customary to start building the *sukkah* (temporary dwelling) immediately, or at least to discuss plans for the *Sukkot* holiday, which begins just four days later. This demonstrates that we go from one sacred act directly to another, maintaining our spiritual momentum.

As we break our fast and return to ordinary time, we do so as people who have been transformed, purified, and renewed for the year ahead.

COLLECTED INSIGHTS

Living the Change

Shira Schechter

Yom Kippur, the Day of Atonement, is one of the most important days in the Jewish calendar. It's a time when Jews around the world seek forgiveness, reflect on their actions, and aim for personal growth. On this holiest of days, we feel a deep connection to something greater than ourselves, whether through fasting, prayer, or a heightened sense of spirituality. But there's something curious about the readings from the Torah on *Yom Kippur* that invites deeper reflection.

On the morning of *Yom Kippur*, the Torah reading, taken from Leviticus 16, focuses on the sacred service of the High Priest in the ancient Temple in Jerusalem. This was the only day of the year when he could enter the Holy of Holies, the innermost and most sacred part of the Temple. The reading highlights the awe and reverence of this unique moment, reminding us of the holiness of the day and its potential for deep spiritual connection and purification, as it says:

For on this day atonement shall be made for you to purify you of all your sins; you shall be pure before the Lord (Leviticus 16:30).

However, in the afternoon, the Torah reading takes a sharp turn. It suddenly shifts to Leviticus 18, a section dealing with forbidden relationships—laws that describe improper and even immoral behaviors. For many, this feels like a strange and uncomfortable transition. After spending the day seeking forgiveness and trying to rise above our flaws, why would we focus on something so negative and base? Why would we bring up such distasteful topics at the very moment when we're striving to be our best selves? Shouldn't we be focusing only on holiness and purity, especially as the day draws to a close?

Yet, there's an important lesson hidden in this juxtaposition. The afternoon reading reminds us that *Yom Kippur* is not just a day of spiritual inspiration and closeness to God. It's a day to prepare ourselves for the real world, the world we step back into once *Yom Kippur* is over, where temptations and challenges await. This section of the Torah is meant to help us guard against falling into the very mistakes that can undo our spiritual progress. Even though on *Yom Kippur* we may feel elevated and pure, the Torah reading gives us a gentle but firm reminder that when it's over, life will test us. We need to be ready for those tests.

Yom Kippur is a model day, a glimpse of what we can achieve when we're at our best. The holiness and purity we experience on this day should be a guide for how we live in the weeks and months that follow. That's why, as the day winds down and we feel most connected to our spiritual selves, the Torah reminds us of our human frailties. It's a reality check. Yes, we've spent the day reaching for something higher, but we still need to be prepared for the challenges we'll face when the day is over.

Once *Yom Kippur* is behind us, the real challenge begins: can we take the lessons of the day—its messages of forgiveness, self-reflection, and spiritual growth—and carry them with us into the days and weeks ahead? Can we face life's inevitable tests with the awareness and strength we gained during *Yom Kippur*?

As we step back into "real life", the challenge is to live up to the potential we glimpsed on *Yom Kippur*. Let's make sure that the commitments we made, the forgiveness we sought, and the spiritual heights we reached stay with us—not just for one day, but for the entire year. As *Yom Kippur* draws to a close, the real journey is only just beginning.

What a Goat in the Desert Taught Me About Forgiveness

Sara Lamm

Most people assume my favorite Jewish holiday must be something festive—maybe the lights of Hanukkah, the joy of Purim, or the family meals of Shabbat. So I always get raised eyebrows when I say it's *Yom Kippur*. Yes, *Yom Kippur*. The one with the fasting. The one where you can't wear leather shoes. The one where you sit in synagogue all day reflecting on everything you've done wrong.

And I love it.

I don't just tolerate it. I wait for it. I count down to it. Because while every other day of the year feels like running—emails, laundry, dishes, kids' snacks—*Yom Kippur* feels like standing still in the best possible way. For 25 hours, I don't have to be anywhere but here. I don't have to answer to anyone but God. It's the one day I am nothing but a soul. A soul with a list of things to clean up, sure—but a soul nonetheless.

At the center of the *Yom Kippur* service in the Torah is one of the most dramatic scenes in all of Leviticus: two goats, one fate. Brought before the High Priest, the goats are nearly identical. One is chosen "for the Lord" and offered as a sin offering. The other is sent into the wilderness, "for Azazel," bearing the confessed sins of the nation.

The Torah describes it like this:

"Aharon shall lay both his hands upon the head of the live goat and confess over it all the iniquities and transgressions of the Israelites, whatever their sins, putting them on the head of the goat; and it shall be sent off to the wilderness through a designated man. Thus the goat shall carry on it all their iniquities to an inaccessible region; and the goat shall be set free in the wilderness." Leviticus 16:21-22

It's strange, isn't it? The animal that carries the weight of our failures isn't sacrificed—it's sent away. The people don't watch it die. They watch it disappear.

That, according to Rabbi Jonathan Sacks and Maimonides before him, is the whole point. The goat ceremony isn't about punishment. It's about purification. Not just kapparah, atonement, but also taharah, cleansing. As the Torah says, "For on this day atonement shall be made for you to cleanse you of all your sins; you shall be clean before Hashem" Leviticus 16:30

Guilt is about what we did. Shame is about who we think we are because of it. Guilt says, "I made a mistake." Shame says, "I am a mistake." And if we're honest, most of us carry both.

Yom Kippur is the one day a year where we lay it all out—everything we've done, everything we regret, everything we were too afraid to name—and we watch it walk away. Not metaphorically. Not hypothetically. But with a real, physical ritual that reminds us: This is not who you are anymore.

Judaism has always insisted on that distinction. We are not the sum total of our missteps. We can return. We can change. We can walk back into the camp cleansed. Not only forgiven by God, but restored in our own eyes.

That's why I love *Yom Kippur*. Because it's not about guilt-tripping. It's not about feeling bad just for the sake of it. It's about clearing space. It's about naming the things that hold us back and then letting them go, one by one, until all that's left is the person God always knew we could be.

And maybe that's why—true story—one of my children was born on *Yom Kippur*. On a day of beginnings, of forgiveness, of wiping the slate clean, I was given new life in the most literal way. It felt like a divine wink.

So yes, there's no food. There's no singing or dancing (well, not until the final *Neilah* service). But there is something better: a whole nation, standing together, honest and unafraid, asking God to see us not at our worst—but as we are at our most sincere.

And year after year, He does.

The Day Hank Greenberg Played for God

Rabbi Elie Mischel

Hank Greenberg was the first Jewish superstar in American baseball and in American sports in general. Now, as you might imagine, when he first came up to the Big Leagues to play for the Detroit Tigers in the early 1930s, antisemitism was a fact of life. But in 1934, Hammering Hank broke out as a superstar, and the anti-Semite Tigers fans had to come to terms with their Jewish hero.

A journalist of the day wrote a poem describing the change:

The Irish didn't like it when they heard of Greenberg's fame

For they thought a good first baseman should possess an Irish name;

And the Murphys and Mulrooneys said they never dreamed they'd see

A Jewish boy from Bronxville out where Casey used to be.

In the early days of April not a Dugan tipped his hat

Or prayed to see a "double" when Hank Greenberg came to bat.

In July the Irish wondered where he'd ever learned to play.

"He makes me think of Casey!" Old Man Murphy dared to say;

And with fifty-seven doubles and a score of homers made

The respect they had for Greenberg was being openly displayed.

That September, late in the season, the Tigers were fighting to win the pennant. And though he initially said he wouldn't play on *Rosh Hashana* (Jewish New Year), Greenberg caved to pressure, and agreed to play on the Jewish New Year:

But upon the Jewish New Year

When Hank Greenberg came to bat

And made two home runs off Pitcher Rhodes—

They cheered like mad for that!

Nine days later, Greenberg once again had a decision to make. Would he play on *Yom Kippur* (Day of Atonement) in a must-win game against the hated Yankees? Or would he go to the Shaarei Tzedek synagogue in Detroit and pray with his fellow Jews?

Came Yom Kippur – holy day worldwide over to the Jew –

And Hank Greenberg to his teaching and the old tradition true

Spent the day among his people and he didn't come to play.

Said Murphy to Mulrooney, "We shall lose the game today!

We shall miss him on the infield, and shall miss him at the bat,

But he's true to his religion—and I honor him for that!"

The awe and power of *Yom Kippur* (Day of Atonement), even for a "secular" Jew like Hank Greenberg, is palpable. *Yom Kippur* is the holiest day of the year, it can't be missed.

But what's fascinating is that *Yom Kippur* didn't always have the same appeal. In fact, we find no mention at all of *Yom Kippur* in the books of the Prophets, the books describing the period of the First Temple.

The historians tell us that in those days, *Yom Kippur* was not like the other holidays when Jews would come to Jerusalem with their sacrifices. Instead, the High Priest would perform the service by himself in the Temple while everybody else stayed home and observed a fast day, the same way Jews observe minor fast days today. There weren't any special prayers, and people didn't crowd into the Temple to watch.

But everything changed in the Second Temple era. All of a sudden, *Yom Kippur* became "popular" and it has remained so to this day. In the Second Temple era, thousands upon thousands of Jews would come to the Temple on *Yom Kippur* just to catch a glimpse of the face of the High Priest on this awesome day. Throngs of Jews would pray together for the success of the High Priest in his mission; getting God to forgive His people. And they would wait with bated breath, straining to see if the High Priest would emerge safely from the Holy of Holies, a sign that forgiveness had indeed been granted.

The question is, what changed? Why were the Jewish people drawn to *Yom Kippur* all of a sudden? Why did the Day of Atonement begin to capture the hearts of the Jewish people in a way that continues to move them to this day?

Rabbi Meir Simcha of Dvinsk explains that in terms of years, the distance between the two Temples was not so great. Construction on the Second Temple began only seventy years after the destruction of the First Temple, and there were Jews who saw the First Temple as children and lived long enough to see the Second Temple as old men and women. But in the most important ways, everything had changed. With the destruction of the First Temple, the era of prophecy, God's direct communication to the Jewish people, came to an end. As did the open miracles that were commonplace in the First Temple.

In the Second Temple era, God's presence in this world was no longer obvious or tangible, and the people felt a profound spiritual emptiness. They were, in the words of Rabbi Meir Simcha of Dvinsk, "thirsty for the word of God" that they could no longer hear.

But one day a year, when the High Priest would enter the Holy of Holies on *Yom Kippur*, there was a moment, a brief opportunity, when God would reveal Himself to His people. For just an instant they again felt that closeness with their Father in Heaven that they had so foolishly taken for granted in earlier generations.

And so, explains Rabbi Meir Simcha, throughout the Second Temple era, thousands of Jews would come to Jerusalem to be with the High Priests on *Yom Kippur* to momentarily feel the presence of God.

Even after the Second Temple was destroyed and the High Priest could no longer perform the *Yom Kippur* service, the magnetic hold of *Yom Kippur* on the hearts of the Jewish people has not diminished. In fact, as the generations decline and we feel more broken and distant from God, our need for *Yom Kippur* only grows.

As our culture pulls farther and farther away from holiness and truth, our yearning for God's closeness and our need for His presence in our lives only intensifies. The superficiality of our society and the endless distractions from what is really important, all divert us from the things that really matter in life and the eternal truths that determine our destiny. Now more than ever we need *Yom Kippur*.

And that is why even the most secular Jews find meaning in *Yom Kippur*. It is our chance to feel the presence of God, to briefly connect with our Creator and to focus on the things which have real meaning in our lives. It reminds us that sometimes we need to rise above our usual selves and think about what is really important, to set spiritual goals and to make space for our Father in Heaven.

A Communal Apology

Sara Lamm

Yom Kippur, the Day of Atonement, is a time when the world quiets down, and a profound sense of calm envelops us. The air feels different, infused with a sacred stillness that invites deep reflection and connection. The liturgy, rich and beautiful, resonates in a way that stirs the soul, drawing us into a collective journey of repentance and renewal.

As we gather in our communities, there is a palpable sense of shared purpose; we come together to acknowledge our shortcomings, to seek forgiveness, and to cleanse our hearts.

In Jewish tradition, this process of teshuva, repentance, is more than just saying "sorry"; it is about taking responsibility for our actions and committing to change.

Historically, *Yom Kippur* began as a day of atonement when the High Priest would enter the Holy of Holies to seek forgiveness for the people of Israel. The ritual, described in the Bible, was precise and detailed. The High Priest atoned first for his own sins, then for those of his family, and finally for all of Israel. It was a solemn moment where even the holiest among the people stood before God in humility, admitting human fallibility. The Torah emphasizes this transformative day:

"For on this day atonement shall be made for you to cleanse you of all your sins; you shall be clean before Hashem." Leviticus 16:30

After the destruction of the Temple, *Yom Kippur* evolved from a centralized, priestly ritual to a personal day of introspection for all. Instead of a High Priest acting on behalf of the nation, each person is now responsible for their own confession and repentance. We stand together in synagogue, reciting prayers that list our wrongdoings. The well-known confession prayers are an alphabetized list of the ways we have missed the mark, allowing us to reflect on the past year and the ways we can do better.

This communal act of confession is one of the most powerful elements of *Yom Kippur*. When everyone admits their failings together, it removes the stigma of personal guilt and shame. The High Priest's admission of his own sins set a precedent for this, reminding us that even the most elevated leaders are not perfect. This creates an environment where we can all feel comfortable acknowledging our mistakes, knowing that no one is immune to error.

Jewish tradition understands that human beings are not expected to be flawless. Instead, we are encouraged to learn from our missteps. The Talmud teaches that true repentance can transform our past mistakes into merits. In this way, the act of admitting wrongdoing is not simply about punishment or guilt; it is about growth and renewal.

What makes *Yom Kippur* so transformative is not the grand gestures of apology, but the sincerity behind them. The prayers we say and the fasting we undertake are meant to create a sense of spiritual awakening, prompting us to genuinely reflect on how we can improve in the coming year. It is a day to be honest with ourselves about where we fell short and how we can do better.

This process of self-examination is not limited to the day of *Yom Kippur* itself. Throughout the year, Jewish tradition offers multiple opportunities to engage in repentance through daily prayers and specific moments of reflection, such as *tachanun*, the Penitential Prayer, and selichot, communal prayers for divine forgiveness said during the High Holiday season and on Jewish fast days. *Yom Kippur*, however, serves as the pinnacle of this spiritual work, giving us a dedicated time to focus solely on our relationship with God, our fellow human beings, and ourselves.

Admitting our mistakes is never easy, but Judaism provides a framework that makes it possible. First, it teaches us that we are always capable of change, no matter how many times we have faltered. Second, it assures us that God is willing to forgive when we genuinely seek to correct our ways. Finally, the collective nature of *Yom Kippur* reminds us that we are not alone in this journey; we are part of a community where everyone is striving to improve.

At its core, *Yom Kippur* is about recognizing our humanity, with all its imperfections, and understanding that the path to spiritual growth begins with honesty. It is a day that calls us to confront our shortcomings, seek forgiveness, and set the intention to become better versions of ourselves in the year ahead.

God is in Our Camp

Rabbi Elie Mischel

Michael Levy was born blind. At his mother's funeral, Michael told the following story:

Since he was not able to see, Michael's mother would walk him to school every morning, and, at the end of the day, she would wait for him right outside the school building to walk him home. As he grew older, this became increasingly humiliating for him; while the other boys were all independent, he had to walk to school with his mommy.

For a long time, he begged and pleaded with his mother to let him walk to school on his own. He had it all worked out; the number of steps to the end of the block, where to hold onto the fence, and so on. They practiced together for weeks until his mother finally said: "Michael, today is the big day, you're on your own!" It was the proudest day of his life. You can't imagine what it felt like to go to school like everyone else.

Michael set off for school and everything went smoothly. As he approached the school building he was exploding in joy. He could hear the tumult of the school as he neared the gate; he had made it!

There was a very nice man who worked on the school grounds, and, as Michael walked to the gate, he said: "Well look at you, Michael Levy!" Michael was beaming with pride, it didn't get better than this!

Until the nice worker said: "and Mrs. Levy, it's so good to see you!" As the words sunk in Michael realized that he had not walked to school alone after all; his mother had been silently following him the whole time. Upset, he turned to cry out to his mother in frustration but all he heard was the sound of her bicycle as she retreated home.

This true story is also a parable of our lives.

God wants us to struggle, accomplish, grow, and learn our own way through the challenges of life. It's not meant to be easy. And so we make our way through life, counting the steps, holding onto the fences and blindly trying our best to get to where we have to go.

But we need to know that, wherever we go in this life, we are never walking alone—someone is silently following us. At every up and down, every time we do a good deed, every time we go to work, every time we fall, and every time we lie down in our beds at night—if someone were to greet each of us at any and every one of these moments—they would say: "Well, look at you, so-and-so, and God, Master of the Universe—it's so good to see You too!"

During the holy days leading up to *Yom Kippur* (Day of Atonement), it's healthy and natural to feel trepidation. We are going to be standing in judgment before God and our fate for the year is about to be sealed, how can we not feel nervous?

But we need to know that we are not alone. God is with us every step of the way. The Bible says in Deuteronomy 23:15 "Since the Lord, your God, moves about in your camp."

God is always "in our camp." He is with us at every moment of our lives.

To be a believer, to live a life of struggle, and to never stop striving for holiness despite all of the brokenness and pain we go through, isn't easy. But with all of our struggles, we also feel the deepest joy; the joy of knowing that we are never alone. Our Father in Heaven never leaves or abandons us in the streets of life, even for one moment.

May we never lose sight of the God who loves us, and may He bless us with health, happiness and joy.

Words of Repentance

Shira Schechter

Why would anyone willingly speak their worst failings out loud? Why put into words the very things you wish you could hide forever? On Yom Kippur, we do exactly that. It's called viduy, and it is the beating heart of the holiest day of the year.

The Confession Prayer, or *viduy*, is one of the most central and powerful prayers of *Yom Kippur*. On this day of judgment and reflection, we stand before God, acknowledging our sins and seeking forgiveness. The Confession Prayer serves as the verbal declaration of our sins, fulfilling the directive found in Numbers 5:7, "he shall confess the wrong that he has done. He shall make restitution in the principal amount and add one-fifth to it, giving it to him whom he has wronged."

The Bible instructs us to confess the wrongs that we have done, but why is it necessary? Why must we put our failings into words at all? Isn't heartfelt remorse enough?

Maimonides, one of Judaism's most profound thinkers, insists that repentance is incomplete without confession.[18] Rabbi Joseph B. Soloveitchik explains why this is so,[19] emphasizing that confession is not merely an add-on to repentance, it is the act that brings it to life. Without confession, the process of repentance remains unfinished. Speaking one's sins aloud transforms our internal feelings of regret into something tangible and concrete, holding us accountable in a way silent reflection never can.

---

18. Laws of Repentance 1:1
19. Joseph B. Soloveitchik, *Al HaTeshuvah* (New York: World Zionist Organization, 1980), 4045, 61-65.

We may feel remorse or regret, but it is only when we put our emotions into words that we truly grasp their depth. Thoughts remain shapeless until they are spoken. As Rabbi Soloveitchik notes, a person himself does not know what stirs even in his own heart until he shapes his emotions and thoughts into verbal expression.

But there is another benefit to verbal confession. Rabbi Soloveitchik explains that before this verbal acknowledgment, a person may only have a vague sense of their failings, but by articulating their transgressions, they bring them into sharp focus. Words have the power to illuminate the seriousness of our actions, and the spoken confession forces us to confront the truth directly.

Of course, this is not easy work. Confession requires breaking through layers of pride, fear, and self-deception. Rabbi Soloveitchik likens *viduy* to a form of self-sacrifice—a personal offering to God. When we confess our sins, we sacrifice our ego, our carefully guarded defenses, and our sense of control. In his words, "Confession forces a person, with great suffering, to recognize the facts as they are and to express the truth clearly." It is not simply admitting wrongdoing—it is a humbling act of stripping away excuses and illusions.

And yet, in that pain lies transformation. It forces us to confront our failings with honesty and humility. This process, though painful, is necessary for true spiritual renewal. As Rabbi Soloveitchik teaches, it is only through this struggle— through the act of speaking the truth about ourselves and the shame that comes with it—that we burn away our pride and our illusions, and in doing so, we find purification and forgiveness. As it says in Leviticus 16:30, "For on this day atonement shall be made for you to cleanse you of all your sins; you shall be clean before Hashem."

These lessons reach beyond our relationship with God. In our human relationships, healing also begins with words of truth. A relationship damaged by hurt cannot fully heal until one party admits their role in causing the harm. By verbalizing our regret and offering sincere apologies, we not only validate the other person's pain but begin to rebuild trust. Just as with *viduy*, reconciliation becomes possible only after this honest acknowledgment.

Confession—whether before God or another person—is the doorway to forgiveness, reconciliation, and the possibility of beginning anew.

Passion and Precision in Divine Service

Shira Schechter

On the holiest day of the Jewish year, when the fate of every soul hangs in the balance, why does the Torah obsess over details? Which garments the High Priest must wear, which animals to sacrifice, even how many times he must wash his hands. For a day meant to transform hearts and souls, Yom Kippur seems remarkably concerned with getting the ritual exactly right.

The answer lies in a tragedy that occurred in the desert, shortly after the Exodus from Egypt. The Torah portion of Acharei Mot begins with a stark reminder: "The Lord spoke to Moses after the death of the two sons of Aaron who died when they drew too close to the presence of the Lord" (Leviticus 16:1). This verse references the deaths of Nadab and Abihu, Aaron's sons, who brought "strange fire"[20] before God and died as a result. What follows, however, is not a discourse on mourning, but detailed instructions for the *Yom Kippur* service and the proper way for Aaron, as High Priest, to enter the Holy of Holies.

Why connect these two events? Why begin the laws of the most sacred day with the memory of such profound loss?

The medieval biblical commentator Rashi offers an illuminating parable. He compares it to a patient visited by two doctors. The first advises, "Don't eat cold food and don't sleep in damp places." The second doctor repeats the same advice, but adds, "so that you won't die like so-and-so did." The second warning, Rashi explains, is far more effective.

The Torah reminds Aaron of his sons' fate not to deepen his

---

20. Leviticus 10:1

grief, but to underscore the gravity of what he is about to undertake. His sons approached God on their own terms rather than God's. On *Yom Kippur*, Aaron would enter the Holy of Holies—the innermost sanctuary where God's presence dwells most intensely. The message is unmistakable: approaching the Divine requires not just spiritual longing, but absolute precision in following God's commandments.

But why would Aaron need such a warning? Unlike his sons, Aaron was known for his faithful adherence to God's laws. What concern could there be?

The answer lies in understanding what motivated Nadab and Abihu. Aaron's sons were young, passionate, and burning with desire to connect with the Divine. Rabbi Naftali Zvi Yehudah Berlin explains that they acted out of a burning passion of love for God.[21]

Their sin was not lack of devotion, but misplaced devotion. In their fervor to approach God, they overlooked what they may have considered "smaller" details—the precise procedures, the required garments, the prohibition against entering after drinking wine.[22] Their spiritual enthusiasm led them to approach God on their terms rather than His.

This is the warning embedded in the *Yom Kippur* service: even when entering the Holy of Holies and reaching an unparalleled level of closeness with the Divine, Aaron must still follow the rules and worship God exactly as He commands. The holiest moment of the year demands the most careful attention to divine instruction.

---

21. Rabbi Naftali Zvi Yehudah Berlin, *Ha'amek Davar*, commentary on Leviticus 10:1
22. Babylonian Talmud Sanhedrin 52a

On *Yom Kippur*, this balance between spiritual intensity and ritual precision becomes the defining characteristic of the day. The High Priest's entry into the Holy of Holies represents the ultimate encounter between human and Divine, yet it is governed by elaborate protocols—specific garments, particular offerings, precise timing, exact words. Every detail matters because the stakes are ultimate: this is the moment when atonement is secured for the entire people.

This speaks directly to our own spiritual lives. How often in our own spiritual journey do we elevate emotional connection over adherence to specific practices? How often do we prioritize feelings of spirituality over religious obligations? The story of Nadab and Abihu, embedded in the very foundation of *Yom Kippur*, reminds us that God desires both our hearts and our obedience.

This speaks to the very essence of *teshuvah*—repentance. True return to God requires not just sincere remorse or spiritual yearning, but a commitment to change our behavior in accordance with divine will. As King Solomon wrote, "Guard your steps when you go to the house of God" (Ecclesiastes 4:17).

Rabbi Aaron Lopiansky, writing to his child about the weight of generational transmission, captured this truth: the treasure our ancestors preserved through centuries of persecution wasn't merely emotional fervor or abstract spirituality, but "a comprehensive way of life—one that encompasses both a sublime connection with God and meticulous attention to His commandments."

On *Yom Kippur*, we inherit this same responsibility. Each year, as we stand in synagogue reciting the ancient prayers, we become links in that unbroken chain stretching back 3,300 years. Like Aaron entering the Holy of Holies, we approach God with both passionate longing and careful adherence to His instructions. We fast not because we feel like fasting, but because God commanded it. We recite specific prayers not because they always move us emotionally, but because they form the divinely ordained path of return.

The lesson of Nadab and Abihu, forever linked to the *Yom Kippur* service, teaches us that approaching the Holy of Holies —whether literally or metaphorically—requires both spiritual fire and disciplined obedience. In this balance, we honor both our deepest yearnings for connection with God and the divine wisdom that shows us how such connection can be safely and properly achieved.

As we emerge from *Yom Kippur*, sealed in the Book of Life, we carry forward this ancient understanding: that true spiritual transformation comes not through abandoning divine law in pursuit of personal religious experience, but through embracing both the spirit and the letter of God's will. In doing so, we ensure that what we pass to future generations is not merely religious sentiment, but the complete framework for living in relationship with the Divine—passionate, precise, and eternally true.

5

SUKKOT – THE FEAST OF TABERNACLES

The final *shofar* blast has sounded. The gates of heaven have closed. The fast is broken.

After forty days of the most intense spiritual work of the year, we might expect to collapse from exhaustion. We might think it's time to return to ordinary life.

Instead, we do something that seems to defy logic: we abandon our comfortable homes and move outside.

This is the paradox of the holiday *Sukkot* (Feast of Tabernacles). Just when we've achieved the ultimate spiritual heights, just when we've been purified and forgiven, we're commanded to make ourselves vulnerable again. To trade security for exposure, permanence for fragility, the solid walls of our houses for the temporary shelter of a hut.

Why? Because *Sukkot* holds the secret to making all that spiritual transformation permanent.

SUKKOT – FROM JUDGMENT TO JOY

The Days Between *Yom Kippur* and *Sukkot*

Picture this: You've just finished the most intense spiritual day of the year. You're exhausted, you're hungry, and you've just broken your fast. What's the first thing you do?

If you're an observant Jew, you grab a flashlight and start building a hut in your backyard. It might sound crazy, but there's something beautiful about immediately channeling all that spiritual energy into something you can touch and build with your hands.

The seven-day holiday of *Sukkot* begins just five days after *Yom Kippur* on the 15th of *Tishrei*. The piercing blast of the *shofar* that concludes *Yom Kippur* still echoes in the air as observant Jews begin their next sacred task: building the *sukkah* (temporary dwelling). By beginning construction immediately, we transition from fulfilling one commandment to another, transforming the spiritual elevation of the Day of Atonement into physical action.

The days between *Yom Kippur* and *Sukkot* buzz with purposeful activity. Families gather materials to construct their temporary dwellings. The *sukkah* walls rise, carefully built to meet the exacting requirements of Jewish law: sturdy enough to withstand normal winds, yet clearly temporary in nature. The covering is then carefully arranged from organic material in order to provide shade while allowing glimpses of sky and stars, creating that essential balance between shelter and exposure that defines the *sukkah* experience.

Children eagerly participate in decorating the *sukkah* with fruits hanging from strings, colorful artwork, and festive ornaments that transform the humble structure into a place of beauty and joy. This decoration serves not merely an aesthetic purpose but fulfills the rabbinic principle of beautifying the commandments. This principle expresses our loving willingness to fulfill God's commands and to demonstrate that we regard them not as burdens but as sources of joy and meaning.

Simultaneously, the search begins for the four species: the *etrog* (citron), *lulav* (palm branch), *hadassim* (myrtle branches), and aravot (willow branches). These are purchased in order to fulfill the biblical command: "On the first day you shall take the product of hadar trees, branches of palm trees, boughs of leafy trees, and willows of the brook, and you shall rejoice before the Lord your God seven days" (Leviticus 23:40). These must be acquired with meticulous care, as Jewish law requires them to be whole, fresh, and beautiful. The *etrog*, in particular, becomes the object of intense scrutiny, examined carefully for any blemishes that might disqualify it from ritual use.

The preparation extends beyond construction and acquisition to the practical necessities of festival life. Kitchens transform as families prepare special foods for the festival meals that will be eaten in the *sukkah*. The temporary dwelling must be cleaned and arranged to serve as the primary living space for the seven-day festival; a place for eating, entertaining guests, studying Torah, and for many families, even sleeping when weather permits.

This flurry of activity serves a deeper purpose beyond mere preparation. It channels the spiritual energy of *Yom Kippur* into concrete acts of religious devotion, demonstrating that true repentance manifests not only in internal change but in renewed commitment to divine commandments. The physical labor of construction becomes itself a form of spiritual practice, as families work together to create a space where they will dwell with the divine presence.

The continuity between the High Holidays and *Sukkot* is expressed through the continued recitation of Psalm 27 throughout the festival. This psalm, which begins to be recited daily from the start of the Hebrew month of *Elul*, contains what the sages identify as a direct reference to Sukkot: *"For He will hide me in His sukkah on the day of trouble; He will conceal me in the secret place of His tent"* (Psalm 27:5). The Hebrew phrase *ki yitzp'neni b'sukko* (for He will hide me in His *sukkah*) links the psalm's themes of divine protection and refuge directly to the festival's central commandment.

Sukkot: The Biblical Command

The biblical foundation for *Sukkot* comes with both clear instructions and deeper meaning:

"On the fifteenth day of the seventh month, when you have gathered in the yield of your land, you shall observe the festival of the Lord for seven days... You shall live in booths for seven days; all citizens in Israel shall live in booths, in order that future generations may know that I made the Israelite people live in booths when I brought them out of the land of Egypt, I the Lord your God." (Leviticus 23:39-43)

These passages connect *Sukkot* to both the harvest season and the historical memory of Israel's desert wanderings. The Torah also commands the taking of the four species, again linking the joy of harvest with celebration before God: "On the first day you shall take the product of hadar trees, branches of palm trees, boughs of leafy trees, and willows of the brook, and you shall rejoice before the Lord your God seven days" (Leviticus 23:40).

Unlike other holidays which commemorate single dramatic moments in Jewish history, *Sukkot* commemorates something different: an ongoing relationship of trust and dependence on divine providence.

The festival asks us to remember not a single pivotal event, but forty years of learning to live with uncertainty while trusting in God's protection. For one week each year, the temporary *sukkah* becomes our primary dwelling, transforming our comfortable homes into a recreation of the wilderness experience our ancestors knew so well.

The Names of *Sukkot*: Reflecting the Holiday's Rich Dimensions

Sukkot goes by many names, and like nicknames that reveal different sides of a person's personality, each name tells us something different about this holiday's character.

The most common name, *Sukkot* (Booths or Tabernacles), directly references the temporary dwellings that define the holiday's observance. This name emphasizes the commemoration of the Israelites' journey through the desert and the ongoing lesson about divine protection and human vulnerability.

The Torah also calls it *Chag HaAsif* (Festival of the Ingathering), highlighting its agricultural dimension: "You shall observe the festival of ingathering at the end of the year, when you gather in the results of your work from the field" (Exodus 23:16). This name reflects the aspect of the holiday which celebrates the culmination of the harvest season and expresses gratitude for divine blessing in the form of material abundance.

Perhaps most significantly, *Sukkot* is known as *Zeman Simchateinu* (the Season of Our Joy). The Torah commands joy during *Sukkot* more emphatically than for any other festival: "You shall rejoice before the Lord your God seven days" (Leviticus 23:40). This joy encompasses both the happiness of a successful harvest and the spiritual joy of dwelling under divine protection.

Finally, the festival is sometimes called simply *Chag* (The Festival), suggesting its importance among the pilgrimage festivals. This designation reflects both its position in the festival calendar as the third and final of the pilgrimage festivals, and its role as the most joyous of the biblical celebrations.

These multiple names reveal how *Sukkot* weaves together themes of historical memory, agricultural thanksgiving, spiritual joy, and divine relationship into a single, comprehensive celebration.

Dwelling in Divine Protection

Sukkot lasts seven days, from the 15th to the 21st of *Tishrei*, followed immediately by *Shemini Atzeret* (Eight Day of Assembly) on the 22nd. Unlike other Jewish festivals that center on specific historical events, *Sukkot* celebrates the ongoing relationship between the Jewish people and their God as mentioned above. The festival's name itself, *Sukkot*, meaning "booths" or "temporary shelters," immediately signals its central preoccupation with the tension between permanence and impermanence.

The holiday centers on two main practices: living in the *sukkah* and taking the four species. The *sukkah* serves as the central focus of life during the festival. Meals are eaten there, guests are entertained there, and many families even sleep there when weather permits. This temporary structure, with its partial walls and permeable roof, creates a unique environment that blurs the boundaries between indoors and outdoors, security and vulnerability.

The command of dwelling in the *sukkah* is understood by Jewish law to mean that the *sukkah* should become one's primary residence during the festival. One should treat it as home as much as possible for the duration of the holiday. This transforms dependence on God from an abstract concept into lived experience, as families experience the same vulnerability and trust their ancestors knew in the desert.

Similarly, the four species are taken each day of the festival (except on *Shabbat*) and waved in six directions, north, south, east, west, up, and down, acknowledging that God is present everywhere. By taking these agricultural products and consecrating them for divine service, we also acknowledge that He is the source of all agricultural and economic success as well, a fitting message for a holiday that celebrates the end of the harvest season.

But the four species carry an even deeper message about the nature of the community that celebrates this festival. Each species represents a different type of person. The *etrog* (citron), with its pleasant taste and fragrance, represents those who possess both Torah knowledge and good deeds. The *lulav* (palm), which produces tasty dates but has no scent, symbolizes those with knowledge but without good deeds. The myrtle, fragrant but not edible, represents those with good deeds but without knowledge. The willow, lacking both taste and scent, represents those with neither knowledge nor good deeds. Yet all four are bound together and waved as one, teaching that the Jewish people in all their diversity form a single unit in divine service, especially after the unifying experience of repentance and forgiveness.

The festival atmosphere is one of profound joy. The Torah commands us to rejoice during *Sukkot* more than any other festival, using the word "joy" repeatedly in its description of the holiday.[1] This isn't surface-level happiness, but the deep satisfaction that comes from fulfilling God's will and experiencing His protection. It is joy rooted in gratitude for the harvest, joy in the successful completion of the High Holiday season, joy of dwelling in God's presence, the joy of unity, and joy in the anticipation of divine blessing for the year ahead.

The Reason for the Holiday

What exactly are we commemorating when we sit in the *sukkah*? The Torah tells us we're remembering the booths our ancestors lived in during the forty years of wandering in the desert. But what kind of booths were they?

Two of the great sages offered radically different answers to this question,[2] and their disagreement reveals something profound about what it means to trust God.

Clouds of Glory

Rabbi Eliezer had a breathtaking answer: The "booths" weren't physical structures at all. They were clouds, the miraculous

---

1. See Leviticus 23:20 and Deuteronomy 16:15
2. Babylonian Talmud, Sukkah 11b

clouds of divine glory that surrounded the entire Israelite camp for forty years in the wilderness.

Picture it: An entire nation traveling through the harsh desert, protected by clouds that provided shade from the scorching sun, protection from enemies and dangerous animals, and a visible reminder that God Himself was hovering over them. These weren't ordinary clouds. According to tradition, they flattened mountains to make travel easier, destroyed venomous snakes and scorpions, and even kept the Israelites' clothes clean and perfectly fitted throughout the entire journey.[3]

From this perspective, when we sit in our fragile *sukkah* exposed to wind and weather, we're not commemorating vulnerability; we're celebrating the ultimate divine protection. We're declaring that the same God who surrounded our ancestors with supernatural care continues to protect us today, even when we can't see the clouds.

Every time the autumn wind shakes our *sukkah* walls or rain threatens to dampen our meal, we remember that our real security has never come from thick walls or sturdy roofs. It comes from the invisible but unshakeable protection of the Divine.

Huts in the Desert

Rabbi Akiva understood it completely differently. The booths were exactly what they seemed: actual physical huts and tents that the Israelites built with their own hands during their desert wanderings. Simple, temporary structures offering minimal protection from the elements.

---

3. Rashi on Numbers 10:34, Deuteronomy 8:4

But Rabbi Akiva's interpretation reveals a different kind of miracle: the miracle of human faith. The Israelites chose to leave Egypt and follow God into the unknown. Egypt, brutal as it was, offered food, shelter, and predictability. In exchange, they followed Moses into an unknown wilderness to live in temporary shelters, completely dependent on divine provision for water, food, and protection.

The prophet Jeremiah captured this breathtaking act of faith: "I remember the devotion of your youth, the love of your bridal days, how you followed Me in the wilderness, in a land not sown" (Jeremiah 2:2).

From this perspective, the *sukkah* represents something equally powerful: the human capacity to choose spiritual freedom over physical security, to embrace uncertainty in service of a higher purpose. Our ancestors' physical shelters were indeed fragile, but they housed a people undergoing the most permanent spiritual transformation in human history.

Two Truths, One Message

So, which rabbi is right? The answer is both, and their disagreement teaches us something beautiful about faith. Sometimes we experience God's protection as miraculous intervention, as the clouds of glory that shield us from dangers we never even see. Other times, we experience it as the strength to build meaning and create holiness even in the most challenging circumstances.

Whether supernatural or natural, whether miraculous clouds or humble huts, the message of the *sukkah* remains the same: We once lived in complete dependence on divine providence, and that experience of trust and vulnerability brought us closer to God than any permanent dwelling ever could.

Today, when we build our own *sukkah* each year, we step into both interpretations at once. We trust that the God who protected our ancestors continues to watch over us—sometimes through miraculous intervention we never notice, sometimes through giving us the strength to find meaning and create sacred moments even when life feels unstable and uncertain.

In a world that promises security through insurance policies, savings accounts, and sturdy homes, the *sukkah* teaches a different lesson: that our deepest security comes not from what we can control, but from our relationship with the One who controls everything else.

Sukkot as a Culmination of the High Holiday Season

The timing of *Sukkot* is no accident. Coming just five days after *Yom Kippur*, it creates a spiritual arc that moves from judgment to joy, from introspection to celebration, from the solemnity of individual reckoning to the communal joy of divine relationship.

The High Holiday season begins with *Elul's* call to self-examination, intensifies through our coronation of God and His judgment of us on *Rosh Hashanah* (Jewish New Year) and the Ten Days of Repentance, and reaches its climax with the spiritual cleansing of *Yom Kippur* (Day of Atonement). *Sukkot* then provides the joyous conclusion to this process, representing the celebration that follows successful spiritual purification.

After achieving forgiveness and spiritual renewal on *Yom Kippur*, we emerge ready to celebrate our relationship with God. The *sukkah* becomes a bridal chamber, a place of intimate connection between the newly purified soul and the divine presence. This transformation is reflected in the mystical tradition's understanding of *Sukkot* as the time when the divine presence (*shekhinah*) comes to dwell in the *sukkah* with the Jewish people, creating a space of unprecedented intimacy between the human and divine realms.

The joy of *Sukkot* isn't arbitrary, it's earned through the spiritual work of the preceding season. It is the joy of reconciliation, the relief of forgiveness, and the excitement of beginning anew with a clean slate. The temporary dwelling of the *sukkah* paradoxically becomes the most permanent achievement of the year, a renewed relationship with the Divine that will sustain the celebrants through all the challenges ahead.

Universal Significance of *Sukkot*

Sukkot may be a Jewish festival, but hidden within its rituals and prophecies is a vision that speaks to all humanity.

This universal dimension appears in several places throughout the tradition. During the Temple period, seventy bulls were sacrificed over the seven days of *Sukkot*, corresponding to the seventy nations of the world. While other nations pursued their own interests, the Jewish people were offering prayers and sacrifices on behalf of all humanity.

The prophet Zechariah envisioned a future when the universal aspect of the holiday would become explicit: "All who survive of all those nations that came up against Jerusalem shall make a pilgrimage year by year to bow low to the King Lord of Hosts and to observe the festival of *Sukkot*" (Zechariah 14:16).

This remarkable verse envisions a future in which *Sukkot* becomes a universal celebration. All humanity will recognize the divine providence that the Jewish people have celebrated throughout their history. The temporary structures that represent vulnerability and dependence on God will become symbols of humanity's proper relationship with the Divine. Nations that once attacked Jerusalem will come as pilgrims to learn the lessons of trust and faith that *Sukkot* teaches.

This prophetic vision gives *Sukkot* both backward and forward meaning. When we sit in our *sukkah* each year, we remember our ancestors' desert journey while also looking ahead to the time of ultimate redemption when all people will recognize God's care and protection.

Sukkot as a Time of Judgment for Rain

Though the High Holidays are over, divine judgment continues. While the High Holidays determine our spiritual fate, on *Sukkot* God determines the amount of rainfall for the coming year.[4]

The connection is both practical and profound. *Sukkot* celebrates the previous year's harvest while simultaneously marking the beginning of the rainy season in Israel. This is when farmers anxiously await the first rains that will determine next year's crops. In addition, the festival's permeable *sukkah* makes us acutely aware of weather conditions - a light rain can transform our temporary dwelling from shelter to exposure, reminding us of our complete dependence on divine mercy for the right amount of precipitation at the right time.

This adds another layer to *Sukkot's* themes of trust and vulnerability. We celebrate God's past provision while placing our hopes for the year ahead entirely in His hands.

---

4. Babylonian Talmud, Rosh Hashanah 16a

Simchat Beit HaSho'evah: The Water-Drawing Celebration

During the Temple period, *Sukkot* featured one of the most joyous celebrations in Jewish life known as *Simchat Beit HaSho'evah*, which literally means the "Rejoicing of the House of the Water-Drawing." Each morning of the festival, priests would draw water from the Pool of Siloam in Jerusalem and carry it in a golden pitcher to the Temple, where it was poured on the altar alongside the wine libation.[5] This ceremony, not explicitly commanded in the Torah but established by tradition, became the focal point of extraordinary celebration.

The Talmud declares that "one who has not seen the rejoicing of the water-drawing has never seen true joy in his life."[6] The Temple courtyard would fill with thousands of celebrants—scholars, priests, and common people—dancing, singing, and celebrating through the night. Great rabbis would juggle torches and perform acrobatics, while Levites played musical instruments and sang psalms. The celebration was so magnificent that its light could be seen throughout Jerusalem.

This water ceremony is connected directly to the prayers for rain that characterize *Sukkot*. By drawing water and offering it on the altar, the people enacted their dependence on God's provision of rainfall. The joy of the celebration reflected not only gratitude for past blessings but confidence in God's continued care.

Though the Temple no longer stands, many communities today recreate aspects of this celebration during the intermediate days of *Sukkot*, gathering for music, dancing, and

5. Babylonian Talmud, Sukkah 48a–48b
6. Babylonian Talmud, Sukkah 51a

celebrations that echo the ancient joy of celebrating our relationship with God.

Reading Ecclesiates: Wisdom for the Season

The custom of reading *Kohelet* (Ecclesiastes) on *Sukkot* presents us with a striking paradox. At the height of our celebration, when joy fills the temporary dwelling and gratitude overflows for the harvest's abundance, why turn to one of the most melancholy books in the entire Bible?

The answer lies in the deep connection between *Kohelet's* themes and those of *Sukkot*. The book's famous opening words, "Vanity of vanities, all is vanity," hit differently when you're sitting in a fragile hut, celebrating in a dwelling that practically shouts the impermanence of everything we build. At the same time, these words speak directly to farmers who've just finished gathering their crops; the moment when it's easiest to feel proud of their accomplishments while forgetting who really controls everything.

Kohelet captures this perfectly: "To everything there is a season, and a time to every purpose under heaven... a time to plant and a time to pluck up that which is planted" (Ecclesiastes 3:1-2). This is the reality every farmer knows. You can work your fields perfectly, but if the rains don't fall at the right time, or if pests destroy your crops, or if a late frost hits just before harvest, all your effort means nothing. The book reminds us that even our greatest successes depend on forces completely beyond our control.

While we're celebrating the abundance of the harvest, *Kohelet* whispers a warning: don't put your trust in what you can accumulate or build. Everything we can touch, buy, or build will eventually crumble. What lasts? Our connection to God,

306 | BEFORE THE KING

the kindness we show others, the wisdom we gain. As the book concludes: "Fear God and keep His commandments, for that is man's whole duty."

In reality, Ecclesiastes is the perfect reading for the perfect moment. Just when we might be tempted to feel secure in our blessings, *Kohelet* reminds us where real security comes from. Just when we might start thinking our sturdy houses make us invincible, we sit in a *sukkah* that lets in the wind and rain. Both the book and the booth teach the same truth: the only foundation that doesn't shift is our relationship with the eternal God.

This wisdom becomes especially powerful following the High Holidays, when we've just spent weeks examining our lives and priorities. *Kohelet* helps us hold onto that clarity, keeping our focus on what actually matters as we move forward into a new year.

SEVEN DAYS OF CELEBRATION: A PRACTICAL GUIDE TO *SUKKOT*

The Eve of the Holiday

The autumn air carries anticipation as *Sukkot* approaches. Like all Jewish festivals, careful preparation allows us to enter the holiday with intention and peace of mind. Since we refrain from work on the first day of *Sukkot*, just as we do on Shabbat, most preparations must be completed beforehand.

Homes should be cleaned and tidied, creating a sense of honor for the approaching festival. Take time for personal preparation too: shower, dress in your finest clothes, and prepare your heart for celebration. The dining table gets special attention, though on *Sukkot*, that table is in your *sukkah*. Set it with your finest dishes, silverware, and glasses. Even if your *sukkah* is simple, treating it with the same care you'd give your dining room transforms it into a palace fit for divine guests.

Food preparation follows the same rules as other festivals— while cooking is permitted on the holiday itself, it's advisable to do most preparation beforehand. Stock up on groceries, prepare ingredients, and think through your menu so you can focus on celebration rather than cooking.

Night-Time Prayers

With sunset, our prayers shift from the ordinary to the festive, marking the beginning of sacred time. We recite the special festival *Amidah* (standing prayer), which celebrates the themes of the holiday and includes the *Ya'aleh v'Yavo* prayer - a request that God remember us favorably on this festival day. This

prayer will be added into every *Amidah* prayer and the Grace
After Meals for the duration of the holiday.

Ya'aleh v'Yavo - May Our Prayers Ascend to You

> e-lo-HAY-nu vay-lo-HAY a-vo-TAY-nu
> ya-a-LEH v'-ya-VO v'-ya-GEE-a v'-
> yay-ra-EH v'-yay-ra-TZEH v'-yi-sha-
> MA v'-yi-pa-KAYD v'-yi-za-KHAYR
> zikh-ro-NAY-nu u-fik-do-NAY-nu v'-
> zikh-RON a-vo-TAY-nu. v'-zikh-
> RON ma-SHEE-akh ben da-VID av-
> DE-kha. v'-zikh-RON y'-ru-sha-LA-
> yim eer kod-SHE-kha. v'-zikh-RON
> kol a-m'-KHA bayt yis-ra-AYL l'-fa-
> NE-kha. lif-lay-TAH l'-to-VAH l'-
> KHAYN ul-KHE-sed ul-ra-kha-
> MEEM l'-kha-YEEM ul-sha-LOM.
> b'-YOM
> For Sukkot: KHAG ha-su-KOT ha-ZEH
> zakhr-AY-nu a-do-NAI e-lo-HAY-nu BO
> l'-to-VAH. u-fok-DAY-nu VO liv-ra-
> KHAH. v'-ho-shee-AY-nu VO l'-kha-
> YEEM. u-vid-VAR y'-shu-AH v'-ra-
> kha-MEEM KHUS v'-kha-NAY-nu v'-
> ra-KHAYM a-LAY-nu v'-ho-shee-AY-
> nu. kee ay-LEY-kha ay-NAY-nu kee
> AYL ME-lekh kha-NUN v'-ra-KHUM
> A-tah

> Our God and God of our fathers, may
> there ascend, come, and reach,
> appear, be desired, and heard,

counted and recalled our
remembrance and reckoning; the
remembrance of our fathers; the
remembrance of the Messiah the
son of David, Your servant; the
remembrance of Jerusalem, city of
Your Sanctuary and the
remembrance of Your entire people,
the House of Israel, before You for
survival, for well-being, for favor,
kindliness, compassion, for life and
peace on this day of:

For Sukkot - This festival of Booths:

Remember us O Lord, our God, on this
day for well-being; be mindful of us
on this day for blessing, and deliver
us for life. In accord with the
promise of deliverance and
compassion, spare us and favor us,
have compassion on us and deliver
us; for our eyes are directed to You,
because You are the Almighty Who
is King, Gracious, and Merciful.

The First Meal: Welcoming Heaven and Earth

After making *Kiddush* (the blessing over wine that sanctifies the festival) and *Hamotzi* (the blessing over bread), we begin a meal that combines an earthly feast with a heavenly encounter. There is a custom to invite the *Ushpizin*, the mystical guests who tradition says visit our *sukkah* each night, at the beginning of this meal. These seven guests include Abraham, Isaac, Jacob, Joseph, Moses, Aaron, and David, each bringing their unique spiritual energy to each of the seven nights of the holiday.

Unlike *Shabbat* which requires three meals, on festivals we are only required to have two. These meals should be enjoyed leisurely with family and friends. It is common to share words of Torah, sing the melodies that have echoed through Jewish homes for generations, and let conversation flow naturally.

Sleeping Under the Stars

Weather permitting and safety allowing, many families sleep in the *sukkah*. There's something profound about falling asleep under the *schach* (the sukkah's roof covering), with only a thin barrier between you and the vast sky. Children often find this the most memorable part of the holiday—camping out in the backyard, but with deeper meaning. If harsh weather or safety concerns make sleeping outside impractical, don't worry. The obligation is to dwell in the *sukkah*, not to put yourself at risk.

The same principle applies to meals: if rain or other conditions make eating in the *sukkah* more uncomfortable than you would reasonably endure in your house, Jewish law permits you to eat indoors.

Morning Prayers: A Symphony of Gratitude

The morning prayers on *Sukkot* follow the familiar structure of regular morning prayers but are enriched with special festival additions. We recite the expanded *Pesukei d'Zimra* (verses of praise) used on *Shabbat* and festivals, and recite the special *Amidah* prayer for festivals. We also add the full *Hallel*, songs of praise taken from Psalms 113-118 that are recited on festivals. These melodies fill the synagogue with gratitude and joy.

Following the Torah reading, we add *Musaf*—the additional service that corresponds to the extra offerings brought in the Temple on *Shabbat*, *Rosh Chodesh* (the new moon), and festivals. This service connects our prayers to the ancient Temple worship and reminds us that even without the physical Temple, our prayers serve as offerings to God.

The *Hoshanot* Prayers: Daily Pleas for Salvation

Each day of *Sukkot*, the morning service includes a distinctive ritual known as the *Hoshanot* prayers, where the congregation circles around the synagogue while holding the four species and reciting special prayers for salvation. The name comes from the Hebrew phrase "*Hosha na*" meaning "Please save us," which appears repeatedly throughout these ancient liturgical poems.

During the *Hoshanot* prayers, the holy ark is opened and a Torah scroll is removed and placed on the reading platform. The congregation then forms a procession around the sanctuary, with each person carrying their four species while reciting prayers that blend requests for physical and spiritual salvation. These prayers ask for God's help in matters ranging from agricultural abundance and protection from enemies to spiritual purification and the ultimate redemption.

The *Hoshanot* prayers are structured as alphabetical acrostics and contain some of the most beautiful Hebrew poetry in the liturgy. They invoke God by numerous names and attributes, recall the merits of the patriarchs and matriarchs, and reference key moments in Jewish history when divine salvation was manifest.

The prayers for salvation acknowledge that despite the

festival's joy and celebration of divine protection, we remain vulnerable and dependent on God's ongoing mercy.

The *Hoshanot* prayers also bridge the gap between the High Holiday season's focus on judgment and *Sukkot's* emphasis on joy. While we celebrate God's past protection and present blessings, we simultaneously acknowledge our continued need for divine help.

The daily recitation of *Hoshanot* builds toward the crescendo of *Hoshanah Rabbah*, when the single daily circuit becomes seven circuits and the prayers reach their greatest intensity.

Opening of the *Hoshanot* Prayers

> ho-SHA na l'-ma-an-KHA e-lo-HAY-nu
> ho-SHA na:
> ho-SHA na l'-ma-an-KHA bor-ay-NU
> ho-SHA na:
> ho-SHA na l'-ma-an-KHA go-a-LAY-nu
> ho-SHA na:
> ho-SHA na l'-ma-an-KHA dor-SHAY-nu
> ho-SHA na:

> Please save, for Your sake, our God,
> please save!
> Please save, for Your sake, our Creator,
> please save!
> Please save, for Your sake, our
> Redeemer, please save!
> Please save, for Your sake, our Attender,
> please save!

The Closing Paragraph of the *Hoshanot* Prayers

ho-SHEE-ah et a-ME-kha u-va-RAYKH
et na-kha-la-TE-kha ur-AYM v'-na-
s'-AYM ad ha-o-LAM: v'-yih-YU d'-
va-RAI AY-leh a-SHER hit-kha-NAN-
tee lif-NAY a-do-NAI k'-ro-VEEM el
a-do-NAI e-lo-HAY-nu yo-MAM va-
LAI-lah la-a-SOT mish-PAT av-DO
u-mish-PAT a-MO yis-ra-AYL d'-
VAR YOM b'-yo-MO: l'-MA-an DA-at
kol a-MAY ha-A-retz kee a-do-NAI
HU ha-e-lo-HEEM AYN OD:

Deliver and bless Your people; tend
them and sustain them forever
(Psalms 28:9). And may these words
of mine, which I have offered in
supplication before the Lord, be
close to the Lord our God day and
night, that He may provide for His
servant and for His people Israel,
according to each day's needs. In
order that all the peoples of the
earth may know that the Lord alone
is God, there is no other (I Kings
8:59-60).

Torah Reading: The Festival's Sacred Narrative

The Torah reading for *Sukkot*, taken from Leviticus 22:26-23:44, brings the morning service full circle. As we stand in synagogue holding our four species, we hear the ancient words that started it all: God's command to "live in booths seven days." There's something powerful about hearing these verses while you know your own *sukkah* is waiting for you at home. This reading reminds us that our temporary dwelling isn't just a charming tradition, it's a living memory of our ancestors' journey through the wilderness and God's protection during their most vulnerable time.

The *haftarah* (reading from the Prophets) for the first day of *Sukkot* is taken from Zechariah 14:1–21. This prophetic passage describes a future, climactic battle over Jerusalem, followed by the ultimate redemption and the universal recognition of God's kingship. One of the most striking elements of this vision is the depiction of all nations ascending to Jerusalem annually to celebrate the festival of *Sukkot*. The *haftarah* includes the well-known verse, "And the Lord shall be King over all the earth; on that day the Lord shall be One and His Name One" (Zechariah 14:9), referring to the future global spiritual awakening.

The prophetic reading envisions a remarkable future: all nations coming to Jerusalem to celebrate *Sukkot*. It's a vision that transforms this very personal, family-centered holiday into something with universal significance. It also reflects the idea that *Sukkot* is not only a celebration of God's past protection, it is a glimpse of the ideal future when the world will live in harmony under God's sheltering presence.

The Four Species

The morning's most distinctive ritual involves the *arba minim*, the four species mandated by the Torah. We take the *lulav* (palm branch), *etrog* (citron), *hadasim* (myrtle), and *aravot* (willow), bind them together as prescribed by Jewish law. To properly arrange the lulav: hold the palm branch with its spine facing you, then place three myrtle branches (hadassim) on the right side and two willow branches (aravot) on the left. It's customary to secure the myrtle and willow branches to the lulav using a holder woven from palm leaves.

We then shake the four species in six directions—east, south, west, north, up, and down—acknowledging God's presence throughout all of creation. This ancient practice connects us to the agricultural roots of the festival while recognizing divine sovereignty over the entire universe.

The four species are held during both the *Hallel* (psalms of praise) and *Hoshanot* (prayers of salvation) prayers. There is deep symbolism in praying while holding these different types of vegetation. The sages teach that each species represents a different type of person, yet the commandment requires that all four species be bound together. This teaches us that we need every type of person to be complete. When we wave the four species together, we acknowledge that our service of God is enriched by diversity, and that every member of the community has an irreplaceable role in the spiritual life of the people. Every person contributes their unique qualities to the service of God.

The Second Meal: Sustaining the Joy

The second meal of the day continues the celebration, again eaten in the *sukkah*. This meal is a continuation of the previous evening's festivities. It's another opportunity to invite guests, share stories or Torah thoughs, and simply enjoy the unique atmosphere of dwelling in this temporary home.

While Jewish law requires only two meals to be eaten in the *sukkah* on the first day of the festival (unlike *Shabbat*, which requires three), you're welcome to eat as many meals there as you'd like throughout the holiday. The general rule for what must be eaten in the *sukkah* is based on the type and amount of food: any meal with bread, and any substantial eating of foods made from the five grains (wheat, barley, rye, oats, and spelt) should be eaten in the *sukkah*. However, casual snacking, drinking water or other beverages, and eating fruits, vegetables, or other non-grain foods can be done anywhere. Some people, out of love for the commandment and desire to fully embrace the *sukkah* experience, take upon themselves the beautiful practice of eating and drinking everything in the *sukkah* during the entire festival.

Intermediate Days: Sacred in Their Own Way

Between the first days of *Sukkot* and the day known as *Shemini Atzeret*, lie the intermediate days known as *Chol HaMoed*. These days hold a special place in Jewish time, as they are more than ordinary weekdays but less than full festivals. We continue to eat and sleep in the *sukkah*, and limit the amount of work that we do. Work that's essential to the festival or that would result in significant loss if postponed is permitted, but the goal is to preserve the holiday atmosphere.

Many families use these intermediate days for outings, visits with extended family, or simply relaxing together. The *sukkah* becomes a gathering place where the boundaries between inside and outside, temporary and permanent, become beautifully blurred. It's time to pause, breathe, and remember that sometimes the most profound dwellings are the ones that remind us that nothing lasts forever, and that's exactly what makes them precious.

Hoshanah Rabbah - The Final Judgment

The seventh day of *Sukkot*, known as *Hoshanah Rabbah* (the Great Hosanna), carries special significance. This day creates a unique bridge between the joyous celebration of *Sukkot* and the approaching conclusion of the extended High Holiday season, carrying both the festive character of the preceding days and the solemnity of final judgment.

On this day, the *hoshanot* prayers, which are recited on each day of the festival, reach their crescendo. While the congregation has circled the synagogue once each day throughout the festival while holding the four species and reciting prayers beginning with "*Hosha na*" (please save us), *Hoshanah Rabbah* transforms this ritual dramatically. The single daily circuit becomes seven complete rounds, creating an intensification of both movement and prayer that fills the synagogue with urgent pleas for divine mercy and salvation.

Hoshanah Rabbah stands at the intersection of judgment and mercy. While the High Holiday season officially concludes with *Yom Kippur*, rabbinic tradition teaches that God, in His infinite mercy, delays the final delivery of divine judgment until *Hoshanah Rabbah*. This day thus serves as a final opportunity for repentance and divine mercy, extending the window of spiritual opportunity beyond the formal end of the Ten Days of Repentance.

According to the Zohar,[7] while our judgment for the new year is sealed on *Yom Kippur*, it is not "concluded" or delivered until *Hoshanah Rabbah*. On this day, "the judgment decided on *Yom Kippur* receives its final seal, the signature that makes it binding," and the parchments containing the decrees are handed over to the angels who distribute them. This represents the completion of the divine judgment process that began on *Rosh Hashanah*.

---

7. Zohar, *Vayechi* 220a; *Tzav* 31b.

Hoshanah Rabbah also marks the time when, according to tradition, God determines the coming year's rainfall.

The day's central ritual involves taking additional willow branches (beyond those included in the four species) and beating them on the ground five times at the conclusion of the *hoshanot* prayers. This ceremony serves as both a prayer for rain and a symbolic casting away of sins.

The willow branch is particularly fitting for this ritual for several reasons. Willows are the most water-dependent of all the four species used in the festival, making them natural symbols for the prayer for rain. Indeed, Scripture refers to them as "willows of the brook" (Leviticus 23:40). In early rabbinic tradition, the willow, having neither fragrance nor taste, symbolizes those who lack both Torah learning and good deeds. Later Hasidic teachers, however, reinterpreted this image more positively. Rabbi Yehudah Aryeh Leib Alter of Ger (1847–1905), known by the title of his work *Sefat Emet*, explained that the willow represents Jews who serve God with simple, unpretentious faith. It is precisely this pure sincerity that gives special power to their prayers.[8]

When we beat the willow branches against the ground, we symbolically express both our humility before God and our urgent need for divine blessing of rain to penetrate the earth and sustain all life.

The customs of *Hoshanah Rabbah* also include staying awake the entire night before, engaged in Torah study and prayer. This vigil reflects the day's gravity and the desire to approach the final moment of judgment with maximum spiritual preparation.

---

8. *Sefat Emet*, commentary on Sukkot, year 5644 (1883).

THE EIGHTH DAY: *SHEMINI ATZERET* AND *SIMCHAT TORAH*

Biblical Source

The Torah concludes its description of the festival of *Sukkot* with a cryptic addition: "On the eighth day you shall observe a sacred occasion and bring an offering by fire to the Lord; it is a solemn gathering; you shall not work at your occupations" (Leviticus 23:36). This eighth day, known as *Shemini Atzeret* (the Eighth Day of Assembly), appears in the biblical text as both connected to and separate from *Sukkot*, leaving us to wonder exactly what this day is supposed to be.

The Hebrew word *atzeret* suggests restraint or holding back, leading to various interpretations of this day's essential character. Some understand it as a day when God restrains the Jewish people from departing, extending the intimate time of the festival for one more day. Others see it as a day of restraint from work, emphasizing the sacred nature of the day. Still others interpret it as spiritual restraint—a day for holding back from the exuberant celebration of *Sukkot* to focus on a more intimate and introspective relationship with the Divine.

The biblical description provides minimal detail about how this day should be observed, mentioning only that it is a "sacred occasion" with prohibitions against work and requirements for special offerings. This brevity stands in contrast to the detailed descriptions of *Sukkot*'s observances, suggesting that *Shemini Atzeret* operates on a different spiritual plane, less concerned with specific rituals than with the quality of relationship it represents.

What is *Shemini Atzeret*?

The rabbinic tradition provides a beautiful metaphor for understanding *Shemini Atzeret.* The biblical commentator Rashi explains the word *atzeret,* which is related to the Hebrew word for "stop" or "detain," with profound simplicity: "I have detained you with Me"—like a king who invited his children to a feast for several days, and when the time came for them to depart, he said, "My children, please stay with me one more day, for your departure is difficult for me."[9]

But why do we have an *atzeret* only after *Sukkot* and not after the other festivals? The medieval commentator *Chizkuni* explains this beautifully. He compares it to a king whose children visit him three times yearly. After their first visit, when they promise to return in fifty days,[10] he lets them go peacefully. After their second visit, when they say they'll be back in four months (from *Shavuot* to *Sukkot),*[11] he again bids them farewell contentedly. But when they tell him after *Sukkot* that they won't return for seven long months, until the next Passover, the king's heart breaks. "If you must be away so long," he pleads, "please stay with me just one more day so I can savor your company a little longer."[12]

This metaphor reveals *Shemini Atzeret* as an expression of divine love, a day when God desires to extend the intimate connection of the festival season. Unlike *Sukkot,* which commemorates the Jewish people's relationship with God in the context of their historical journey and agricultural cycle, *Shemini Atzeret* represents pure divine-human intimacy, without any of the symbols or historical commemorations that define other holidays.

---

9. Rashi on Leviticus 23:36
10. There are fifty days from Passover to *Shavuot* (Feast of Weeks)
11. From *Shavuot* to *Sukkot*
12. Chizkuni on Leviticus 23:36

This understanding transforms *Shemini Atzeret* from an appendage to *Sukkot* into its own unique spiritual experience. While *Sukkot* celebrates divine protection and providence through the symbolism of temporary dwelling and agricultural thanksgiving, *Shemini Atzeret* celebrates the relationship itself, the love between Creator and creation that underlies all the specific kindnesses and protections.

One More Day for the Jewish People

The universal elements of *Sukkot*, the seventy bulls offered for the nations, the prophetic vision of all peoples coming to Jerusalem for the festival, give way on *Shemini Atzeret* to a focus on the particular relationship between God and the Jewish people. This transition is dramatically illustrated in the Temple service itself. The Talmud[13] explains that the seventy bulls offered during the seven days of *Sukkot* corresponded to the seventy nations of the world, with Israel serving as priests offering sacrifices on behalf of all humanity. But on *Shemini Atzeret*, only one bull is offered, representing God's desire for an intimate celebration with His chosen people alone.

Rabbi Elazar captures this beautifully: "The seventy bulls correspond to the seventy nations. The single bull—for the unique nation." He compares it to a king who hosted a great feast for all his subjects for seven days, then said to his beloved friend: "Make me a small meal so that I may enjoy your company alone." This day belongs exclusively to Israel, representing the unique covenant that binds God and Israel.

This special focus on the Jewish people doesn't diminish the universal significance of the season but rather grounds it in the specific relationship through which universal blessing flows.

---

13. Babylonian Talmud, Sukkah 55b

The Jewish people's particular calling as a "kingdom of priests and a holy nation" (Exodus 19:6) enables their universal mission to bring divine light to the world. *Shemini Atzeret* celebrates this foundational truth: God's love for all humanity is expressed through His special relationship with Israel.

The day represents the intimate connection that sustains Israel's mission to the world. Just as individuals need private time with loved ones to sustain their public relationships, the Jewish people need this day of exclusive divine intimacy to sustain their role as a light to the nations.

This understanding helps explain why *Shemini Atzeret* lacks the elaborate rituals and symbols that characterize other Jewish holidays. The day is not about performing specific actions but about being in relationship. It requires no *sukkah*, no four species, no elaborate ceremonies. Its essence lies in the quality of presence and attention that the Jewish people bring to their encounter with the Divine.

Part of *Sukkot* or a Separate Holiday?

The relationship between *Sukkot* and *Shemini Atzeret* is complex. The Talmud[14] debates whether *Shemini Atzeret* is an extension of *Sukkot* or its own unique holiday. The answer is that it is a bit of both.

The Talmud indicates that in six key ways, *Shemini Atzeret* stands as an independent holiday: A new lottery determines which priests serve that day, the *Shehecheyanu* blessing marks it as a new time, it gets its own name as a festival, it has its own special sacrifices, its own psalms, and its own prayers. But in other ways it is an extension of the *Sukkot* holiday.

---

14. Sukkah 47b

Jewish law reflects this ambiguity in practical terms. The *sukkah* is no longer required on *Shemini Atzeret* and the four species are not taken, yet in holiday prayers it is called "the time of our joy" which is the description used for *Sukkot*. It is treated as a separate holiday for certain purposes but as a continuation of *Sukkot* for others.

The eighth day thus represents both conclusion and new beginning, both culmination and fresh start.

Observing *Shemini Atzeret*

While *Shemini Atzeret* lacks the dramatic rituals that define other Jewish holidays, this apparent simplicity is deceptive. The day's power lies not in what we do with our hands but in what we do with our hearts, expressed through our prayers.

The Familiar Framework

Shemini Atzeret begins like any Jewish festival, with candles flickering to life at sunset and the familiar rhythm of evening prayers. We recite the festival *Amidah*, sanctify the day with *Kiddush* over wine, make a blessing over two loaves of bread and settle into the comfortable patterns of holiday observance. The morning service similarly unfolds with its familiar elements—the full *Hallel* (Psalms of thanksgiving) filling the synagogue with songs of praise, the Torah reading connecting us to our sources. Yet in addition to this familiar structure, there is one prayer addition that makes the prayers of this day unique.

The Prayer for Rain

During the repetition of the *Musaf* service, the cantor recites *tefillat geshem*, the prayer for rain. This prayer marks the beginning of the winter rainy season in Israel, when the country transitions from the dry summer months to the season of life-giving rains essential for the coming year's crops. In many communities, the cantor dons a white kittel, the same garment worn on *Yom Kippur*, signaling that what follows is no ordinary petition but a matter of life and death for the world.

The prayer invokes Abraham, who dug wells in the desert, Isaac, whose life was saved by water, and Jacob, who rolled away the stone from the well so Rachel's flocks could drink. Each line weaves together our ancestors' stories with our desperate need for the rains that will sustain us through the coming year.

In addition to asking for rain, this prayer acknowledges our utter dependence on forces beyond our control. We've just finished celebrating *Sukkot,* which reminds us of our vulnerability. Now we turn that vulnerability into prayer, asking the One who controls wind and weather to remember His covenant and send the rains in their season.

Following this prayer, we begin adding the phrase "*mashiv haruach u'morid hagashem*" (He causes the wind to blow and the rain to fall) to every *Amidah* prayer throughout the winter months. This addition, recited until Passover, serves as a daily reminder of our dependence on divine providence for the water that sustains all life.

A Celebration of the Torah

The celebration of *Simchat Torah* (Rejoicing in the Torah) was added to the holiday of *Shemini Atzeret* during the medieval period. *Simchat Torah* marks the completion of the annual Torah reading cycle and its immediate renewal, celebrated with joyous dancing, singing, and processions with Torah scrolls. While this pairing might seem like a historical coincidence, it reveals profound spiritual connections that make the combination feel almost inevitable.

After the destruction of the Second Temple in 70 CE, the Jewish people were scattered in exile throughout the world, cut off from their homeland and the central focus of their religious life. In this new reality, the Torah became the portable homeland that traveled with Jewish communities wherever they went. By the medieval period, Jewish communities in Babylonia, living in exile for centuries, had developed the custom of reading through the entire Torah in one year, unlike communities in the Land of Israel, where the cycle took three and a half years. They chose to celebrate the completion of this annual cycle on *Shemini Atzeret*, creating one of Judaism's most joyous celebrations.

But why this particular day?

On one level, it was a convenient day to celebrate since it was a holiday with no other unique celebrations. But the connections between the Torah and *Shemini Atzeret* are profound.

The Torah reading cycle concludes with the final verses of Deuteronomy, which describe Moses' death: "Moses the servant of the Lord died there, in the land of Moab, at the command of the Lord" (Deuteronomy 34:5). These verses mark not only the end of the Five Books of Moses but the conclusion of the most detailed account of divine revelation in human history. Immediately afterward, the cycle begins anew with Genesis: "In the beginning God created the heavens and the earth" (Genesis 1:1). This transition from ending to beginning mirrors the spiritual journey from the solemnity of the High Holidays to the joy of *Sukkot* and beyond.

In addition, *Shemini Atzeret* is the day when we begin praying for rain, the life-giving water essential for survival. Jewish tradition has always seen Torah the same way. As the Talmud teaches: "There is no water except Torah," and Isaiah calls out, "Ho, everyone who thirsts, come for water" (Isaiah 55:1), which the Sages understood as an invitation to Torah study. Moses himself established that Torah should be read at least every three days, recognizing that people cannot survive spiritually without it, just as they cannot survive physically for more than three days without water.[15] So on the very day we pray for life-sustaining rainwater, we celebrate our life-sustaining Torah, which is compared to water.

The timing also reveals something deeper. *Sukkot* carries a universal message, and its sacrifices represent all nations. But *Shemini Atzeret* shifts focus to the unique relationship between God and the Jewish people. Torah perfectly embodies this transition. While Torah's ethical teachings have influenced all of civilization, the Torah itself represents the specific covenant that shapes Jewish identity and enables the Jewish mission to the world.

Finally, *Simchat Torah* represents what the Jewish people offer back to God on this day of divine intimacy. *Shemini Atzeret* and *Simchat Torah* form a "conversation between God and the Jewish people." *Shemini Atzeret* represents God's invitation: "Stay with me one more day." *Simchat Torah* becomes the Jewish response: a joyful declaration of loyalty and commitment to God.[16]

15. Babylonian Talmud, Bava Kama 17a
16. Rabbi Moshe Taragin, "Shmini Atzeret and Simchat Torah: A Duet Between Hashem and Man," Orthodox Union, https://www.ou.org/holidays/shmini-atzeret-and-simchat-torah-a-duet-between-hashem-and-man/.

Torah as Survival

During the long centuries of exile, the connection between Torah and survival became a matter of life and death. Jews lost everything: their land, their Temple, their political independence. But they kept their Torah. As one liturgical poem from *Yom Kippur* laments: "Nothing remains but this Torah." The medieval philosopher Sa'adia Gaon understood that Torah was essential to Jewish survival. The Torah didn't just preserve Jewish teachings. It preserved the Jewish people themselves.[17]

This truth found its most dramatic expression in Soviet Russia. Practicing Judaism was forbidden. Yet thousands of Jews would risk everything to gather in the streets outside synagogues on one day each year: *Simchat Torah*. They came to celebrate not just a book, but their identity. Their refusal to disappear. Many had never studied the Torah they celebrated, yet this single celebration was enough to awaken Jewish identity and inspire emigration to Israel.

The power of *Simchat Torah* to sustain Jewish identity in the face of oppression would be tested again in our own time, though in ways no one could have imagined.

A Shadow Over Joy

Rabbi Jonathan Sacks once observed: "A people that can walk through the valley of the shadow of death and still rejoice is a people that cannot be defeated by any force or any fear."

This dimension of *Simchat Torah* became heartbreakingly relevant in our time. October 7th, 2023—*Simchat Torah*—witnessed the largest massacre of Jewish people since the

---

17. Rabbi Saadiah Gaon, *Beliefs and Opinions, 3*

Holocaust. Hamas terrorists invaded Israel and brutally murdered over 1,200 people, including entire families, children, and the elderly, while taking hundreds more as hostages into Gaza.

This tragic convergence creates a permanent association between one of Judaism's most joyous celebrations and one of its darkest modern tragedies. The day meant to celebrate the eternal nature of Torah became a day of profound loss that reverberates through every Jewish community worldwide.

The attacks occurred during a festival celebrating divine protection and Jewish endurance. Families were murdered in their homes. Young people were slaughtered at a music festival celebrating peace. Entire communities were devastated. The contrast between *Simchat Torah*'s joy and October 7th's horror seems too great to bear, yet somehow the Jewish people must find a way to hold both realities together.

This painful contradiction reveals something essential about Jewish religious life. Jewish tradition has always held that joy and sorrow exist together, not in opposition. The Jewish calendar itself teaches this; fast days follow festivals, mourning periods appear within seasons of joy, and in modern times, Israel's Independence Day follows immediately after its Memorial Day. Faith must encompass both security and vulnerability, both divine presence and apparent absence.

This isn't new to Jewish experience. Jewish tradition teaches that even in the darkest moments, Torah continues to offer light and meaning. The annual cycle ensures that every ending leads to a new beginning. Every conclusion opens into a fresh possibility.

Simchat Torah will forever carry the weight of October 7th. But it will also continue to affirm the eternal values that no act of hatred can ultimately destroy. The dancing with Torah scrolls, the joyous processions, the excitement of beginning the cycle anew—these will continue because they represent truths that transcend any particular historical moment. The Torah that teaches "Choose life" (Deuteronomy 30:19) remains the Jewish people's guide and strength.

Previous generations celebrated *Simchat Torah* in ghettos, concentration camps, and under Soviet oppression. This generation will find meaning in the celebration despite, and perhaps because of, October 7th. The very act of continuing to dance with the Torah becomes resistance against those who would destroy the Jewish people and their joy.

In choosing to celebrate life, learning, and hope in the face of unspeakable loss, the Jewish people once again prove Rabbi Sacks' insight: that a people capable of joy in the valley of the shadow of death cannot be defeated by any force or fear.

COLLECTED INSIGHTS

Nature's Divine Lens

Rabbi Yaakov Wolff

A few months after our wedding, my wife and I embarked on a brief vacation in the Swiss Alps. At each stop on our itinerary, I found myself awestruck by the breathtaking beauty that surrounded us. The towering mountain ranges, glistening glaciers, cascading waterfalls, and the array of wildlife all brought to mind the verse, "and you shall love God, your Lord" (Deuteronomy 6:5). Maimonides explains that the path to loving God involves appreciating the marvels of creation, as expressed in Psalms 8:4-5: "When I behold Your heavens, the work of Your fingers, the moon and stars that You set in place, what is man that You have been mindful of him, mortal man that You have taken note of him."

As we sat atop one of the mountain peaks, immersing ourselves in this divine splendor, a small commotion caught my attention. Turning, I observed a group of approximately 50 individuals approaching the lookout. For a moment, I questioned whether we were at a mountain summit or a press conference as cameras clicked away with remarkable fervor, as though the mountains might vanish and the photo opportunity would be forever lost. The group ascended to the lookout, continued to snap their shutters, and then promptly departed.

Reflecting upon these photo-hungry tourists, I wondered: why do some people perceive the beauty of nature as a spiritual encounter while others remain unaffected, seeing it only as a fleeting, picture-worthy moment?

The answer to this question can be found in the observance of the holiday of *Sukkot* (Feast of Tabernacles), a week during which we are commanded to engage with the natural world. *Sukkot* distinguishes itself significantly from other Jewish holidays, as it necessitates our departure from our permanent dwellings to reside in temporary huts. Additionally, we bring various plant branches and citrus fruits into the synagogue, holding them during parts of the morning prayer service.

These two distinctive practices hold a unique position in Jewish tradition throughout the year. By vacating our homes, we eliminate the artificial barriers that separate us from God's natural world. We behold the sun and stars, and feel both warmth and chill, all intended to evoke a sense of proximity to God. Subsequently, by incorporating various elements of the natural world within the synagogue service, we affirm that all aspects of creation are intended for the service of God.

The question then arises: why is this practice observed specifically on the holiday of *Sukkot*? We find no comparable practices in scripture with regard to the other holidays or daily rituals.

I believe the answer lies ironically in the observance of *Yom Kippur* (Day of Atonement). On this day, Jews spend the entire day in the synagogue engaged in prayer, introspection, and repentance. However, in order to partake in these spiritual activities, we are instructed to "afflict our souls" (Leviticus 23:32), necessitating abstinence from physical pleasures. *Yom Kippur*, the holiest day of the year, occurs a mere five days prior to *Sukkot*, both falling in the Hebrew month of *Tishrei*.

Thus, we encounter *Yom Kippur*, a day characterized by abstaining from physical indulgence, immediately preceding *Sukkot*, a celebration of nature. This juxtaposition conveys the message that to discover God within the physical world, spiritual preparation is indispensable. Only by strengthening our souls within the sanctuary can we authentically connect with God through the wonders of nature. People who encounter the beauty of nature, without proper spiritual preparation, will therefore fail to be inspired.

This understanding transformed my memory of that day in the Swiss Alps. Those tourists with their cameras weren't wrong to capture the beauty; they simply lacked the spiritual preparation to truly see God's majesty in it.

The lesson of *Sukkot* is that the natural world is waiting to reveal the Divine to us, but only if we first prepare our hearts to truly see.

God's Favorite Memories

Rabbi Elie Mischel

The holiday of *Sukkot* (Feast of Tabernacles) has become my favorite holiday of the year. I love sitting outside in the *sukkah* (temporary dwelling) with a good book and some hot coffee, feeling connected to God.

But for such a beautiful holiday, *Sukkot* has a rather weak rationale. The *sukkah* is meant to remind us of the miracle of the Clouds of Glory that led the Jewish people through the desert so many years ago. This is certainly very beautiful, but there were many miracles that took place in the desert. God provided manna from heaven and water from a rock, He sweetened the waters at Marah (Exodus 15:22-25) and ensured the Israelites' clothes would not wear out during the forty-year trek through the desert. The whole desert experience was one great array of miracles!

Why, then, did God establish the holiday of *Sukkot* to remember the Clouds of Glory in particular? What is unique about that miracle that makes it more memorable than any other aspect of the desert experience? Why is this miracle worthy of a holiday?

As a kid, whenever I would hear about a house burning down, after it was clear that nobody was hurt, the first question was always: "Were the photo albums destroyed? Were they able to save their pictures?" Photo albums, and particularly old photo albums, are so precious and valuable because we cherish the memories of our youth. They bring us back to some of our most beautiful moments.

If this is true of human beings and the relationships that we share with each other, this idea must be rooted in something even deeper – in the relationship that we share with our Father in Heaven.

God, of course, remembers everything that has ever happened in human history. But which "photo albums" from the history of our relationship with Him does He love to look at most? What are God's favorite memories?

The holiday of *Sukkot* is the answer to that question. The defining words of this holiday are the words found in Jeremiah 2:2: "Go proclaim to Jerusalem: Thus said the Lord: I accounted to your favor the devotion of your youth, Your love as a bride — How you followed Me in the wilderness, In a land not sown."

God recalls with great love how the people of Israel followed Him out of Egypt and into the desert. We left Egypt with little food or water and followed God into the barren wilderness, entrusting our very lives to the Clouds of Glory which guided us through the desert.

What, specifically, does God praise us for? God does not praise us for our lofty intellectual or spiritual accomplishments. He doesn't talk about the great levels of prophecy that every Jew achieved at Mount Sinai. Instead, He praises us, and establishes the holiday of *Sukkot*, to commemorate the faith we had in Him in our "youth," when we were still in a state of immaturity at the lowest of the forty-nine levels of impurity. He praises us for following Him into the desert at the very beginning of our relationship with Him.

When God opens up His picture album, he goes right back to the earliest photos. The ones in which we are still awkward and unsure of ourselves. The faith we showed in God when we were just beginning our spiritual journey as a nation means more to God than all of our attainments and achievements that followed.

In a similar vein, Rabbi Yehudah Aryeh Leib Alter, a Hasidic rabbi known for his main work called the *Sfat Emet*, teaches us that the worship of God we do when we are in a "desert" is more precious to God than anything else.

What does it mean to serve God in a "desert"?

When we do something for the first time, it is always more challenging. When a commandment is new to us, at that moment we are still in a "desert." When our path to serving God is not yet clear and defined, but we still find a way to squeeze in some time for studying the Bible or fulfilling a commandment, in a certain way that gives God the greatest possible joy.

The Sages teach that the moment of greatest joy on *Sukkot*, the happiest celebration in the Temple, was the water drawing ceremony. All year long, we would bring wine libations in the Temple, but these offerings to God did not bring the same joy that the water offering on *Sukkot* would bring. Why not? Shouldn't wine be more joyous than water? After all, wine represents the highest levels of wisdom and symbolizes the great Torah scholar and advanced levels of serving God.

Based on what we have been saying until now, the answer is clear. Wine is very holy and is used in many of Judaism's rituals. But it represents a more sophisticated and established form of worship. Water is the simplest liquid. It represents simplicity, the beginning of our relationship with God, and those first awkward steps forward in serving Him. Water represents the simple service of the "desert" celebrated on the holiday of *Sukkot*.

Our routine worship of God is important. But equally important is to take a new step forward in serving God every once in a while. When you take a step out of your comfort zone, your first step into the "wilderness" is likely to be wobbly. But there is something so sweet and beloved to God when we serve Him in the "desert." Though those steps will likely be awkward and uncomfortable, God says, "I remember the great love of that moment, the moment when you followed Me into the desert, to a land that was not sown." These are the pictures of us that God treasures. These are His favorite memories!

Sukkot's Sacred Guests

Shira Schechter

The holiday of *Sukkot* (Feast of Tabernacles), referred to as "the season of our joy," is one of the most unique and meaningful holidays in the Jewish calendar. One of the features of the holiday is dwelling in booths, as it says: You shall live in booths seven days; all citizens in Yisrael shall live in booths (Leviticus 23:42).

As the weather turns cooler and people prepare to retreat indoors for the winter, Jews leave their comfortable homes and step outside to dwell in fragile, temporary huts, the *sukkot*.

But we are not meant to dwell in these huts alone. One of the traditions we perform on this holiday is welcoming the *ushpizin*, the spiritual guests, into the *sukkah*. Why do we invite these guests, and what do they represent?

The *ushpizin* are the seven "patriarchs" of the Jewish people — Abraham, Isaac, Jacob, Joseph, Moses, Aaron, and David — who are symbolically invited to join us in the *sukkah*. On each of the seven days of the festival, one of these spiritual forefathers is honored as the primary guest. According to Rabbi Norman Lamm,[18] their presence in the *sukkah* is far more than a ceremonial gesture. These figures, who all experienced profound moments of displacement, wandering, and exile in their lives, embody one of the core lessons of *Sukkot*: how to maintain spiritual resilience in a state of impermanence.

The *sukkah* itself is a symbol of this impermanence. A temporary structure, it commemorates the temporary shelters

---

18. Rabbi Norman Lamm, "The Booth of Alienation," sermon delivered on Sukkot 1966, Rabbi Norman Lamm Sermon Archives, Yeshiva University.

338 | BEFORE THE KING

the Israelites built during their forty years of wandering in the desert, a time when they were neither in the land of their bondage, Egypt, nor in their promised home, Israel. Thus, the *sukkah* embodies transience or, as Rabbi Lamm put it, the *sukkah* teaches us "how to live in exile — and to survive."

In the modern world, the feeling of displacement, or alienation, is not foreign. Many people, regardless of their circumstances, experience a sense of not fully belonging, of being strangers in their own lives or environments. This universal experience of alienation is something that the *ushpizin* deeply understood. Abraham was called to leave his homeland and wander in search of his destiny. Isaac, after the binding on Mount Moriah, became a stranger even in his own household, misunderstood by those closest to him. Jacob fled from his brother and spent years in exile working for Laban. Joseph was sold into slavery by his brothers and rose to prominence in a foreign land, never fully at home in Egypt. Moses had to run away from Egypt and was a refugee in Midian. Aaron, abandoned by Moses who had ascended Mount Sinai, stood helpless as the people worshiped the Golden Calf. David spent years running from Saul and even from his own son. Each of these figures lived through experiences of alienation, yet they did not lose their sense of purpose or their connection to their spiritual identity.

By inviting the *ushpizin* into our *sukkah*, we are reminded of their struggles and their ability to maintain faith and integrity in the face of exile. Their presence in the *sukkah* teaches us how to survive both our national exile and our personal moments of alienation. In a world where displacement, whether emotional, physical, or spiritual, is a common experience, the *ushpizin* offer us a model for how to remain grounded and connected to our values, even in the midst of turmoil.

Moreover, the presence of the *ushpizin* in the *sukkah* extends an essential lesson about hospitality and empathy. Just as we invite these spiritual guests, we are also expected to invite human guests, particularly the poor and the lonely, into our *sukkah*.

The *sukkah*, fragile and open to the elements, serves as a powerful reminder of human vulnerability. By welcoming the *ushpizin*, we acknowledge that every person, like our forefathers, carries their own burdens of exile and alienation. Yet, just as our ancestors overcame these challenges, we too can rise above them and thrive. They are timeless guides reminding us that exile, whether personal or communal, physical or spiritual, can be endured with grace, strength, and faith. And they remind us of the moral obligation to extend kindness and generosity to the vulnerable. True joy is only complete when it is shared with those in need.

Through this sacred ritual, we learn that the key to survival, both physically and spiritually, lies in our ability to carry our values with us wherever we go and to share them with others.

Rooftop Reflections

Rabbi Elie Mischel

I remember the day I turned twenty years old. In Jewish thought, turning twenty is very significant because it is only at the age of twenty that we become fully responsible for our actions. Though girls and boys become Jewish adults at the ages of 12 and 13, respectively, we are not fully responsible for our sins until the age of twenty.

I understood that turning twenty was a big deal, but I didn't know how to properly celebrate this significant birthday. A rabbi of mine directed me to a book of letters by Rabbi Moses Feinstein, in which Rabbi Feinstein addressed a twenty-year-old who had exactly the same question that I had. What was his advice? Rabbi Feinstein told this boy to "be careful to honor your mother."

I'll be honest, I was looking for something more exciting or profound than simply being careful to honor my mother. I thought he might tell me to study the Bible all night or do something "spiritual." Honoring my mother is incredibly important, of course, but what did that have to do with turning twenty?

Regarding the holiday of *Sukkot*, the Bible tells us: "You shall live in booths seven days; all citizens in Israel shall live in booths" (Leviticus 23:42).

The Bible commands us to build small huts and live in them for seven days. According to Jewish law, when you build your little hut, called a *sukkah*, you can build the walls out of anything you want – wood, metal, plastic, canvas – as long as the walls are sturdy enough that they won't flap in the breeze.

But there are very specific rules about what can and cannot be used for the roof of the *sukkah*. In order to be "kosher," the roof has to fulfill the following 3 requirements:

- It must be made out of something that grows from the ground, like tree branches.
- The branches or leaves must be cut off from the tree and not attached to the ground.
- The materials used for the roof must be unfinished items that have not been processed into objects with specific functions like a ladder or door.

What is the reason behind all of these laws that govern the roof of the *sukkah*?

I once read an article written by Lisa Morguess, a frustrated mother. She described a classic scene: After her kids were all ready for school she would turn on the TV. But like all good moms, she had a rule – the kids could only watch certain channels. The rule was that mom sets the channel, and no one could change it without permission.

The problem was that her daughter, Annabelle, never stuck to this rule. The moment her mom walked out of the room she would start changing the channel. One particular morning, after reminding Annabelle not to touch the TV, she found her daughter channel surfing again and totally lost it.

Morguess writes about her reaction that morning:

"I'm not excusing my losing it this morning. I'm ashamed. I wish I held it together better, I really do. But this is why people say that motherhood is a hard job. Not because it's especially intellectually challenging or physically demanding – I mean it is those things, but there are certainly other pursuits that require far more intellectual and physical effort than motherhood. It's because it's so incredibly thankless so much of the time. It's because I feel like I've sacrificed so much of myself for them, and they don't appreciate it. It's because I do and do and do for them, constantly, and it often seems like all I get in return is complaining that it's not enough – or just outright ignored. I'm not looking for accolades or awards or fanfare. But how about a thank you?"

This, to me, captures the greatest challenge of motherhood. It's not the constant work or the incredible juggling it requires. More than any of these things, it's the feeling of thanklessness, the sense that everything you do is "expected" and therefore ignored.

This is why, I believe, Rabbi Feinstein told the twenty-year-old boy who reached out to him for advice to honor his mother. Because it's precisely at the age of twenty, when a young man enters the age of responsibility and a new level of maturity, he must stop and reflect upon all the little things that his mother did for him while he was growing up that he never properly appreciated.

As Lisa Morguess said, "How about a 'thank you'?" At twenty, when you become a full-fledged adult, it's time to wake up and say 'thank you.'

Why do we have these strange laws when it comes to the roof of the *sukkah*? All three of these restrictions ensure that the materials we use for our *sukkah* roofs will be things that we don't generally value. Leaves, branches, grass, weeds – there is no end to things that grow from the ground. Because we have so much of it, we treat it like it's worthless. And they have to be cut from the ground. We appreciate beautiful, living trees with strong branches. But when the leaves fall off the tree and the branches are broken, we totally ignore them. Similarly, the roof can't be made out of a vessel or anything that has been made into something that we value.

When we build our *sukkah*s, we are commanded to build them out of materials that we take for granted all year long. A few weeks before Sukkot we hardly notice the branches lying in the corners of our backyards. But when we build the *sukkah*, our perspective changes – what we didn't see or value before becomes the essence of the commandment.

The message of the *sukkah* roof is to pay attention and take notice.

On the holiday of *Sukkot* we are commanded to live in the *sukkah* as much as possible. For seven days, we look up at the broken branches and leaves that we step on all year long. Once a year, we are commanded to stop, notice and appreciate all the little kindnesses that we ignore the rest of the year.

Whether it's our mothers who spend so many years of their lives doing mundane yet invaluable things that enrich our lives in so many ways; or whether it's the small blessings our Father in Heaven rains down upon us every moment of every day, *Sukkot* is the time to sit in the *sukkah* and to pay attention.

Sukkot's Joyous Judgment Day

Rabbi Tuly Weisz

According to Jewish tradition, *Sukkot* is one of four "Judgment Days" that occur during the year, and on this festival, God determines the world's water allocation for the coming year. In ancient times, life and death hinged directly on the amount of rainfall that fell in Israel, and so, *Sukkot*'s prayers concerning the judgment of rain are taken extremely seriously.

Despite the seriousness of God's judgment, many of *Sukkot*'s water-related prayers and rituals are celebrated with festive joy. The waving of the four species that grow along the water and the nightly parties commemorating the Temple's water libations are joyous occasions in light of Deuteronomy 16:13-15:

"After the ingathering from your threshing floor and your vat, you shall hold the Feast of Booths for seven days. You shall rejoice in your festival, with your son and daughter, your male and female slave, the [family of the] Levite, the stranger, the fatherless, and the widow in your communities. You shall hold a festival for the Lord, your God, seven days, in the place that the Lord will choose; for the Lord, your God, will bless all your crops and all your undertakings, and you shall have nothing but joy."

How do you reconcile joy and judgment? No one looks forward to Judgment Day. Given the fact that the Land of Israel is very dependent on rainfall, it seems that *Sukkot* should be a solemn time and not one of joyous celebration. What is the reason for such festivity?

We can learn a very important Jewish principle from a story about a father and his two sons.

A father had two sons, and while he agreed to support both of them, he took two very different approaches. The father gave his older son a very generous amount of money and told him to return again the following year when he ran out or needed more. He turned to his younger son and only gave him a tiny fraction of what the older brother received. When the younger son complained, the father told him to come back for more tomorrow.

At first blush, the younger son felt hurt and disappointed that he received such a smaller amount, and felt that his father must love or trust his older brother more. "On the contrary," the father explained, "it's precisely because I love you so much that I want you to return often, for I want a meaningful relationship with you."

Israeli Prime Minister Golda Meir once quipped that after wandering in the desert for forty years, Moses dragged Israel to the one place in the entire Middle East with no oil and no natural resources. Egypt's Nile River made it the superpower of ancient times, and in the modern era, Saudi Arabia's oil wells turned the kingdom into one of the wealthiest nations on earth. Israel seemingly got dealt a losing hand, the short end of the stick.

The Torah explains the purpose for such unequal distribution of resources: "For the land that you are about to enter and possess is not like the land of Egypt from which you have come. There the grain you sowed had to be watered by your own labors, like a vegetable garden" (Deuteronomy 11:10)

Unlike Egypt, where agricultural success came so easily thanks to the spillover from the Nile River, Israel would depend on constantly seeking out the Lord through prayer just to make it through the day. This wasn't a sign of God's disinterest in the

Jewish People. Just the opposite! God seeks a relationship with Israel and intended that His People develop key spiritual qualities such as faith, prayer, and trust. By making His people dependent on rainfall, which comes from heaven, God ensures that Israel must maintain a close connection with Him through prayer at all times.

The secret behind the joyous judgment day of *Sukkot* is that we are looking beyond the verdict, and seeking out a deep relationship with the Judge. It is this constant connection with our Father in Heaven, by virtue of His children's continued dependence on Him, which is the cause for great celebration on *Sukkot*.

Sukkot and Sluggers: Life Lessons Beyond the Ballpark

Rabbi Yaakov Wolff

Great baseball players are often celebrated for their remarkable feats on the field, such as hitting towering home runs, throwing blazing fastballs, or making spectacular defensive plays. However, there exist a few baseball players who have left an indelible mark not only for their athletic prowess but also for their unique accomplishments beyond the actual game. Cal Ripken, known for playing in an astonishing 2,632 consecutive games, never missed a single contest in 16 years. Bo Jackson, an All-Star outfielder, achieved an unparalleled distinction by also excelling as a Pro Bowl running back in the NFL. And Armando Gallaraga, who came agonizingly close to a perfect game, only to have it slip through his fingers due to an umpire's mistake, displayed remarkable grace and understanding with his response: "Nobody's perfect." These athletes impart valuable life lessons, and the convergence of these lessons becomes evident on the holiday of *Sukkot* (Feast of Tabernacles).

"On the first day you shall take the product of hadar trees, branches of palm trees, boughs of leafy trees, and willows of the brook, and you shall rejoice before the Lord, your God, seven days" (Leviticus 23:40). On *Sukkot*, we are commanded to take four species, one of which is a citrus fruit called an *Etrog*. Although the precise identification of the *Etrog* is a matter of tradition, the Jewish sages taught that the *Etrog* tree has three identifying attributes. One is that there are fruits on the tree all year round. The second is that the tree can survive on various sources of water. Finally, not only the fruit but even the branches of the tree have flavor to them.

Rabbi Samson Raphael Hirsch (1808 – 1888) pointed out that these three attributes contain important moral lessons. Having fruit year-round is a sign of unwavering consistency. The ability to survive on different types of water represents versatility. And the flavor in the branches represents internal morality that is consistent with outward expressions.

These are also the three lessons that we learn from the baseball players mentioned above. Cal Ripken taught us how to be consistent; to show up every day and give our best effort. Bo Jackson taught us versatility, performing with greatness on different fields. And Armando Gallaraga taught us the importance of having a good heart that is consistent with our public behavior.

The lessons from these baseball players and the symbolism of the *Etrog* fruit used on *Sukkot* converge to offer valuable insights into life. As we celebrate *Sukkot* and reflect on the symbolism of the *Etrog*, let us remember the inspiring stories of Cal Ripken, Bo Jackson, and Armando Gallaraga. Just as these athletes demonstrated unwavering consistency, versatility, and internal morality, we too can apply these principles to lead more meaningful and fulfilling lives. These lessons remind us that greatness isn't just about physical prowess but also about the character we exhibit and the values we uphold.

Prayers for Salvation, Branches of Unity

Shira Schechter

Some of my most cherished childhood memories are of visiting my grandparents' house in the Bronx. My grandmother always had her cookie jar filled and ready for us, and my grandfather never ran out of stories to tell. We looked forward to every visit, eager for the treats and the tales.

But once a year, our visit had a different purpose. My grandfather grew *aravot*, willow branches, in his yard, and during the *Sukkot* holiday, we would drive to the Bronx to cut the branches, bundling them into sets of five to sell at the synagogue on *Hoshanah Rabbah*, the seventh day of the holiday. At the time, it felt like a fun holiday tradition, but I didn't fully grasp the deeper meaning behind those willows until much later on.

While *Sukkot* is often associated with celebration and joy, *Hoshanah Rabbah* introduces a more solemn tone to the otherwise festive holiday. According to the sages, this day marks the final opportunity to influence the divine judgment for the coming year, which begins on *Rosh Hashanah* (Jewish New Year) and continues through *Yom Kippur* (Day of Atonement). Jewish tradition teaches that God's judgment is not fully sealed until *Hoshanah Rabbah*, making it a critical moment in our spiritual journey. Additionally, we are judged for water on *Sukkot*, with that judgment also being finalized on this day. As a result, extra prayers for salvation are added to the morning prayer service.

On *Hoshanah Rabbah*, we circle the synagogue seven times, reciting the ancient *Hoshana* prayer, which begins: "Please save, for Your sake, our God, please save!" While these prayers are recited every day of *Sukkot*—one prayer for each day—on the seventh day, the ritual reaches its climax as all seven prayers for salvation are repeated, with additional prayers added to the liturgy. At the end of the recitation, we symbolically beat the willow bundle on the ground five times.

But what is the meaning behind this unusual custom?

One interpretation suggests that beating the willow branches is a silent prayer for rain. The willows are referred to in the Bible as "river willows," or "willows of the brook," reflecting their reliance on water:

"On the first day you shall take the product of hadar trees, branches of palm trees, boughs of leafy trees, and willows of the brook, and you shall rejoice before the Lord, your God, seven days." (Leviticus 23:40).

Because they are so dependent on rain, the branches become a fitting symbol in our prayers for water recited on this day.

Additionally, the four species of *Sukkot* are thought to represent different parts of the body: the *lulav* (palm branch) represents the spine, the *hadassim* (myrtle branches) represent the eyes, the *etrog* (citron) represents the heart, and the *aravah* (willow) represents the mouth, which is linked to prayer. In this context, the willows, representing the mouth, are beaten on the ground, emphasizing the central role of prayer in seeking divine favor.

While one interpretation connects the willow to the mouth and the centrality of prayer, another interpretation compares the four species to four types of people. The *etrog*, with both taste and fragrance, symbolizes those who possess both Torah knowledge and good deeds. The *lulav*, which has taste but no fragrance, represents those who study the Bible but may lack in good deeds. The myrtle, fragrant but tasteless, corresponds to those who perform good deeds but lack Torah knowledge. Finally, the *aravah*, which lacks both taste and fragrance, symbolizes those who have neither knowledge of the Bible nor good deeds. By bringing these four species together, the ritual highlights the unity and interdependence of all, regardless of their individual strengths or weaknesses.

Based on this interpretation, Rabbi Abraham Isaac Kook, the first Chief Rabbi of Israel, offers a unique perspective on the ritual of beating the willow branch. He suggests that using the willow branch, rather than any of the other species, represents the quiet strength of those who are simple and unlearned. According to Rabbi Kook, the true strength of the Jewish people lies not in the intellectual brilliance of scholars, but in the unwavering faith and devotion of those who, though not learned, follow the commandments with humility and steadfastness. It is their humility and steadfastness that sustain the community through difficult times.

The simple *aravah*, which seems so ordinary, carries profound symbolic weight. Whether seen as a humble prayer for rain, a symbol of unity, or a representation of the quiet strength of the simple-minded, the willow branches remind us that every individual, no matter their level of observance or learning, plays a crucial role in the fabric of the community. As we beat the branches on *Hoshanah Rabbah*, we acknowledge both our vulnerability and our collective strength, turning to God in a final plea for a year of blessing and salvation.

Stay With Me

Sara Lamm

One of the most insightful "concepts" I've learned as a parent is the idea of Connection Capital. Coined by child behavioral psychologist and parenting expert Dr. Becky Kennedy, it refers to the idea that the more time you spend connecting with your children—through play, conversations, and shared experiences —the more likely they are to cooperate and trust you. It's not a guaranteed formula, of course. Any parent who has put in the effort to bond with their kids knows that even the most well-connected child can still throw a tantrum, or two (or 100). Yet, the underlying truth is profound: relationships are built in the small moments of connection. Naturally, this idea doesn't just apply to children; it extends to our relationships with our spouses, friends, and even our relationship with God.

Of course, these moments are often hard to carve out in our fast-paced, distraction-filled lives. But they're crucial, and this idea is at the heart of *Shemini Atzeret*, the holiday following *Sukkot*. Known as "The Eighth Stop," or "Eighth Day of Assembly," it's an invitation from God to stay a little longer, to pause, and to share an intimate moment together.

Imagine the quiet of the night after a long day. The kids are asleep, the house is still, and the day's noise has faded. You sit with your spouse in the dim light of the living room, a cup of tea in hand, and talk about everything and nothing. There are no interruptions, no phones buzzing, no to-do lists running through your mind. It's just the two of you, sharing the quiet. These conversations—often about little things like the events of the day or a shared memory—are when you feel closest, when you remember why you chose each other. It's not about grand gestures or big plans; it's about being together, undistracted and present.

During the day, conversations with your spouse might be scattered between errands, chores, and work. Even though you're together, your attention is divided. But in these late-night moments, when the world has quieted, you're fully present with each other. And it's in these simple moments that the depth of your relationship truly shines.

This is how we can understand the essence of *Shemini Atzeret*. *Sukkot* is a vibrant and bustling holiday filled with communal gatherings, festive meals, symbolic gestures, and public prayers. During the time of the Temple, 70 oxen were sacrificed on behalf of the 70 nations of the world, representing the universal focus of the holiday. It was a big event. But when *Sukkot* ends, God asks us to linger a little longer, for just one more day of connection. *Shemini Atzeret* is that moment of quiet after the celebration—a day just for us and God to be together.

On *Shemini Atzeret*, the offerings in the Temple are scaled down dramatically. Instead of many sacrifices, we offer just one ox. The Talmud explains this difference with a beautiful parable. A king holds a weeklong feast for all his subjects, but when the feast ends, he turns to his closest friend and says, "We've celebrated with everyone. Now, let's enjoy a small, simple meal —just the two of us." This is what God says to the Jewish people at the end of *Sukkot*. After the public festivities, He invites us to spend one more day with Him in an intimate setting, where it's just us and Him.

"On the eighth day you shall hold a solemn gathering; you shall not work at your occupations" (Numbers 29:35).

The simplicity of *Shemini Atzeret* reflects the beauty of quiet moments. There's no need for grand gestures—just the act of being together is enough. It's like those quiet conversations with a spouse after a long day, or a bedtime story with your child, where the connection grows not because of what is said, but because you've taken the time to be fully present.

The Torah's description of *Shemini Atzeret* uses a term of affection: *Atzeret*, which means to gather or hold back. As the sages explain, it's as if God is saying, "Your departure is difficult for me. Stay a little longer." It's not about ritual or obligation; it's about love.

We often think that meaningful connection requires large amounts of time or elaborate plans. And sometimes, those grand gestures are truly meaningful. But *Shemini Atzeret* reminds us that the most profound type of connection happens in the quiet, undistracted moments. In the same way that our relationships with our loved ones deepen when we spend time together without distractions, our connection with God grows stronger when we pause to simply be with Him.

Let Us Dance Even More: The First Anniversary of the Hamas Slaughter

Rabbi Elie Mischel

For most people, the Hamas massacre of over 1,200 innocent Israelis is known simply as "October 7th." And so, on October 7, 2024, thousands of Jews, Christians and other good people gathered together at ceremonies across the world to mark the day and memorialize the victims of Hamas' brutal assault.

But for traditional Jews, the true anniversary of this attack is the festival of *Shemini Atzeret* and *Simchat Torah* that marks the end of the *Sukkot* festival. October 7th is the secular anniversary of the attack, but according to the traditional biblical calendar, *Simchat Torah* is the "yahrzeit," the anniversary of the attack. Hamas did not choose a random day to overrun the border. They chose to attack and slaughter Jews on the day of "The Joy of the Torah," when we traditionally dance for hours while holding Torah scrolls and celebrate the completion of another year of reading the Five Books of Moses.

For months, traditional Jews have asked themselves: can we possibly dance on *Simchat Torah* this year? Is it possible, or even appropriate, to joyously hold the Torah scroll in our arms as thousands of families observe the first anniversary of their loved ones' deaths?

The answer, I believe, is a resounding YES.

The Hamas attack on October 7th was not only an act of unbelievably evil physical cruelty. It was also an attempt to destroy Jewish identity – Judaism itself. Hamas immediately named their war against Israel the "Al Aqsa Flood." Al-Aqsa is the name of the mosque that sits atop the Temple Mount in Jerusalem, the holiest site of the Jewish people, about 50 miles away from the Gaza border. Though Israel liberated the Old City of Jerusalem after Jordan invaded the Jewish state in 1967, Israel allowed Jordan to maintain control over the day-to-day administration of the Al-Aqsa Mosque through the Jordanian Waqf, a branch of Jordan's Ministry of Awqaf Islamic Affairs and Holy Places.

After its brutal attack, Hamas leaders issued a document listing its many grievances against Israel and justifying the October 7 slaughter. The first reason listed is "The Israeli Judaization plans to the blessed Al-Aqsa Mosque, its temporal and spatial division attempts, as well as the intensification of the Israeli settlers' incursions into the holy mosque." In other words, Hamas' goal is to prevent the Judaization of the Temple Mount and all of Israel. They wish to wipe not only the Jews, but Judaism itself, off the face of this earth.

But if their goal was to destroy the Jewish spirit and Jewish identity, they have failed – and failed miserably! Hamas attacked us on the day we celebrate the Torah, with the goal of destroying the Torah itself. But the opposite has occurred. In defiance of our enemies, Jews across Israel and throughout the world are returning to the Torah, the Hebrew Bible. Assimilated Jews who know little about their heritage are awakening and embracing their Jewish identity. Our enemies awakened the sleeping lion within, and God's people are fighting back.

Today, we will not cry in despair. We will not stop dancing. No – we will dance with more passion and fire than we have ever danced before! This year, more Jews than ever before will gather together to hug and hold the Torah scrolls that are the secret to our strength and which guarantee our victory. There is no better way to observe this day than to dance with joy while holding tightly the Torah scrolls that have preserved us through all the generations.

On August 24, 1929, Arab mobs attacked the Jewish community of Hebron, slaughtering 69 Jews while raping and wounding many others. Many Jews were also murdered in other parts of the country. Understandably, the Jews of Israel were deeply traumatized by these events, and many sank into despair. One month later, the Jewish community of Jerusalem, still in mourning, celebrated *Simchat Torah* together with their illustrious leader, Rabbi Abraham Isaac Kook. Even as they began dancing together with the Torah, the sadness was evident and their hearts weren't in it.

Suddenly, Rabbi Kook began singing, loudly, over and over again, the following words:

"O nations, acclaim His people! For He'll avenge the blood of His servants, Wreak vengeance on His foes, And cleanse the land of His people" (Deuteronomy 32:43).

For over an hour, Rabbi Kook and the congregation sang these words with great intensity, calling out to God to destroy the evil doers who had murdered His people. With every step, their sadness was transformed into resolve, and ultimately into joy. For they knew that if they hold onto God's Torah, the Jewish people cannot be defeated. Days are coming. God will avenge His people and bring joy and peace back to His land.

INTO THE FIRE:

STORIES OF HEROISM FROM OCTOBER 7TH

Step inside the tragedy - and into the hearts of ordinary Israelis who chose courage over fear when everything was on the line.

SCAN NOW TO GET YOUR COPY!

Or visit israel365store.com

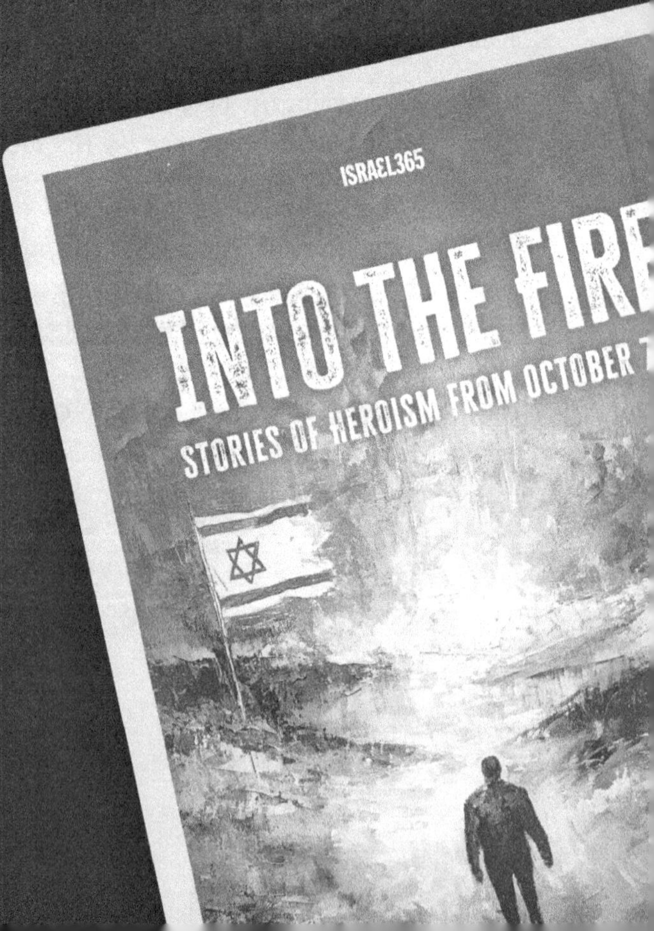

Shut Off the Noise. Turn On the Divine.

Shabbat Revolution:
A Practical Guide to Weekly Renewal
shows you how to step away from the chaos, unplug with purpose, and create sacred space for God, family, and real peace - ***every single week.***

SCAN NOW TO GET YOUR COPY!

Or visit
israel365store.com

From Texas to the Temple

The Return of the Red Heifers: Paving the Road to Redemption tells the true story of five rare red heifers, ancient purification laws, and the extraordinary Christian-Jewish partnership bringing prophecy to life in our time

SCAN NOW TO GET YOUR COPY

Or visit
israel365store.com

TWO ENEMIES.
ONE MISSION:
ERASE THE BIBLE.

*Islamic radicals and Western progressives couldn't be more different - except in their shared war on biblical truth. **The War Against the Bible: Ishmael, Esau and Israel at the End Times** reveals the prophetic roots of this modern-day spiritual battle.*

SCAN NOW TO GET YOUR COPY!

*Or visit
israel365store.com*

www.ingramcontent.com/pod-product-compliance
Lightning Source LLC
Chambersburg PA
CBHW061552120626
46550CB00004B/1458

* 9 7 8 1 9 5 7 1 0 9 8 9 3 *